Hyperdimensional You

Endorsements

"Ground-breaking, unprecedented theories. I have sheer astonishment at your ontological understanding." —**MB**

"Adeptly progresses the reader from narrative to Truth, from clever to wise, in a way that's definitely thought-provoking and potentially life-changing!" —**Dr. Lisa C-Navarra**

"Logical, practical advice for a Source-leaning, upgraded life." —**LMB, Sacramento, CA.**

"Good reading with elegant insights" —**Professor Zeus Y.**

"I so enjoyed your book!" —**Rev. Janée Marth**

"A very insightful and interesting read." —**AC**

"Your book had a deeply profound effect on me. It challenged me to revisit my controlled narratives and sense of self at a deep level. I am experiencing positive effects in my spiritual growth as well as with family, friends, work, and community. I am deeply grateful!" —**Jeff F-P**

"I thoroughly enjoyed this book… I could feel the truth within the pages. If you want a boost on your path to enlightenment, read and contemplate this magnificent book." —**Meg**

Also, by Bob Cochran

- Emerging Imaginal You, 2021 [book, Rated[1] 5 out of 5 stars!]
- Bob's Blog: Articles, Videos, and the free *Blessings Co-Op* crowd-sourced experiment at https://clever2wise.com
- Podcasts on Podbean: https://bcochran52.podbean.com/
- On social media, search for #clever2wise
- Science journal writing: https://tinyurl.com/yc7mfa2s
- Dozens of computer technology patents[2]

Hyperdimensional You

Surfing the Shift Toward Mastery

Bob Cochran

Independently Published, 2023
ISBN: 979-8-218-19115-3

Cover art: *Leave the lights on*, by permission of Carla Linder

Dedication

*To courageous "red pill" people, wherever
and whenever they may be found.*

Disclaimer

The author is not a medical professional and does not diagnose, recommend, treat, heal, cure, or dispense medical advice. Readers should consult certified medical professionals before making any health-related decisions. The information in the book represents only the author's opinion as opposed to statements of fact. The author/publisher disclaims all responsibility for any and all liability, loss, or risk, personal or otherwise, incurred as a consequence, directly or indirectly, of the use and application of any of the contents of this book.

Table of Contents

Acknowledgments

This book would never have materialized without the support and inspiration of my amazing wife, family, friends, and social media encouragers. I'd like to specifically thank those who provided pivotal input and feedback, such as:

Yaana Allen, Gregg Braden, Lee Carroll, Penny Clement, Angela Cochran, Carolyn Cochran, Connie Cochran, Makayla Cochran, Roy Cochran, Rev. Deborah Phillips, Jeff Ferreira-Pro, Lee Harris, Elaine Laroa, Cynthia Sue Larson, Dr. Lisa Cochran-Navarra, Peggy Campbell Roberts, Rev. Janée Marth, Regina Meredith, Dr. Julia Mossbridge, Rev. Jamie Sanders, Dr. Zeus Yiamouyiannis, etc.

Since truly unique and new ideas are much rarer than one might think, I especially thank and acknowledge all the courageous Truth seekers and tellers, upon whose shoulders we all stand.

> *No matter how long you live, never cease to stand like curious children before the great mystery into which we were born.* —Albert Einstein

Introduction

In order to provide context for this book, I first need to provide a quick overview of myself and my prior book, *Emerging Imaginal You,* published in 2021. Having a grasp of the concepts of my first book (*rated five out of five stars*) allows one to jump right in at the current book's higher level. In order to facilitate this, some of the first book's "greatest hits" have been included and noted with a (📖) symbol in the essay title.

I'll first provide a glimpse into how I was maneuvered by life events from an initial position of viewing reality only through the limited, black-and-white lens of mainstream science to the more complete (full color) view of reality available at the *corner of science and spirituality.* Most of my writing occurs at that intersection.

> *The first gulp from the glass of natural sciences will make you*
> *an atheist, but at the bottom of the glass, God is waiting for you.*
> —Werner Heisenberg (quantum mechanics pioneer)

From the perspective of my logical, *left*-brain, science-type self, I'm a retired engineer and inventor after 42 years working with a prominent Silicon Valley technology giant. Much of that time was spent as an engineer and team leader in a computer research and development lab, where my name became associated with dozens of high-technology patents.

From the perspective of my *right*-brain self, I'm also a graduate of massage school, Reiki Master training, Quantum Touch energy training, and Bengston Energy training.

Although I once thought these very different parts of me would never meet, I ultimately combined my left-brain and right-brain skills, plus intuition, to conduct experiments. These experiments involved successfully accessing and altering the past[3], the future, and objects at a distance. My results were published[4] in the 2019 scientific journal *Syntropia* under the title: *Exploring Syntropic Intent Effects across Nonlocal Time.*

You may have noticed that science-only types occasionally find themselves becoming more spiritual—that is, suddenly living at the intersection of science and spirituality. This is often due more to undeniable experiences than any life plan. What this book details is a similar transformation in my life, which has made it increasingly obvious to me that an accurate scientific view of reality must consider what can be learned (and unlearned) from spiritual inquiry, which is the ancestor of scientific inquiry.

The trick is to unknow long enough to clearly perceive*.

I was pretty much a science-only person until age 16, when my grandma appeared to me as a sparkling energy cloud, moments after her death nearly a thousand miles away. My takeaway from this experience was that *we are indestructible energy with temporary access to an avatar body*—an eternal mind with temporary access to a transducer brain.

The brain is to consciousness what a TV is to a TV station. The death of the TV has no impact on the TV station other than having one less vehicle of expression.

I couldn't help but wonder why science had so poorly prepared me for this conclusion. Later in life, my *remote viewing* and remote Reiki experiences involved many instances of data collection and energy delivery at great distances, apparently by way of energetic (quantum) entanglement. My takeaways from these experiences were that distance is an illusion within our holographic universe,

---

* Epigraphs between horizontal lines, with no source cited, are the author's.

and people heal themselves but may benefit from being offered supplemental energy with a wellness template. Again, I was perplexed as to why mainstream science had so poorly prepared me for this realization.

I've had compelling experiences with hyperdimensional (hyper-D for short) beings in various forms, including individual and group experiences with one particular being I can only describe[5] as an angel. My takeaways from these types of experiences have been that *we constantly share the space around us with hyper-D realms and beings* (mostly unseen, as confirmed in a CIA document[6]). Again, I was perplexed as to why mainstream science had so poorly prepared me for this.

> *The world of spirit has been painted as a foreign world, which couldn't be further from the truth. Humans are walking through it every single day.* —The Z's

You may have heard the term "bilocation," as in being in two places at once. Friends and family have told me on at least three occasions that a convincing facsimile of me interacted with them in one location while I slept in another location. Just like we often don't remember dreams, I don't remember these interactions. That said, these were all significant people in my life, and I may well have been concerned about them as I fell asleep.

> *There are multiples of you in different places.* —Kryon[7]

On one of those occasions, my physical body was asleep on an airplane in the process of flying between states. This didn't seem to deter my astral body from traveling many miles to intervene in a heated argument my daughter was having with her spouse. My takeaways from these experiences are that *emotion plus focused intent* can sometimes alter what we think of as the "normal" laws of physics. Again, science had not prepared me for this.

> *When the vibration of desire supersedes the vibration*
> *of doubt, BAM! IT HAPPENS!* —Abraham[8]

I once participated in a group that traveled to Egypt to meditate for peace in the Middle East. On a Friday afternoon, we were allowed private access to both the queen's and king's chambers, deep within the great pyramid[9] on the Giza plateau. Our only sources of light were small tea candles.

Within the king's chamber is a so-called *sarcophagus*[10] that countless people have laid in, including Napoleon and Alexander the Great. After taking my turn lying in it, I sat down by the far wall to begin meditating for peace. I was amazed to notice (as I looked down) that I could see clouds and stars in the night sky, all the way through the planet! My takeaway from this experience was that things are not nearly as solid as they appear and that (as documented by Dr. William Tiller), once a space is charged by meditation and intent, that which normally *can't* take place *may* take place. Again, science had not adequately prepared me for this.

> *Humans will increasingly walk with one foot in hyper-D. Beyond the mindless charging of a space by a group, group intent will personalize the energy of a space. Previously unsolvable or unhealable things will be solved and healed.* —Kryon

Regarding science, I'd like to make it clear that I'm a <u>big</u> fan when it lives up to its promise. Unfortunately, science all too often seems to lose its courage and integrity when it ignores findings that might impact special interests or contradict well-entrenched dogma.

> *If you think science is advancing…it's only…mundane science that doesn't upset anyone too much. The game changers must wait for an entire fearful generation or two to pass away before being accepted.* —Adapted from Max Planck (originator of quantum theory)

In *real* science, when the prevailing theory can't explain unexpected and inconvenient data, instead of discounting the data, we improve the theory.

One concept I refer to in this book is that of the "red pill" vs. the "blue pill." If you recall the 1999 film "The Matrix," Morpheus offers Neo a choice of a blue pill or a red pill. If he had chosen the blue pill, he would have been returned to his former life to rejoin the sleep-walking masses, insulated from (capital T) True reality. This would have been a choice of convenience over Truth.

> *In the long run, the most unpleasant truth is a safer companion than a pleasant falsehood.* —Theodore Roosevelt

On the other hand, choosing the red pill meant choosing Truth over convenience. Quite simply, my writing is for red pill people and calls for blue pill science to be upgraded to red pill science. For those who think today's science is obviously superior to and separate from spirituality, let's look at the lineage that birthed science:

Spirituality: *For tens[11] of thousands of years, the continued pursuit of deeper and deeper understanding about higher and higher truths by way of contemplation and experiment*

Science: *For ~300 years, the continued pursuit of deeper and deeper understanding about higher and higher truths by way of contemplation and experiment*

Comparing science and spirituality in this way, it's apparent that the two have more in common than most would admit, with the differences sometimes coming down to semantics. For instance, a scientist may say they believe in hyper-D places and things but are not the slightest bit spiritual. On the other hand, a spiritual person, believing in hyper-D places, things, and sentience, may say, "Keep going; you're more spiritual than you know!"

> *The notion that science and spirituality are somehow mutually exclusive does a disservice to both.* —Carl Sagan

As it turns out, their similarities make sense. *Spiritual inquiry* birthed *philosophy*, which birthed *natural philosophy*, which birthed *science*. In truth, scientific inquiry (as the great-grandchild of spiritual inquiry) shares a lot of common "DNA" with its ancestor.

What is spirituality? Have you ever been so engrossed in the sights, sounds, and emotions of a movie that you temporarily forgot you were in a theater? If a movie engaged <u>all</u> the senses, plus emotion and thought, most could become lost in that movie for life. This is a metaphor for the "blue pill" world in which most reside. The universe shakes some, until they again notice the theater and screen, remembering that they are so much more than the movie. This is "red pill" territory and the path to spirituality.

In fact, science may have much to learn from spirituality since, as the mother of inquiry and discovery, spirituality had an enormous head start.

Spiritual experiences such as those I've described are not uncommon, so even though they contradict mainstream scientific dogma, the data leads where the data leads. As someone who's made a living with intuition, I don't make this prediction lightly when I say that extremely important breakthroughs will take place at the intersection of science and spirituality. This is one of the reasons why my writing often arises from that place.

The spiritual path leads from narratives to reality.

My first book was a 10-year labor of love, in combination with a hyper-D being I refer to as my *muse*. If you have any experience with a genuine muse, I'd have to offer both my congratulations and condolences. On the one hand, muses tend to deliver great ideas. On the other hand, muses prompt you until you put those ideas into action. If you've ever been relentlessly tapped on the leg or stared at by a pet before feeding time, you might get the general idea, especially if that pet started in on you 10 years before feeding time!

One concept I employed in approaching my first book was the notion of "If I could send a letter to my younger self, what would I say?" Although this might have started out as a literary device, I had enough success with altering the past that having that book delivered to my younger self shifted to a serious intent. I eventually stopped doubting that the book would be delivered to my younger self in *some* timeline. I just didn't know if that would include my current timeline.

As it turned out, within hours of hitting the "publish" button, I experienced noticeable upgrades and changes, as if I had begun my spiritual path years earlier. One change was to suddenly have a (new…old) memory of a book-sized parcel wrapped in brown paper on the walkway leading up to what used to be my front door. So, perhaps it was delivered!

We're all familiar with the notion of *causality,* when something in the future is believed to be caused by something in the past. Cutting-edge science is currently studying *retro*causality, where something in the past is caused by something in the future. Writing a book in my future that impacts the information and *energy* available to me in my past may be an example of retrocausality.

> *Thoughts alter the course of your future but also your past,*
> *in that (because all time is now) they can heal, reorganize,*
> *and rebalance past events.* —The Z's

Another concept in my first book was that of *stacked premises*. When a stage acrobat stacks chairs one on top of another and climbs to the top, how many of those chairs need to be faulty or non-load-bearing before the whole stack comes crashing down? Just one.

Your assumptions [premises and information sources] are your windows on the world. Scrub them off once in a while. —Isaac Asimov

As the older me eventually discovered, the younger me built his life around premises, on top of premises, that were not nearly as load-bearing as I thought. So, guess what? Pretty much every aspect of my life, when placed under sufficient strain, came crashing down.

> *It ain't what you don't know that gets you into trouble. It's what you know for sure that just ain't so.* —Josh Billings[12]

Another concept used in my first book was that of the process involved in a caterpillar becoming a butterfly. Everything *seems* fine for the caterpillar until it turns into *goo*, where it might feel its entire world is ending. Perhaps only its imaginal cells know that the caterpillar's world is being dissolved as part of a grander plan so a butterfly can emerge. This is why my first book was titled "Emerging Imaginal You."

For anyone, such as myself, who's come through what is often called "the dark night of the soul," the butterfly metaphor may seem all too familiar. In fact, the whole point of writing my first book was so it could be delivered to my (decades younger) mid-30s self just prior to *my* dark night of the soul, where pretty much everything in my tidy and well-constructed world dissolved around me.

What made me think it reasonable and logical that my first book could be delivered back in time to my younger self? Even if the invention of time travel takes another 10,000 years, you can bet that time-traveling historians and tourists will be visiting times and places of interest during our lifetime. So, to whomever apparently left that parcel containing my first book (from the *future*) on my front walkway in the past—*thanks!*

Although my first book was intended for an audience of one (the younger me), it was also written in a way that could bring benefit to just about anyone of the red pill variety. In the first section of that book, called "Deconstruction – Welcome to the Goo," I identify my 16-level stack of foundational life premises and then use logic to test each of them for their ability to hold up under load. As it turned out, few did.

Although your premise stack might differ slightly, if you take the trouble to go through a similar exercise, you're likely to reach similar conclusions. Since these foundational life premises hold each other up, like the stacked floors of a parking garage, how many do you think must be faulty before you'll eventually have a big problem? Just one, any one! Thus, you can be forced to replace the faulty ones in the middle of a major life crisis (like me), or you can do it at your leisure. Having tried the first way, I don't recommend it.

This leads to the next section, where I moved from "Welcome to the Goo" to "Rebuilding for what's true," where improved, load-worthy premises were substituted for the flawed ones.

The first step to growing what you know is to grow your "I don't know."

That led to the next butterfly-themed section, called "Building Flight Muscles," where I laid the foundation for a more sustainable, reality-based life lived at the intersection of science and spirituality. An important concept I referred to in that book is that of self-sovereignty. A self-sovereign requires nobody's permission to notice the extent to which their mind has been "hacked" by (often well-intentioned) hand-me-down *controlled narratives* and pseudo-truths. This is viewed by some as the first step to enlightenment.

Controlled narratives should be approached like kitchen knives, since they're capable of great good, great harm, and everything in between.

Correcting the situation involves prioritizing Truth over narrative by way of research and intuition. A self-sovereign may also make use of

15

unseen, universally available information and energy sources that most leave untapped, such as in the *quantum field*. This led to the last two sections, called "A Self-sovereign IS" and "A Self-sovereign DOES."

Toward the end, I used an ice hockey term, "skate to the puck," regarding how a self-sovereign may correctly anticipate coming societal changes. That term refers to the difference between *good* ice hockey players, who skate to where the puck seems to be going, and *great* players, who intuitively skate to where the puck is actually headed. I invoke that metaphor regarding an approaching societal *wave* called "The Shift."

> *Shift: What happens when what society*
> *is convinced of encounters what's True.*

As with any wave, those who align with it have the opportunity to *surf* it, while those who ignore it are likely to be destabilized by it. The multi-generational wave that's building right now involves a *new normal* for integrity, transparency[13], fairness, tolerance, compassion, and cooperation. In short, our win-lose (survival mode) paradigm, based on fear-based controlled narratives, will increasingly give way to a win-win (beyond survival mode) paradigm based on Truth.

Old thinking often assumes we must choose between compassion for others and our own survival. *New* thinking realizes that compassion for others may be the best way to ensure one's own survival. In the old, win-lose energy, every thought and action had to be weighed against survival within a false context of separateness, or, "What thought or action most facilitates my continued, separate existence?"

> *We are here to awaken from the illusion of*
> *our separateness.* —Thich Nhat Hanh

In the new, *beyond survival* mode, win-win energy, we increasingly realize that we're unharmable consciousness, so our continued existence and oneness are a given. Hence, every thought and action can be weighed against: "What thought or action most facilitates staying in peaceful *balance* and allows the highest or best outcome for this body and planet?"

> *Balance is the key for guiding this new*
> *consciousness into the future.* —Onyah[14]

Changing to a win-win mindset, one person at a time, is how personal and global conflict and drama will become rarer.

For those looking for reasons to care, this is how we make war obsolete. Another reason to care is that the shift may impact those invested in or employed by segments of society that rely on the *old normal*. Those who are impacted while ignoring the shift may be in for an unnecessarily rough ride. Another reason is that when we individually reach a point where unkindness to others hurts our hearts, we become more kind, if only out of self-interest. Enough of us reaching that point will change the world.

After millennia of existing in the old, dark energy, the balance has finally shifted from *light workers* having to buck a strong wind of darkness toward an increasingly strong wind at our back. This is a game-changer. Those who first sense this shift can benefit the most from resetting their figurative sails, while those of compassionate consciousness increasingly gain control of the rudders of society.

This book, *Hyperdimensional You*, as the second in the *Emerging You* series, picks up where the first book left off. It reiterates some book-one themes around the increased <u>realization</u>[15] of universal Truth (bottom-left triangle below). Represented by the center triangle, we then move deeper into new themes, such as the increasing *shift* in the <u>availability</u> of universal Truth. Finally, the book moves into new themes[16] around our increased <u>utilization</u> of universal Truth (the bottom-right triangle) on the road to mastery.

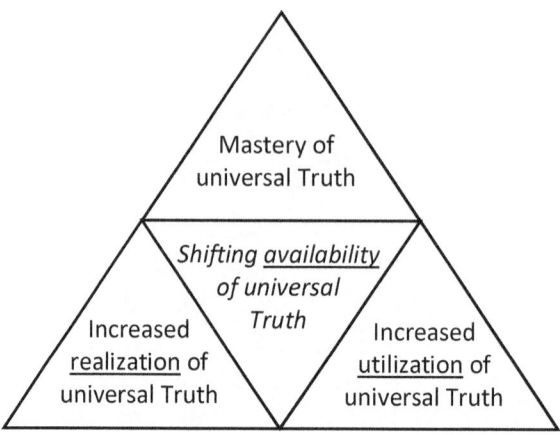

Stages in the Pursuit of Truth

In combination, we'll focus on how a hyper-D-aware, self-sovereign light worker may do better than just survive the shift at the trailhead toward mastery. This ongoing shift is from an old energy of *judgment,* escalation, and separation (which can devolve relationships) toward a new energy of discernment, compassion, and collaboration.

Judgment may be just an unproductive way of saying,
"I believe in your ability to aim higher."

It's a shift from centuries of tearing apart toward centuries of putting together to the point of lasting peace.

It's a shift from everything being about matter in a 4D world to everything being about (conscious) energy in a 4D+, or hyper-D, world. *Hyper-D* refers to that which goes beyond the typical four dimensions of height, width, depth, and linear time. As such, the multi-generational shift is *toward* hyper-D thinking and the out-of-the-box solutions that feel most right to those of a "higher vibration" consciousness.

I placed *higher vibration* in quotation marks in that its use, much like "increased light," "higher consciousness," or "quantum," although common in spiritual circles, may be more metaphorical than scientific. For instance, a vibration frequency measuring device would not necessarily tell us if we're more ascendant this year than last. Linear terms and measuring devices don't necessarily apply well to that which is nonlinear or hyper-D, such as spiritual progress. A more accurate metric may be where we currently are on the *amnesia-to-Truth* continuum.

That said, I may use such terms in the sense that they may connect the reader to contemporary concepts. For instance, I may use either *quantum, hyperdimensional, hyper-D,* or *broader-dimensional* in regards to leaning into higher or broader dimensions. Why do I mention *higher* and *broader* dimensions? The decision to add intuition to our linear left brain may be seen as a *broadening* of our 4D experience. At the same time, noticing or accepting the presence of a departed loved one may be an example of leaning into a *higher*-dimensional experience.

As with my first book, I'm requesting that this second installment be delivered to my younger self, backward in time. While this current book also has a target audience of one (younger me), others are cordially invited to follow along as I use short essays to document my journey on the path from *clever* to *wise*.

The clever answer questions, while the wise question answers.

As my writing may reflect, an essay may come *to me*, or *through me*, when I least expect it. Per Lee Harris, our unseen guides *surge* our energy when something should catch our attention. This causes things to selectively jump out or glow as I hear or read them. When this occurs, a "riff" on that which caught my attention often becomes a muse-inspired essay.

While I assume these unseen nudges are without flaw, I wish I could say the same for the writing that results. As I re-read some of my essays, sometimes I think, "I was really inspired." Other times, I can almost hear Paul Simon singing, "All my words come back to me in shades of mediocrity." Either way, I've done my very best to document my journey of discovery and very much appreciate your company along the way. According to James Redfield, writing a book involves sharing with the world a part of one's soul. With a choice of virtually countless books to spend time with, I'm very grateful that you've chosen mine. I genuinely hope it adds real and lasting value to your life.

In this second book, the journey begins at the point of individual spiritual emergence and continues from there. Given the short essay format, some themes may be repeated so that each essay can better stand alone.

This book lends itself to a multidimensional reading approach, such as a "read a few essays, put the book down, and think about it" approach or even an "open to a random page" approach, as well as the traditional "read it front to back" approach. It's said that a book is a friend that stays quiet while you think. It is my hope that this particular book will become one of your most valued friends.

Let's begin!

Context for a New Normal

There is magic occurring, a shifting of the light, as the dreamers awaken, and the lovers unite. —Creig Crippen

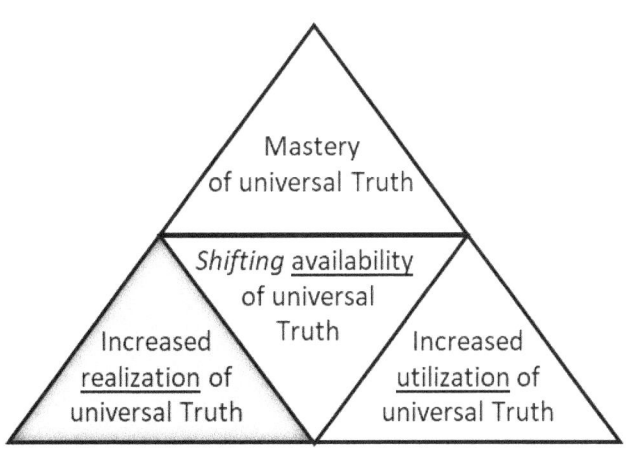

*The world is shifting toward hyper-D.
Welcome to the transition team!*

Ch. 1: Players in the game of life

Whether one consults ancient Toltec, Mayan, Aztec, Egyptian, or Native American wisdom, a common prophetic theme involves humanity greatly changing in one of two ways. One way was for humanity to terminate itself prior to December 2012. While astronomers called that date the midpoint of a ~26,000-year Earth wobble called the *Precession of the Equinoxes*, ancient cultures may have referred to it as the transition midpoint from one *Great Year* to the next.

Since we've survived past that critical point, the alternate way for humanity to greatly change, per ancient prophecies, is now in effect. That way involves a slow, yet inevitable (two steps forward, one step back) dance in the direction of planetary ascension. The most common term for this change is simply "the shift." That is, a shift from millennia of human *competition*, rooted in a false, fear-based notion of separateness, to millennia of increased *compassion*, rooted in empathy, love, and the truth of our oneness.

> *Move through these changing times…be easy on yourself and one another…learning a new way…voyage deeper into yourself… As yang-based habits and decaying institutions… begin to crumble…Feel the sun on your wings.* —Council of 13 Indigenous Grandmothers

If the first line of this next quote approximates where we're collectively coming *from,* the second line approximates where we're collectively shifting *toward.*

> *Jealousy says, "Compete." Envy says, "Destroy."*
> *Empathy says, "Help," Love says, "Empower."*
> —Matshona Dhliwayo

At some point, even the approaching era of compassion will eventually become our "from" as we move toward an even more enlightened era of *mastery*. As evidenced by masters that lived thousands of years ago, every era has some fraction of the population that's way ahead of the crowd. However, in contrast to the historical pattern of those who are ahead of their time having a *rough* road, leaning into the coming era of compassion may provide the *smoothest* road through the long arc of the shift.

Society's long arc toward oneness will reportedly[17] involve an upward shift in human nature, an upward shift in the vibratory rate of human consciousness, and an upward shift in how many dimensions the average person perceives as relevant. This shift will likely be so significant that historians will one day separate those of our current day into two camps:

- The larger camp of those believing four dimensions to be all there is—within a context of separation (the 4D camp)
- The smaller camp of those who realize we live in many more than four dimensions—within the context of an entangled, unified, spiritual universe (the hyper-D camp)

The 4D, non-spiritual camp, may become known for their non-lucidity within the illusion of being awake. They will be known for their blue pill[18], fear-based outlook that tends to show up in "us vs. them," "win-lose," and "as long as I get mine" ways—ways that often embrace controlled narratives to prioritize winning over truth. Those who've seen no reason to grow beyond this paradigm may become increasingly *confused* and disturbed as we move ever deeper into the shift.

Be confused, it's where you begin to learn new things. —S.C. Lourie

On the other hand, the hyper-D, spiritual camp may be known by our future for sufficient lucidity to not be taken in by the illusion of being awake—known for their red-pill, love/oneness outlook that may show up in win-win ways that seek (despite ubiquitous fear-inducing *media*) to prioritize and maintain balance and a high personal vibration.

Start to be far more selective about what you will or won't watch… Anything can move you {vibrationally} from one point to another…get adept at noticing. —The Z's

Hyper-D people who've already spent years getting comfortable with the shift, besides being ideally positioned to navigate it with grace and ease, may now be positioned to go even further ahead of the curve as they lean toward mastery.

Some of my hyper-D experiences were detailed in my prior book. For instance, I've experimented with altering the past (*retrocausality*), the future (*causality*), and objects at a distance (*remote causality via quantum entanglement*). These experiments, which I considered to be successful, were documented in a scientific journal[19]. In addition, I've been seen in two places at once on multiple occasions. While this type of thing may seem unusual to those steeped in the old energy of our past, the new energy of our future will find such things to be more common.

My first book focused on why the 4D world will be increasingly unsustainable and how to lean into where the world is headed. This current book picks up midway into the first book before diving deeper into both hyper-D territory and *Leaning Toward Mastery* territory.

This first section explores the "Increased realization of universal Truth" triangle by starting from a context of scientific and spiritual basics. The second section highlights the "Shifting availability of universal Truth" (as part of the shift) triangle. The third section focuses on leaning into mastery. That is, the "Increased utilization of universal Truth."

Mammal-human 📖

Although there are many models for how humans can be sorted into categories, I have simplified it to three types: *mammal*-humans, *clever*-humans, and *wise*-humans.

Of the three, mammal-human is the least evolved. Other than a few isolated pockets, this has not been the predominant type of human for a long time. This group's worldview tends to lean toward survival amidst separation via unquestioned loyalty to some alpha leader. How many mammal behaviors could one spot in daily life that might also be found in a pack of dogs? Surprisingly, quite a few.

- Striving to be the top dog
- Courtship and attacking those who would take our mate or resources
- Picking on those who seem different
- Seeking power and control, or making war
- Wanting to be accepted by the group
- Might makes right

The list could go on and on. The point is not that mammal behavior is necessarily bad, but that it's a part of us. That said, most of us have the choice to either consciously live from the place of our inner mammal-human or rise above it. Given the type of weapons available today, acting at this level could cause humanity to go extinct. While mammal-humans may have accounted for most of humanity thousands of years ago, individuals whose actions are controlled by strict allegiance to a gang leader are getting harder to find outside of prisons, cults, and perhaps politics.

Clever-human 📖

One layer up from mammal-humans, on the scale of increasing levels of order and functionality, are *clever*-humans. Clever-humans represent most of humanity today. This group's views tend to concentrate on how to maximize self and family interests, often within a context of win-lose separation. The attributes of the less developed *mammal*-human are still enfolded within and are always accessible to clever-humans when they are emotionally triggered or afraid.

Clever-human represents the highest level one can attain by utilizing the logical left brain, and instinct alone. In Eastern terms, this is indicative of having only chakras one, two, and three (out of seven+) active. Albert Einstein[20] (in his early years) and Sigmund Freud might be considered examples of clever-humans.

Wise-human 📖

A *wise*-human infers perceiving and making decisions with a synergized heart-brain complex in a way that becomes possible when the fourth chakra (heart energy center) is functional. Max Planck, Carl Jung, and Nelson Mandela might be considered wise-humans.

To adapt a saying from Dr. James Doty, the brain knows a lot, but the synergistic heart-brain combination knows much more. This is why the wise-human should be consulted as mankind's best hope for survival. In addition to logic, he or she often benefits from reliable intuition or inspiration by way of chakras four through seven (plus).

> *Those with the internal stillness to hear inspiration often speak when spoken through.*

Wise-humans currently represent only a small fraction of humanity. That said, it's an increasing fraction, which others would be *clever* to consult. This group's worldview often focuses on how to optimize for interconnectedness, global survival, and win-win outcomes.

Imagine a fishing boat with a steering wheel on each of the three deck levels. When most fearful about the weather, one might steer from the lowest-level wheelhouse that's most protected but has the poorest visibility. This corresponds to having fewer intuitive senses available when fear has caused wise-humans to retreat all the way to the level of mammal-humans.

Ironically, due to poor visibility, we often make ourselves most vulnerable when we think we're most protected. This fact is not lost on those whose agendas are furthered by our fear. How much extra fear do controlling interests need to sprinkle on the news in order to keep most of us hunkered down in our lowest, least intuitive, and most vulnerable wheelhouse? It seems like surprisingly little, especially when applied consistently.

> *This is the reclamation age...first reclaim yourself [self-sovereignty], then collectively reclaim your planet from the controlling few.* — The Z's

At the other extreme, when least fearful about the weather or when courage has compensated, one could steer their boat from the highest-level wheelhouse that's least protected from the weather but with the best visibility, making it ironically the safest. This corresponds to having the courage to not retreat out of fear and prioritizing emotional balance in order to keep intuitive senses online and available.

Wise-humans could more accurately be called *mammal-clever-wise-humans*[21] because, depending on the level of fear or courage in any given moment, they can easily find themselves on the slippery slope to thinking or acting at one of the lower levels. Ideally, this is a temporary condition in that wise-humans have the best tools for recognizing and correcting many situations.

Inter-human communication 📖

While communication and understanding may readily propagate in an upward direction, propagation may not occur in a downward direction. This hurts us as a society. It's like a wise-human is communicating in the language of calculus. That is, a type of math that neither clever-humans nor mammal-humans understand or appreciate, even though it will solve a problem more efficiently and with fewer undesirable side effects.

At the same time, it's like clever-humans are communicating in the language of algebra, which wise-humans understand but mammal-humans do not. Consequently, the lower levels of humans might only implement a solution from a higher-level human if there was a strong sense of blind respect and trust, which our current culture makes unlikely. The tragic result is that while the solutions to world problems generated by wise-humans are most likely to work while creating a minimum of new problems, the masses aren't likely to seek out, appreciate, or trust those solutions.

> *The thing about smart people is that they seem like crazy people to dumb people.* —Stephen Hawking

Hence, creating a shift in our culture to honor the advice of the wise and spiritual while encouraging people (especially leaders) to lean into their higher nature might be the change that makes all the difference.

We are easily programmed 📖

Author and speaker Gregg Levoy writes[22] of being in a college psychology class where the students secretly decided to use what they had learned to experiment on their teacher. Although their professor's normal lecture style involved evenly pacing left and right across the full expanse of a lecture hall stage, the students secretly agreed to subtly act *less* interested when their professor paced to their left and *more* interested when their professor paced to their right.

By the end of a single 50-minute class, the professor was virtually glued to the far-right wall. This happened without the professor being aware that he was being subconsciously programmed to alter not only his behavior but perhaps also his *beliefs* about what holds the attention of a classroom. In a similar way, we, without being aware, are *subconsciously* programmed with preferences, premises, and beliefs from the day we're born.

> *At the core of all well-founded belief lies belief*
> *that is unfounded.* —Ludwig Wittgenstein

This programming from family and institutions covers all aspects of life, including what's acceptable, what's desirable, and what's thought to be true. Prior to this programming, people around the world tend to be similar. After programming, differences arise not so much between people as between the incompatible controlled narratives that have been instilled within them.

> *It's not a question of whether your mind is being controlled; it's*
> *only a question of who, at the moment, is doing the controlling.*

A *controlled narrative* (as opposed to Truth) is a story told from an agenda-serving angle. We all operate from underlying premises, preconceived notions, and assumptions. History has shown that while some of our underlying premises will still be seen as true far into the future, the vast majority will (sooner or later) be known as false. It was not long ago that any *rational* person knew (falsely) that the sun orbited around a flat Earth, man could not possibly travel any faster than a horse could run, and bloodletting was the way to treat most ailments.

The premises that drive our decisions and actions are largely taught to us by well-meaning others. Whether family, teachers, or other trusted figures, they're the proverbial *man-in-the-middle* between Truth and us. These premises are *precarious* in that, though we tend to act as if they're unassailable, the future will not be kind to most of them. The context provided by our precarious premises influences how we perceive, experience, and interact with the world and the rate of our personal and collective growth. In fact, to understand the underlying premises of any person, society, religion, government, or business is to understand much about what drives them, how they keep score, and how they're likely to show up in a given situation.

Our underlying premises (the "why?" behind our actions) tend to be piled in load-bearing stacks, like floors in a building or the many levels of a painter's scaffold on the outside of a building. Hence, if we examine and change *even one level* of our underlying "why?" premises, a complete reassessment of everything they support is required. For instance, is it your underlying premise that you are a body with temporary access to consciousness, or a consciousness with temporary access to a body?

The camp we belong to can hugely affect how we interact with others and our host planet. Ironically, people from these two camps often have diametrically opposed views when the final answer, as is so often the case, may come down to being more about *and* than *or*. Perhaps we're a cosmic consciousness with temporary use of a body, which comes equipped with some built-in body-centric consciousness? As is the case in so many disagreements, finding common ground may be facilitated by softening our entrenchment and adjusting our semantics.

Be the rare person whose "We disagree" doesn't translate to "You and I have been programmed with conflicting narratives."

Chakra power levels 📖

The Bible speaks of manna (nourishment) falling abundantly from the sky. One way to view manna is as a metaphor for how an intelligent universe is always offering energy and information to those who've positioned themselves to receive it.

Irony: We're manipulated via fear-inducing falsehoods into <u>not</u> accessing the very energy and information circuits that would allow us to spot fear-inducing falsehoods.

It's our birthright to tap into these various energies as sources of vital nourishment, energy, and information. This essay is about how to maximize available power and information by way of a fully activated and powered chakra (energy center) ensemble.

> *Everything is energy. Your thought begins it, your emotion amplifies it, and your action gives it momentum.* —Unknown

Why should we care about not forfeiting helpful energy and information? They are more than a birthright; they are key to success and growth in life. Although a fully actualized human avatar body has all chakras powered and activated, the vast majority of us have only two or three out of seven (plus) in full operation.

This level of disempowerment is least optimal for us while being most optimal for controllers and exploiters. Why might controlled narratives encourage us to be empowered just enough to be obedient workers but no more? While it's not news that some increase their relative power by disempowering others, it *may* be news that some employ this technique on a large scale. People with minimal personal power tend to live a *me*-centric life that (ironically) is in service to someone else's reason for being.

The diagram illustrates the minimal power connections that are activated for a disempowered person. At the opposite extreme, *fully* actualized humans, with access to maximum personal power connections, tend to lead a *we*-centric life—in service of their *own* reason for being while finding ways to be in service to others. Below, I will attempt to explain the usefulness of open and operational chakras by way of cellphone-like electronic circuit block diagrams.

The 2-chakra, *ungrounded*, *unpowered* human

A fully empowered individual (skipping ahead to Fig. 1.3) has a healthy relationship with fear while accessing much of the truth, sovereignty of mind, information, and personal power available to them. The multiple connections shown in Fig. 1.3 refer to the power and data available to that *cellphone* (person).

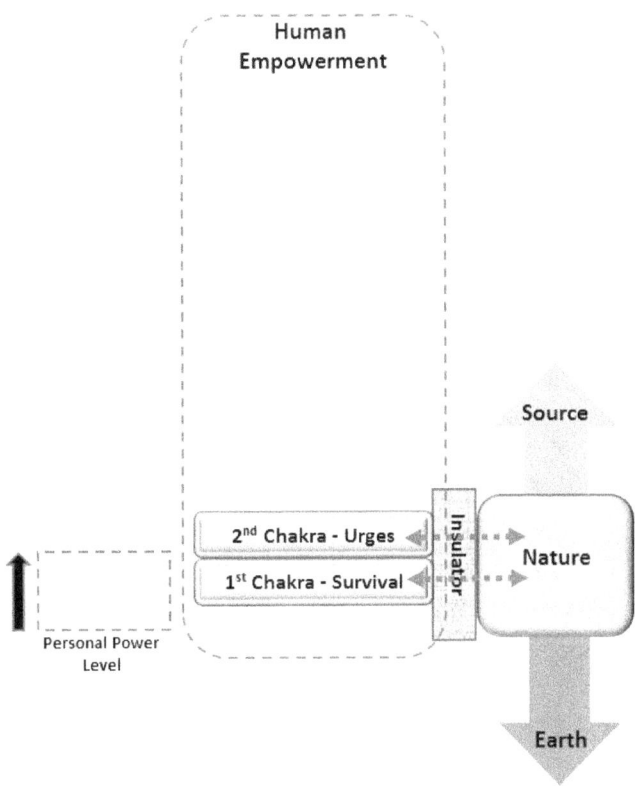

Figure 1.1: A human with only 2 of 7+ energy
centers operational (ungrounded).

The opposite extreme is illustrated in Figure 1.1, where the human energy system represented by the cellphone-shaped dotted line box is missing the top five of its potentially seven active and empowering chakra energy centers. The world of the *2-active-chakra* human tends to center around survival and urges. This disempowered and uninformed circuit diagram (person) unfortunately represents a good deal of Earth's current population. This type of human is maximally power and information handicapped because they're forfeiting several available information, power, and ground connections.

Sovereignty of mind: Without sufficient internal thought control to notice or filter outside thought control, sovereignty of mind at this stage tends to be minimal.

Personal power: These largely disempowered humans, as illustrated by the virtual zero reading on the personal power meter (bottom-left of Fig. 1.1), must settle for the *table scraps* of power and information they can derive from the Earth. They should prioritize walking barefoot on the grass until additional, higher chakra energy sources can be activated.

Fear control: Because the self-esteem chakra (not shown) is disabled, these people are more easily controlled by fear. Even though this level of human is about as far from ideal as one can get, this example (and the next) represent most humans—empowered just enough to be useful workers who don't ask too many questions. In contrast, an ideal human benefits from a dedicated connection to earth ground as well as multiple birthright power and information chakra connections.

The *3-chakra*, ungrounded, partially powered human

At this level of development, the top 4 traditional chakra levels (not shown in Fig. 1.2) remain disabled. The *thought cloud* indicates that these people have the first inklings of sovereignty of mind in that their preponderance of thoughts is self-controlled enough to activate the "on" switch to enable a single, modest connection to birthright Source power and information. This may be indicative of someone making early attempts at clearing system-clogging emotional baggage.

Unlike the *In the Now* and *Attitude* life force valves (described later), which change in small increments with each passing thought, the switches shown in this and the next diagram are more solidly *on or off* based on the vibratory level of our preponderance of thoughts.

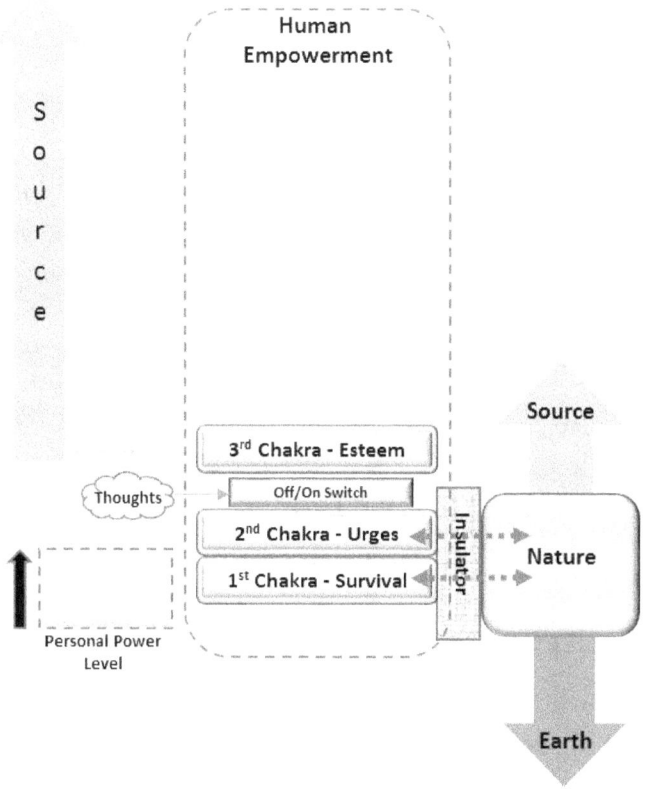

Figure 1.2: A human with 3 of 7+ energy
centers operational (ungrounded).

This level allows the 3rd (self-esteem) chakra to become intermittently powered by way of an independent connection to universal Source power, as shown by the dotted line. Getting access to a higher level of power and information can be a game-changer.

Sovereignty of mind: This person's worldview tends to rest upon premises that are largely pre-decided by others. Internal thoughts may be only sporadically monitored and controlled.

Personal power: Although these people are still missing a dedicated connection to earth ground, they enjoy a sporadic connection to Source power by way of a straw-thin power and data pipe. By "data," I mean these people may receive sporadic gut instinct (3rd chakra) intuitive information. Notice the minimal reading on the cumulative personal power meter in Figure 1.2.

Fear control: These people are often controlled by their fears. Although this common human level leaves massive amounts of power and intuition untapped, this still marks an important first step toward self-empowerment.

Examples: This level of human empowerment is typical of *average* employees and lower levels of management.

> [*Note: For descriptions of those with 4, 5, and 6 active chakras and four other (very important) on/off switches, controlled by our preponderance of thought, consult the first book in this series.*]

The *7-chakra*, grounded, *multi*-powered human

Jumping way ahead, the people illustrated in Figure 1.3 have access to virtually all the conventional[23] circuits, all the power, and all the quantum field (and unseen guide) data available. They possess sufficient sovereignty of mind to have consistently constructive thoughts such as "I trust my intuitive inner knowing," although fully owning and internalizing these words may take some time.

Activating the 7th (intuitive knowing) chakra often involves the courageous process of owning that *we know what we know*, even if we can't explain how we know. At this level, virtually all engine *cylinders are firing*, so to speak, with access to the accumulated power of all five, increasingly thicker lines, each capable of carrying more Source power and data. By "data," I mean that in addition to gut instinct, heart, hearing intuition, and seeing intuition, these people may be capable of claircognizance, or *knowing abilities* beyond what the brain could possibly know.

Whether it's intuition, the "Clair" senses, guidance, remote viewing, or channeling, much of what comes through our imagination is more than just our imagination… until our imagination distorts it. #The_First_Hit_Is_The_Best_Hit

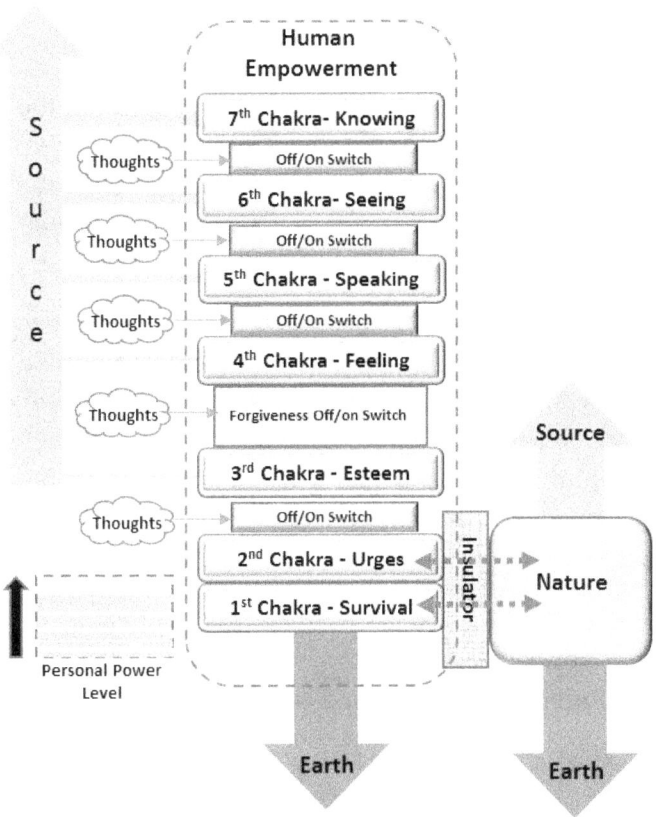

Figure 1.3: A human with 7 of the 7+ energy centers operational (grounded).

As a job and survival advantage, this is the birthright-owning situation for which we should strive.

Personal power: The enviably high reading on the cumulative personal power meter of Figure 1.3 can likely be further increased by way of meditation, etc.

Fear control: This person's Truth-sensing gut, heart, hearing intuition, and knowing intuition are often able to identify the falseness of many (if not most) fears and controlled narratives, offering a very significant career and evolutionary advantage. Having seven (or more) chakra sensors online can make all the difference in potentially dangerous situations. For instance, should I walk down this street or that one?

When my brother Roy was a U.S. Marine, on patrol in the jungles of Vietnam, he became known as an intuitive who knew when something didn't feel right. He could energetically sense the air displacement of approaching bullets before they could be heard, seen or felt.

If you recall the mass sniper shooting at an outdoor music concert in Las Vegas, my friend was centered in the massive crowd when the shooting began. Her fully activated chakra sensors allowed her emergency 360-degree perception to see, in spite of the poor light, with a firm knowing as to which way was away from the sniper. An explicit inner voice ("Go left, go right, go faster, stop!") allowed her to lead some directly to safety, as others were shot within a few feet of her.

Examples: Prophets, consultants, and futurists, who sometimes just *know* how potentials are likely to turn out.

Takeaway: Putting in the effort to improve our birthright power and data connections can be more than worth the effort. It can provide a significant career and evolutionary advantage.

Ch. 2: Game pitfalls

If life is a video game, which *you* is you? 📖

If you've ever participated in a multi-player video game, how many times would you play the same game—hundreds of times? How often did you play the same game level over and over? As a player and observer, how much sleep would you lose over your video game avatar ending one particular incarnation and starting again? None.

There are no victims in this scenario. There is only you as a semi-distant *neutral observer* playing a multi-incarnation long game, perhaps sacrificing short term goals or even lives in order to figure out the game well enough to accomplish a longer-arc goal.

In other words, neutral observer "you" is *doing it to* virtual avatar "you," which is taking turns being the bad guy, the good guy, the perpetrator, and the *victim*—the one who "died" too soon and the one left behind to deal with it in a destructive or constructive way. What if this is a close metaphor[24] for our higher self (as an aspect of either our soul or our far future self[25]) observing and guiding our various Earth avatar incarnations?

Because our higher self may be simultaneously observing us in countless parallel (past, present, and future) timelines, it already has a pretty good idea regarding how we will likely use our free will to respond to specific positive or negative circumstances. Life can deliver crushing blows. In my experience, those who embrace the video game metaphor (and the view that everything that touches our lives is handpicked by our higher self) have access to something akin to a *suffering volume control.* Such a volume control can theoretically (when necessary and appropriate) allow us to adopt the perspective of a semi-distant neutral observer[26].

Perhaps the super-conscious, higher self, or soul part of you wants to experience something that the conscious part of you would never choose in a million years. What the conscious mind wants (like healing), either our subconscious, our higher self, our ancestral programming, or our societal programming may veto. In a universe where the most dominant thought can alter quantum potentials, the strongest *intent* appears to win.

Windshield Wiper Wisdom: Our experience of what's happening on the outside can be modified from the inside.

Therefore, unless you want your life to appear like a boat without a rudder, developing sufficient sovereignty of mind to overcome those other factors may be well worth the effort.

Earth incarnation: the game 📖

Theories come and go, but we tend to believe what we've experienced. Most things mentioned in this book represent my direct personal experience. In the video game of life, you'd be surprised how much is determined by how well we maximize *potential* and minimize *pitfalls*.

This would apply equally whether we're temporarily directing the actions of a video game avatar, constructed of only energy and information, or whether (for the length of an incarnation) we're walking around in a human avatar (meat suit) body, ultimately constructed of only energy and information. That is, an energy being (soul) influencing the actions of a human avatar in a full-emersion virtual reality game we refer to as an Earth incarnation. If this is the case, a wise incarnated soul, like a wise video game player, would:

- Optimize their avatar's energy level—taking pains to keep their avatar's energy and vibratory level as high and balanced as possible. This is because it has a direct impact on our avatar's health as well as whether the avatar is up to challenges and opportunities, which impacts life's progress and destination.

- Optimize their access to useful intelligence and abilities.
- Avoid pitfalls and snares.
- Play the long, multi-life game, making every avatar life count toward figuring the game out while eliminating karmic[27] debt.

Like a video game, there are multiple ways in which we, in real life, can either take advantage of or forfeit vital energy units. Unfortunately, *Earth: The Game* will not tell us that:

There is a game. It will let us believe that before and after an incarnation in our avatar body, there is nothing. Those who believe this game-generated, controlled narrative are at a massive disadvantage.

Most enter the game as babies with amnesia. Known as "The Forgetting," controlled narratives within the game are designed to keep us from trusting our intuition enough to navigate our way out of the *forgetting*.

The game offers baited traps. Beyond obvious pitfalls and baited snares, many seemingly innocuous things within the game are weaponized. Since progress in the game often comes with the wisdom of age, unhealthy food, entertainment, and diversions, if not avoided, can cut our game (life) short.

We're not alone in the game. Invisible friends and foes (without amnesia and often from a different dimension) enter the game with us. The game will try to keep us at a low enough power and vibratory level that our intuition and subtle senses do not alert us to their potentially helpful or unhelpful presence.

The same loving heart, pure intent, and controlled thoughts (via sovereignty of mind) that may make unseen high-vibration beings notice us and want to assist tend to make unseen low-vibration beings want to stay away, which can be a game changer. On the other hand, fear, lower-nature thoughts, and poor thought control may cause unseen high-vibration beings to steer clear of us, while energy-sapping, trouble-causing, low-vibration unseen beings may notice and seek to exploit us.

> *Any time you are interacting with other dimensions,*
> *you are having an [ET] contact experience.* —The Z's

The game responds to our thoughts. Depending on our power and vibration level, the game responds to our thoughts with different levels of delay and fidelity. Early in the game, the delay is long enough and the fidelity of results is low enough that most miss the connection between thoughts and results. For those who've figured out the connection and have learned via sovereignty of mind to control their thoughts, the game may seem like their best friend. For those who've not yet figured out that their thoughts impact not just *how* they experience but *what* they experience, the game can seem like their worst enemy.

The game may lure us into mass hypnosis. The game may entice us (for an entire lifetime) to follow the (*blue pill*) sleepwalking crowd, largely experiencing only the first three chakras (survival, sex, and force) as a hollow substitute for true empowerment.

> *Whoever supplies [the masses] with illusions is their master; whoever*
> *attempts to destroy their illusions [is punished].* —Gustave Le Bon

All seems perfectly normal until we realize our life is nearly over, and somewhere along the line we were lulled into giving up the hero's quest that may have been our very reason for incarnating.

It's not enough to survive the game's polarity. This refers to good/bad, right/wrong, true/false, love/fear, male/female, etc. The quest is to avoid being lulled to sleep while working through the confusion brought about by those polarities so they may be transcended.

The game may misdirect, divide, and misinform. Since humans are more capable of helping each other awaken in groups, the game creates controlled narratives to *separate* and divide us. The game will use misdirection to keep us arguing as polarized groups over symptoms (the proverbial *shadows on the wall*), so we don't pay attention to the underlying causes.

> *Many truths were shielded inside religious constructs designed to keep you separate…less than…cloaking the truth…but truth is rising.* —The Z's

Arbitrary separators such as race, religion, politics, and wealth are prominent, with the most harmful separator being a belief in separation or the false notion of *other*.

> *There is no "other." There's only self and other-self[28]. Empathy and compassion (compass-action) are symptoms of being on course and living in the real world.*

The game may distract and disempower. The game distracts with controlled narratives that encourage constant busyness, so we won't have time to sit in silence long enough to have awakening realizations.

> *Irony: We don't have the time to demand Truth and fairness from those who distort Truth and fairness, so we don't have enough time.*

The game won't tell us how to progress. Finding our way out of the game starts with deciding to combine intuition with the noticing of details, from micro to macro. This leads to noticing the patterns and connections most people miss. This leads to confusion about why we see things differently. This leads to firsthand realizations, conclusions, and experiences most never have. This leads to the lightly traveled spiritual path toward the game's exit door.

> *More Spiritual than Religious: Possessing sufficient courage to give more weight to personal experience and intuition than hand-me-down narratives.*

The game won't help us activate vital information/energy circuits. Fully functional game avatars maximize their information and energy inputs by way of body energy centers, or chakras. In that these are key to making progress, the game may try to keep us from realizing that these circuits exist, from taking them seriously, or from activating them.

The game encourages us to downgrade our birthrights. The incarnation game is about originating from a place of Joy, Oneness, Love and Truth and embarking upon an *away mission* in which we find ourselves not only with amnesia, but subjected to constant programming that seems designed to throw us off the scent for finding our way back home.

Instead of *Joy*, we're programmed for somberness, as in, "How dare you smile when so much is wrong with this world?" Instead of *Oneness*, we're encouraged to participate in separation games such as competition and various forms of "As long as I get mine" warfare. We're encouraged to downgrade the quest for Oneness to a quest for "the one." We're encouraged to downgrade the quest for *Love* to a quest for self-gratification. We're encouraged to downgrade from head-*with*-heart to head *without* heart and from conscious self to self-conscious. We're encouraged to downgrade our quest for (capital-T) Truth to controlled narratives composed of pseudo-truths. We're encouraged by black-and-white linear thinking to forget our birthright of hyper-D thinking, sensing, and being.

> *Black and white views have taken us out of hyper-D thinking, sensing, being…your connection to other dimensions…scrubbed out of history… Higher dimensions are available to you. Evidence … is all around…* —The Z's

Those who find themselves on a spiritual path toward home are those who, like going lucid amidst a dream, have managed to shake themselves awake amidst society's constant programming. In steps, they first increasingly awaken, then increasingly pull back veils to expose light, then increasingly let that light in to become more enlightened. Such "lightworkers" are the trailblazers to our more ascended future.

Like houseplants, some of us are compelled to seek and grow toward the light. Others… not so much.

Entering the game 📖

Between incarnations, we understand our amazingness as unharmable energy beings interconnected within an aware, holographic universe. What happens during each amnesia-handicapped incarnation counts as a *visceral* experience through which our soul adds breadth to its academic knowledge.

Mystics and sages throughout time have suggested that Earth humans are a "veiled" species. That is, souls that volunteer to take part in the Earth human experiment, insert themselves into human mammal avatars and attempt to overcome countless handicaps designed to keep them from finding and staying on the path toward successfully completing and exiting the game.

Once the Earth game is entered, some say souls tend to be in it for the duration. For every lifetime in which we play the role of the figurative hammer, we may need to live other lifetimes in the role of the nail. *Historically*[29], these lifetimes were thought necessary to balance our karmic scorecard while coming to viscerally understand all sides of situations. Part of this game is realizing there *is* a game while overcoming obstacles and avoiding game pitfalls, snares, and slippery slopes.

In addition, what we seek within the game may elude us behind mismarked doors, with *peace and healing* behind the door marked "Forgiveness," *Truth* behind the door marked "Courage to Explore Alone," and *growth* behind the door marked "Discomfort."

A time-tested perspective on unseen agents 📖

Agents of the game come in many forms and have many agendas. Some are humans, some are not. Some are corporeal and visible, some are not. Some have amnesia regarding their true essence; some do not. Some are from our 4D time/space dimension, some are not.

Despite those variables, agents of the game tend to sort into a few general categories; they tend to interact with us in either a neutral fashion, a win-win fashion, or a win-lose fashion. That is, unseen beings may be classified as *observers, helpers, tricksters, exploiters,* or *predators*, much like 4D beings.

Saint Hildegard, a very intuitive and perceptive Benedictine abbess, came to similar conclusions about helpful and unhelpful unseen beings around 900 years ago, except her painting sorted our possible interactions into five categories (Fig. 2.1). She was recently named by Pope Benedict to be a *Doctor of the Universal Church*, a title given by the Catholic Church only to saints of special importance. This infers that the Pope agrees with her description of helpful and unhelpful unseen agent interactions, as described below.

As a visionary/intuitive mystic rebel, her pull-no-punches writings and paintings exposed unseen agents of the *game* that could either hold humans back, take part in a light-vs.-dark tug-of-war, or facilitate us in finding our upward path.

Regarding the three types of unseen agents she illustrates, I categorize them as lower astral, higher astral, and celestial beings. I recognize all three types from personal experience, not by appearance but by vibration level and motives.

Figure 2.1: St. Hildegard's astral/celestial agents of interaction[30]

Most beings, whether they know it or not, have the ability to utilize universal energy as their supplemental, if not sole, form of sustenance. This is why keeping our energy chakras closed or offline leaves enormous amounts of life-sustaining and life-improving energy (and information) on the table. To borrow a quote from Vivian in the movie *Pretty Woman*, "Big mistake. Big. Huge!"

As it turns out, the ability to access free universal energy applies not just to humans but also to higher astral and celestial beings. Because lower astral beings appear to be, by choice, cut off from sustaining universal energy, they may need to go elsewhere for energy sustenance. Unfortunately, elsewhere includes us. The energy they actively encourage in us as food is *fear*.

St. Hildegard's painting[31] (panels 1–5, bottom to top, Fig. 2.1) describes five categories of humans and how unseen agents (*within the confines of our free will and cosmic law*) may interact with each category of human.

At the bottom of the painting, St. Hildegard's humanity level one[32] is the lowest vibrational level of *free-range, imprisoned,* suffering humans. At this level, lower astral beings seem to have their (uncontested) way with humans, who seem completely controlled. Besides being unable to spot the manipulating, untrue, and fear-inducing controlled narratives artificially injected into their world, those at this level are more vulnerable to addictions in the form of grievances, bigotry, hate, substances, etc. A significant part of sleepwalking humanity still resides at this level—non-lucid within an endless work, eat, entertainment, and sleep cycle.

Since fear is a poor substitute for divine energy, lower astrals reportedly must continually encourage our fear, called *loosh,* as their energy food. Do we willingly participate and buy into their fear-inducing controlled narratives, thoughts, and media? For most of us, I'd have to respond with an emphatic… Yes.

Not only does fear lower our personal and collective vibration, keeping us away from much of the good that awaits, but it can also literally feed and strengthen unseen chaos agents. Hence, what we consider to be inconsequential lowbrow fear-based entertainment may be anything but inconsequential.

To humans of a higher vibration, it may seem obvious that any payoff we might receive from tolerating fear or seeking it out as entertainment is not worth the consequences of feeding unseen trans-dimensional chaos agents. For those of a lower vibration, this conclusion may seem nonsensical.

Are lower-vibration people interested in the higher-vibration advice that could greatly lessen their suffering? In my experience, no, in that this advice does not seem to make sense. Therefore, the best that people of higher vibration can do is raise their own vibration so that the metaphorical vibrational *tide* goes up, causing all *boats* to rise.

Many are here to hold, be, generate, and experience light…You don't have to be on the front line, or perfect. Those sitting in their house, meditating, expanding their heart, connecting with heart consciousness…emanating that, are changing the vibration of the planet. —The Z's

What percentage[33] of higher-vibration people could make a tide-raising difference? According to studies, something less than 1%[34] of the population is all it takes. All points in space and time are connected. Hence, everything done in the spirit of love sends a vibrational upgrade transmission everywhere and to every *when*. *Not* indulging in the constant supply of fear and outrage bait may allow a person's vibration level to migrate upwards.

In Saint Hildegard's human level *two*, lower astral beings are still completely uncontested as they have their way in causing suffering to humanity in their daily lives. This level of *free-range imprisoned* human is shown in something akin to a grape press, except what is being squeezed is humanity, and what is coming out is the fear (*loosh*) that lower astral beings reportedly utilize as food. That fear-food-inducing book, newspaper, TV show, or movie may be neither harmless nor without consequence. Combined, Hildegard's human levels one and two may loosely correlate with what I've described as *mammal*-human.

In Saint Hildegard's human level *three*, darker lower astral beings (left) are finally contested by lighter, higher astral beings (right) as they have a moment-to-moment, human thought by human thought, tug-of-war for each human that falls into that vibrational range. The lighter-colored, higher astrals seem especially able to assist when humans are focused on high-vibration thoughts or make a direct request for assistance.

A Native American Cherokee legend speaks of two wolves inside us that are always at odds. One is a white wolf, which represents higher nature aspects like kindness, bravery, and love. The other is a black wolf, representing lower-nature aspects like greed, hatred, and fear. The wolf that wins is the one we feed, moment to moment.

I once had a pleasant close encounter with what I took to be a higher astral being, whom I'll call the professor[35], that you would likely enjoy meeting. Years ago, I had a very physical and unpleasant encounter with what I took to be a barely visible lower astral[36] being, whom you would definitely not[37] enjoy meeting.

St. Hildegard's level *three* (loosely correlated with my previously described *clever*-human) is typical of white-collar professionals who are not particularly in touch with their heart or spiritual side. This is as high as the typical atheist, materialist, or reductionist is likely to ascend. Who wins the tug-of-war is determined moment by moment and thought by thought. This is not lost on the agents of the game, who are constantly finding ways to suggest how we should think.

> *Thoughts have power, so controlling our thoughts is a demonstration of power.*

Saint Hildegard's level *four* envisions the Holy Spirit as a green[38] energy curtain that appears to be restraining lower astral troublemakers. In my interpretation, the rainbow-type arch represents fountains of energy (perhaps free universal energy) that we're able to bathe in. At this level, humans are not only less *o-pressed* by fear but are also remotely guarded by what appears to be the wing of a huge, higher astral being. This is the typical vibrational level of non-atheist professionals, in touch with their heart and spiritual side.

This correlates with the beginnings of what I describe as a *wise-human*.

Saint Hildegard's level *five* human enjoys high-vibration sovereignty of mind by way of controlled, mindful *thoughts*, emotions, and responses. This is the typical vibrational level of a non-atheist, intuitive mystic in touch with a balanced male/female heart, mind, and spiritual side.

> *If technology allowed us to hire someone to control our thoughts, and you're pretty sure it would result in an improved life, why not up your own thought game?*

As shown, the darker lower astrals are still shooting arrows of potential trouble, suffering, and chaos, but the celestially maintained (warmed inner chamber) tent is protective and supportive for those who go *within*, as in meditation.

> *Things look up when we look in, because IN is the way out.*

One might draw a correlation between the protective tent and the aura that often shows up in humans of higher vibration. Again, the rippled curtain associated with the Holy Spirit is shown providing comfort as a warm robe and space heater. The tent within a tent, within an insulated room, may allude to the warm and protected inner chamber of meditation. Whether walking or sitting, meditation provides the career, evolutionary, and cosmic advantage of noticing and discerning what most miss, both within and without, revealing the true nature of people and things. Meditation in our daily lives can cause one to be the most intuitively awake, relaxed, and fearless person on the block.

What we might call "angels" may be the celestials shown helping. One I've met (and you would *like* to meet) I call *Myriad* (as in *many*), in that *she* did not seem inclined to be confined to a single name or concept. The combination of Saint Hildegard's human levels four and five may be loosely correlated with my previously described *wise*-human.

Now, let's identify some game pitfalls.

The "not here and now" addiction pitfall 📖

For every second our attention departs from the here and now, we forfeit a game advantage that comes from significant amounts of life force energy. Consequently, the game will supply endless inducements to *not* be in the here and now.

Traditionally, the most common and powerful (not here and now) addictions have been worries, regrets, and grievances. Like designer drugs, people lose decades ensnared in these addictions.

Recently, we've added another powerful, *not here or now,* pitfall in the form of video screen addiction, which already claims an average of ten hours[39] out of many Americans' days. Allowing video screens to reduce our attention span is more than just another game pitfall. Without a normal attention span, we have little hope of making progress in the research and intuitive introspection necessary to sort Truth from controlled narrative.

The "appeal to authority" fallacy pitfall 📖

Those who are innately susceptible to the *appeal to authority* fallacy[40] may automatically accept narratives from authority figures as Truth. No mind control needs to be applied to this segment of the population in that groupthink in the form of "If you tell me what to believe, I'll believe and defend it" appears wired into their makeup.

Somewhat related is the "you convinced me I was seeing it wrong, so you must be seeing it right" pitfall. Entire political parties and nations have experience with this one.

The normalized faux-truth pitfall 📖

Saying, "We've been conditioned by the game," doesn't sound too bad. It seems more serious when we substitute equivalent terms such as purposeful *conditioning* or mind control.

We've been conditioned to let slogans substitute for information, information substitute for knowledge, knowledge substitute for intuition, force substitute for power, and cleverness substitute for wisdom.

When I say our vulnerability to mind control is greater than most suspect, I'm specifically referring to people in the 20–50 year old range who, while having some level of sovereignty of mind, are still far more susceptible to mind control than they realize.

The TV show *Derren Brown: Mind Control*[41] features a mentalist who demonstrates the susceptibility of that age range. An internet video shows him playing his voice in a loop for thirty minutes over a shopping mall public address system. After a period of subliminal mind control programming that went largely unnoticed, he snapped his fingers and said, "Now!" over the sound system. To their bewilderment, a sea of strolling mall shoppers suddenly froze in place and held one arm up over their heads.

What was the mechanism that allowed all those unsuspecting mall shoppers to be pre-programmed and mind-controlled?

If you listen carefully to the words coming over the sound system, some words are out of place. This confused the subconscious of the shoppers to the point of, "I'm confused; just tell me what to do, and I'll do it," meaning that even though these people are not necessarily in the *appeal to authority* fallacy camp, they're suddenly unconsciously willing to execute whatever direction was offered.

This harmless example makes one wonder how advertisers and political types may be exploiting this human vulnerability in an equally real but more harmful way. It may be worth considering before casting our next vote or making our next impulse purchase!

If confusion is part of that type of mind control, can we find any examples of national events that seem specifically designed to confuse? Plenty. On alternating days, we may hear, "The media and government are trustworthy," "Neither are trustworthy," and "One is far more trustworthy."

Another common example may be when our intuition tells us a news report or a person's story is true, but someone in authority says it's false, or vice versa. It makes one wonder whether such things are random or purposefully engineered to cause confusion. When millions are subconsciously confused to the point of, "I'm confused; just tell me what to do," one can only guess what instructions may come next.

If every computer in the world (except yours) secretly had the same computer virus, everyone would be calling their computer *normal* and yours in need of being fixed. Hence, there may be no perception of anything being askew without an "outside the problem" point of view. In the same way, the ones most capable of perceiving how far society's norms have become distorted are those with an outside-the-*programming* vantage point that comes from combining low-brow media detox with intuition, research, and silent contemplation.

A properly kept silence is the father of very wise thoughts. —Diodicus

Right-brain intuition may be an essential tool for knowing the difference between controlled narratives and Truth. If we're not familiar with how to access our right brain to allow the experience of profoundly deep peace, joy, intuition, mental silence, and universal inter-connectedness, according to Dr. Jill Bolte Taylor, we've learned what we were taught. Self-sovereign individuals *re-mind* themselves to claim their full brain birthright.

Ten seconds of absolute quiet mind is more powerful than any actions you've ever offered, put together. The leverage of nonphysical is [so significant] like that. We suggest 15-20 minutes [of meditation] because it usually takes that long to get...that ten seconds. —Abraham

If we look into what we've been carefully taught, some things may dawn on us. For instance, the placebo effect may just be a way of tricking ourselves into overriding the part of us that's been carefully taught that we can't heal ourselves with the part of us that can. Science may eventually follow that thread to discover that the laws of physics are subordinate to the *law* of conscious intent, which is itself subordinate to the *law* of cosmic oneness.

Likewise, dowsing, tarot, and pendulums may just be ways of tricking ourselves into overriding the part of us that's been carefully taught about what we can't possibly know with the part of us that knows. Science will eventually follow that thread to discover that we are hyperdimensional.

The herd or nerd pitfall 📖

Humans are herd mammals, capable of being controlled and exploited as a group. No one needs to tell us that being in the herd is preferable to being an outsider. Watching how those in the herd *appear* to be rewarded by the game while those with the courage to stand outside the herd are punished is enough for most of us to come to the conscious or subconscious conclusion that thinking and acting independently as our authentic selves should be postponed, if not completely avoided.

> *The most courageous act is still to think*
> *for yourself. Aloud.* —Coco Chanel

We may use normalizing terms for herd behavior like fad, fit-in, consensus, movement, trend, groundswell, in-crowd, mob, or tribe, but they're still herd behavior. Those with the courage to stand outside the herd as free thinkers are often picked on by herd enforcers (bullies) and given labels like nerd, geek, and loser. Unless we understand these dynamics, we may not notice and resist the many herd-controlling pitfalls we may encounter on an average day.

Without deviation from the norm, progress isn't possible. —Frank Zappa

Herd membership involves forfeiting some free will, free thinking, individuality, and (likely) progress in the game for the *appearance* of group safety. Safety from what? Since we can find food and water on our own and are not on the Serengeti Plain being hunted by lions, herd membership ironically only protects us from herd enforcers, who somehow perceive our non-conformity as a threat. To put it more succinctly, we often fall into the game pitfall of joining the herd for protection *from* the herd. Rather than safety, we ironically end up vulnerable to group manipulation, along with reasons to postpone our solo hero's journey.

The "force versus power" pitfall 📖

Confusing force for power is like confusing cleverness for wisdom; one is a hollow imitation of the other. Growing up, my siblings and I recognized that our towering, imposing, sometimes scary father represented a lower-nature *force* in our home. On the other hand, our quiet, intuitive, loving, and healing mother represented higher nature *power*.

You need [force], only when you want to do something harmful, otherwise love is enough to get it done. —Charlie Chaplin

This is an example of a larger issue in that the game will try to trick people, especially men, into settling for (disempowered) *force* as a hollow substitute for our birthright of *power*.

The monetizing agent pitfall 📖

Many agents of the game employ an age-old technique I'll call "multi-touch monetizing." That is, first they extract money from us as we take some form of bait, and again later *because* we took that bait.

A win-win, non-weaponized example of multi-touch monetizing might be to extract money from those responding to an advertisement for a dental college and then extract money multiple times more as they need books, uniforms, equipment, insurance, etc.

One of the game's snares involves impacting our health, so we *check out* before we get old enough to figure things out. A win-lose, "It's not personal, it's just business" example of a weaponized snare is to monetize people as they ingest satisfying but unhealthy things into their bodies. The next step is to monetize the same people as they seek out businesses that cater to those who don't feel well or don't feel good about themselves.

Other examples of weaponized snares might include those who sell our media-watching *attention-seconds* to advertisers as we consume fear-enhanced news and then monetize us again as we support the industries and politicians that help us feel less afraid.

> *The day we require complete, unfiltered news is the day we realize how overwhelmingly neutral or good the news is and how much we've confused controlling narratives with being informed.*

Even if one catches on and avoids weaponized snares, to be resentful of agents of the game creating and profiting from such things is to fall into yet another snare. The low-vibration, low-energy snare of resentment exemplifies why compassion and forgiveness are important for self-care as well as for making progress toward exiting the game.

How could compassion and forgiveness apply here? The win-lose agents of the game are still on the low-compassion, low-vibration part of their long cosmic arc. Their actions, based on their stack of premises, will seem completely reasonable to them. Compassion and forgiveness are not about the ones our compassion and forgiveness are *supposedly* directed toward. It's about what will allow us to become energetically unhooked from them so we may progress in our version of the game.

I'd follow the lead of Toto from the film "The Wizard of Oz" when catching on to the wizard behind the curtain. Toto didn't confront or try to change the wizard; he simply pulled the curtain back. Likewise, this book seeks to pull back a few curtains.

The declined consciousness upgrade pitfall 📖

Although my friend and I own the same cellphone hardware, perhaps only one of us takes the time to download all the latest operating system (OS) software updates, making the capabilities and features of each cellphone *very* different. By analogy, my friend and I may have similar human avatar *hardware*, but only one of us pursues self-actualization, meditation, and enlightenment to access the latest human consciousness OS upgrades available for cosmic download. Consequently, humans end up with vastly different capabilities.

As part of the shift, it appears a conscious universe is making cosmic upgrade downloads available with exponentially increasing frequency, as if in hopes that humanity will progress in wisdom and stop harming our ecosystem. Available OS upgrades tend to be refused most often in order to minimize short-term discomfort. This is ironic in that ending up on the wrong side of change may result in long-term discomfort.

The twisted narrative pitfall

Part of the game involves noticing that many, if not most, of society's narratives have been twisted, somewhere between partially and completely upside down—twisted systematically by agents of the game. What if the actual "original sin" or evil was when agents of the game purposely twisted the universal oneness Truth of "All are interconnected and therefore equal" to "All are separate, isolated, and unequal?" According to Sean O'Laoire (Pd.D., an ordained Catholic priest), "sin" is an infraction of a culturally created precept, whereas "evil" is a cosmic conspiracy, utilizing human intermediaries, to separate souls from Source. By that definition, all that promotes separation (and its many children) might be in support of that original evil.

> *Isolation [separation] is a trick played on humans. Separation is a war against oneness. Humanity has been successfully confused...to isolate you in your own minds...separate from each other, creating fear. Fear is a human construct, present when [a false sense of] disconnection is* present. —The Z's

While I don't think the Z's (in the quote above) are saying that fear exists nowhere else in the universe, humans on Earth may experience an Earth-specific type of fear. If F.E.A.R. stands for *False Evidence Appearing Real*, the way to create an Earth-specific type of fear is to get Earth humans to buy into a specific form of false evidence. In this case, humans have been sold the false narrative of separation. Hence, the game, in a nutshell, may come down to a tug-of-war, with one side pulling us toward the constructive oneness Truth of our ascended future. Those pulling on the other end of the rope would (wittingly or unwittingly) pull us back by reinforcing the false, destructive separation narratives of our past.

> *Oneness is the highest octave, with components such as joy, bliss, love, and connection. This is the home to which you are constantly trying to*

return. Joy is five times more powerful than fear, yet fear is 5 times more sewn into your culture. When you buy into the separation/fear game, you forfeit your power—the lights go out. —The Z's

Don't be surprised if the game supplies the most prominent separation narratives by way of the organizations claiming to promote the opposite. For instance, separation narratives like *worship, prayer, intercession, and judgment* may all tug on the separation end of the rope. Rather than a traditional worship service, watch for people to increasingly seek out that which tugs on the Oneness end of the rope, such as a *Oneness Experience Service.*

Prayer to "other" can erode the soul. A false sense of separation is the cause of physical/emotional/mental disease. —The Z's

To the false narrative of separation, we complicitly applied the manifestation power of our divine free will, making separation-based fear seem extremely real. Having been duped into misusing our free will to cast a shadow over the light of universal oneness, we experience that shadow as fear. The more intensely we buy into the illusion of separation, the more intense the shadow and our fear. This tells us how to overcome fear. The more we, as individuals and as a planet, withdraw our divine free will from sustaining the false narrative of separation, the less intense Earth-specific fear will be, until it eventually vanishes.

The more real you get, the more unreal the world gets. —John Lennon

Why would agents of the game try to trick humanity? Earth is reportedly a contested planet that's been embroiled in an eons-long struggle between light and dark. If so, that original twisting of Truth may have been a weaponized narrative to keep us as disempowered, easily manipulated, free-range inmates. The seeds of that original upside-down narrative germinated into layers upon layers of twisted offspring narratives. Narratives that have normalized us living in our low empathy and compassion, judging, fearful, war-tolerating, lower mind—to what end?

> *Multidimensional beings are working with...Earth... Why? If it was full of open-hearted, connected people, it may be powerful enough to bring harmony to the entire universe. Hence, [separateness] seeds of war were purposely planted on Earth to jeopardize the balance of the entire universe.* —The Z's

How could buying into separateness destabilize our world? That original false notion spawned the false notion of scarcity, which spawned the false notion of competition in order to safeguard the false notion of our one and only incarnation. These ingredients influence the low self-esteem and disempowered masses.

> *Self-judgment was implanted to keep you small, as an energy that can cloud judgment, possibility, and potential. The more you excavate that energy, the more you allow the higher in.* —The Z's

Over the centuries, a system consisting of the disadvantaged masses serving the advantaged few became self-reinforcing. The advantaged few, either directly or indirectly, have historically neutralized those who would correct the twisted narratives that offer them an advantage. This practice persists to this very day. Countless false narratives have become so institutionally entrenched, normalized, and defended that the untwisted, truthful versions may sound unhinged to the masses.

> *When a society has been programmed to normalize insanity, the sanest might be found among those labeled otherwise.*

This is likely not an accident. Twisted-truth programming may have wrapped our internal "truth detectors" in sufficient subconscious foreboding that many will consciously respond to Truth by saying,

"That's baloney, and not for me," while subconsciously thinking, "Beware! Truth has been bad for my health in past lives."

However, to those living in their higher, empowered, high empathy and compassion minds, the falseness of many narratives (due to a lack of Truth resonance) is often obvious. As part of the shift, children are now coming in with increased awareness and Truth-seeking abilities. While these young people offer hope for our future, the pain caused by society's twisted narratives reportedly makes it difficult for some to stay. This may account, at least in part, for the dramatic increase in teen suicides in the last decade, especially among the indigenous community. Between the crucial ages of 14 and 20, sensitive teens may need extra support.

> *How you suffered for your sanity. How you tried to set them free. They would not listen. They did not know how. Perhaps they'll listen now.* —Don McLean (edited)

Being steeped in a constant bath of false narratives can result in being unknowingly programmed. For instance, westerners assume that we're all born with self-esteem issues. When the Dalai Lama[42] first visited the west, he was mystified by a question about self-esteem issues because the concept did not exist in the east. Self-esteem issues, rather than being inborn, seem to be systematically programmed into those in the west.

Why is it important to avoid being triggered into entering our imbalanced, mammal-human lower mind? People, in their lower minds, are easily manipulated. Decisions made with our *lower* minds tend to increase our troubles. Wise-humans try to spend as much time as possible in their balanced, *higher* mind. Decisions made with our higher mind tend to decrease our troubles. Clever-humans, based on their most recent thought or exposure to weaponized narratives, tend to jump between their higher and lower minds, resulting in a mixed bag of decisions that both increase and decrease their troubles.

Strategies to avoid game pitfalls 📖

What's the best way to avoid game pitfalls? First, move most everything in our premise stack, especially *pre-decided by others'* viewpoints and controlled narratives, from the *true* pile to the pile marked "to be determined." Those premises that pass the scrutiny of our best logic and intuition can then be moved to the *working theory* file. Those that do not pass should be replaced with something more load-bearing and sustainable.

> *Re-examine all that you have been told…dismiss*
> *that which insults your soul.* —Walt Whitman

In addition to taking steps to maximize our sovereignty of mind while minimizing our fear, we should cultivate and develop any *Truth-sensing skills* at our disposal, whether logic, intuition, kinesiology, pendulums, dowsing rods, etc. Concentrating on our self-care and growth encourages a brighter future for us and our planet, if not our entire universe.

You might be astonished that there could be any possible connection between rational science and the use of a pendulum or dowsing rod to answer questions. According to *The Biology of Belief* by Dr. Bruce Lipton[43], the conscious mind can process around 40 bits of information per second, as opposed to the subconscious mind processing 11 to 20 <u>million</u> bits of information per second. Given that the subconscious mind may be controlling the movement of the pendulum or dowsing rod in response to a question, those utilizing pendulums and dowsing rods may be *crazy like a fox* in that they're answering the same questions as everyone else but with up to 500,000 times more processing power. That could offer a huge advantage.

We should get into the habit of being intuitive, self-sovereign free-thinkers who attempt to validate the many supposed Truths and untruths we encounter. Expect some Truths to be actively concealed by the game, while others are hidden in plain sight but fenced off with a ridicule factor designed to fend off the faint of heart. Next, we should limit our exposure to mass-programming controlled narratives that would keep us disempowered. Better yet, substitute our own constructive and empowering self-programming mantras.

> *To become News Sober, don't get your*
> *news from the news.* —Glennon Doyle

Next, respect the synergy of group energy, whose combined coherent thought may go beyond additive to exponential. If thoughts and the *group effect* can impact reality at a quantum level, what happens when millions watch fear-based content? As one of the pitfalls, the game may first bait us to fear something in large groups and then utilize that collective group energy to manifest (at a quantum level) the very thing we've been caused to fear. As sneaky and diabolical as this sounds, it's an all-too-effective formula, perhaps used for centuries.

In a barrel of apples, the best place to hide the perfect apple is behind a less-than-perfect one. Knowing this, game agents may hide spiritual Truth, useful if not vital for game progress, in unexpected places. For instance, looking for the fire of accurate spirituality under the smoke of a coopted, corrupted, or compromised religion is the last thing many would do unless guided by intuition. This is one way the game limits the progress of individuals, if not entire populations, that have been outfoxed into using their free will to cut themselves off from vital game power and information assets.

Religion and science: Learn doctrine, assuming it to be truth.
Spirituality: Unlearn doctrine on the path to Truth.
While learning may take us to the trailhead to Truth, it's
the courage to unlearn that allows the most progress.

Ch. 3: Welcome to the new normal

Dimensionality versus consciousness level 📖

I'll define our level of dimensionality as the number of dimensions we choose to notice. Since most of us choose to notice only the length, depth, and height of objects in our world, most of us are initially three-dimensional, or 3D people.

> *You are also in other dimensions. Third-dimension Earth is becoming less and less normal reality… the higher dimensions are beginning to permeate. — The Z's*

Accounting for the flawed belief that time is unchangeable and progresses in only one linear direction makes most of us 4D people. The rare few that actively monitor more dimensions[44], even if only by taking care to remain in the eternal *now* dimension of time, might be called hyper-D people.

> *There's far more power and magic in adjusting our sails for what we're for in the now, rather than adjusting our anchors for what we're against, especially in the past or future.*

In addition to knowing the power of staying in the now, hyper-D people may know *time* to be more malleable, manageable, nonlinear, bi-directional, and varied than most suspect. Multiple examples of successful hyper-D thinking and experiments may be found in my science journal publication, and first book.

Since multiple levels of dimensionality exist within the human species, it's logical that *agents of the game* (regardless of species) might have risen to levels of dimensionality, whether by evolution or technology, that could make them unseen to us while occasionally sharing our space and time. That said, a being's level of dimensionality should not be confused with its level of consciousness.

I've had direct experience with a male (exploiter) being that was dimensionally high enough to be mostly invisible while demonstrating a decidedly nefarious and forceful nature that I'd associate with a lower vibratory level of consciousness. On the other hand, I've also had direct experience with a female (helper) being of high vibration consciousness that was of sufficient dimensionality that she was only visible to myself (and others in the room) in our minds' eye.

The point being that those who encounter unusual beings with advanced capabilities should not assume too much about their motives, goodness, or vibratory level.

Like *seen* beings, I believe unseen beings will eventually come to a point where selfish exploitation can no longer progress them further. Like it or not, further progression beyond that point will require that they abandon win-lose thinking in favor of unity consciousness and loving acceptance of what is. Life at that level is more about balance, peace, and synchronicity-filled illumination. That consciousness level understands that *other*-helping or *other*-harming is ultimately self-helping or self-harming.

Where's true north on our compass? 📖

When duality, such as in a win-lose relationship with others, is the *true north* of our guiding compass, compassion might be seen as an inefficient personality defect. When unity, such as a win-win relationship with others, is our true north, a *lack* of compassion might be viewed as a personality defect.

As individuals, nations, and as a planet, our choice of true north and our relationship to compassion (compass-action) will likely determine our future. In the near term, we can utilize this knowledge to create generations of *unity*-inspired harmony or *duality*-inspired pain. Ultimately, we will conclude that the only path that progresses humanity beyond a certain point is one that leans toward oneness.

Between duality and oneness, only oneness is in alignment with the ultimate nature of our divine Source. This is because the universe begins and ends as the oneness of a single consciousness, with only the illusion of multiple (individualized free will[45]) points of consciousness interacting with each other in between. For those who seek a sense of individual and collective oneness, this quote tells us what to work on:

We are all one. Only egos, beliefs, and fears separate us. — Nikola Tesla

Although the duality road may be good for many[46] miles, it eventually becomes a dead end, while the oneness road continues toward home. So, it's not a question of whether duality is a dead end, but only of how much needless pain must be experienced by those on the losing side of the win-lose equation before we collectively notice the dead-end sign and try a more sustainable road.

Only two root emotions – love and fear 📖

Elizabeth Kubler-Ross noted that all emotions boil down to either love or fear. When we (or our leaders) lean into love, it takes forms such as joy, happiness, compassion, trust, helping, healing, softening, forgiveness, etc.

> *A good way to assess a leader is to see if they speak from, or with their heart.* —The Z's

When we (or our leaders) lean into fear, it takes forms such as judging, shunning, disgust, distrust, wariness, outrage, bigotry, hate, defensiveness, insecurity, protectionism, etc.

Earlier in my life, when I was more religious than spiritual, I spent far too much time under the influence of disguised and normalized fear, with names such as worry and concern. This was before I came to realize that, unlike the supportive *love* road, the destructive *fear* road is ultimately a dead end.

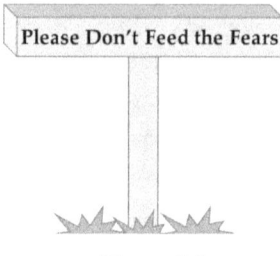

Figure 3.1

After researching the smoke versus fire of religious franchises and realizing that the underlying fire tended to come from love-based spirituality, I became more spiritual than religious. For me, it became less about structure and more about perpetually leaning toward *Love/Truth/Compassion*. I join these three together as an example of hyperdimensionality, in that each has the others enfolded within it while also leading to the others while being distinct.

The cosmic switchboard 📖

How does our cellphone know how to reach our friend's cellphone? Telephone network switching centers are the automated version of the old human-operated switchboard. How does a mother suddenly awaken with a strong feeling that something's happened to her child? Let's call it the cosmic network switching center, or *cosmic switchboard*.

How is it that just as you're thinking about your friend, they call? You, or they, may have received a *psychic text* message by way of the cosmic switchboard. If the cosmic switchboard performs the routing, what supplies the power? We do, because "where attention goes, energy flows."

Experiment[47] after experiment has demonstrated that a conscious, holographic, quantum-entangled universe has the ability to figure out how to complete an energy and information connection between us and whatever we hold in mind, even if we don't know its current location.

While the "how" of this has not always been apparent, the ability continues to be demonstrated in controlled scientific studies. I personally have seen consistent evidence that the cosmic switchboard allows us to connect with and transfer energy and information to and from beings or things across great spans of distance and time. In "Conversations with The Z's – Book Two," Lee Harris identifies the "how" as one of our guides (the Oracle). Like a cosmic switchboard, this particular guide is reportedly able to connect us with any being, anywhere.

Dream school and astral dimensions 📖

While most believe that dreams originate from electrical activity in the brain, some believe that dreams originate in our higher-self mind, showing up as electrical activity in the brain. Given how often my dreams seem to feature specifics not available to my brain, I lean more toward the second group.

My dreams *used* to be of the garden variety, in which I played all the characters in a scene that might as well have been created by my brain. My dreams eventually evolved into nightly *trans-dimensional* astral-body field trips to teaching dimensions, where I (*while apparently being monitored, interacted with, and evaluated*) am obviously not playing all the parts.

> *The higher dimensions are coming in higher than ever. Become a powerful conduit for those energies. Access the future and past… {via} astral traveling. Live from a more hyperdimensional standpoint. [To] generate light is the crucial next step.* —the Z's

At what I'll call "dream school," I'm routinely given the opportunity to learn as I sleep. Over the last 25 years, I've learned countless valuable things. Most of my early lessons focused on compassion for people I had recently judged. After making progress in that area, new lessons began to emerge.

Of all the dimensions my astral body has visited in dream school, I gauge most (if not all) to fall into the two general categories of either higher vibration, higher nature astral realms (*higher astrals*) or lower vibration, lower nature astral realms (*lower astrals*). It's not until I notice people leaning into their higher or lower nature that it's clear which category of dimension I'm currently visiting.

In lower astral realms, residents and visitors often exploit others or maximize self-interest at the expense of others. Beings appear to secretly steal energy, information, or both from visitors by way of physical proximity[48] or contact. Walking across a crowded train station in a lower astral dream, one *man* seemed to go out of his way to walk near me. In a moment of lucidity, I grabbed[49] his arm and asked, "Are you a being of the light?" After some protest, he said, "No," as part of his face disappeared to reveal a large insect eye. My takeaways were that wherever I was in my astral dream, I was not alone, and there are circumstances in which deceitful beings are obligated to tell the Truth.

The physics of the lower astral realms seem *wired* to frustrate visitors' goals, regardless of effort or attention to detail. That is, except when I become lucid enough to change lower astral physics. This is accomplished by creating a localized high-vibration bubble in order to strengthen the connection between intent and results. Employing this technique while holding hands with an untrustworthy old woman, I saw her transform into an innocent child. Even after waking from a lower astral visit, I still flood my dream location with divine love in hopes of leaving it better than I found it.

On the other hand, the higher-vibration physics of the higher astral realms seem more *wired* to accomplish dream goals in spite of what might appear to be insufficient levels of effort and attention to detail. As opposed to lower astral dimensions, goal attainment (such as flying) in higher astral dimensions seems biased toward success.

Residents and visitors of these realms tend to pursue self-interest in a way that's not at the expense of others.

How might dream wisdom translate to the waking world? Imagine a Venn diagram of two overlapping circles representing the polarized characteristics of the lower and higher astral dimensions. The area of intersection between the two circles might provide an approximation of our current waking world. Characteristics specific to lower and higher astral realms may foreshadow what our world could become if we consistently and collectively lean into either our lower or higher natures.

Whether we call it temptation or inspiration, some thoughts are not our own, *which should be considered before acting them out*. As with dreams, our thoughts (which set the frequency of our localized vibration energy bubble) may alter the physics of our waking world. Since it often takes a while for the universe to respond, our thoughts and intent should ideally remain aligned and consistent.

> *Like a guided missile's instantaneous corrections, each of our ~70,000 daily thoughts are either love or fear sourced, instantly correcting us toward our best or worst selves.*

The same types of positive and negative hyper-D, unseen beings that may be near in our dreams may also be near in our waking state. How do we vote for which type of unseen being will be attracted to us to help shape our experience? We vote by way of the vibration level of each and every thought.

> *If all of us knew that the smallest...thought has such far-reaching effects...how [carefully] we would think.* —Irina Tweedie

Each thought *vote* raises or lowers the collective consciousness *tide* that determines what passes for normal and acceptable. With this knowledge comes responsibility. A self-sovereign works at staying positive, so only helpful unseen beings come near.

Just as being near a charging pad can charge our cellphone, nefarious trans-dimensional exploiters may extract energy from us by being near us, especially if our thoughts fall within a certain low-frequency range. Higher vibration rates associated with gratitude, compassion, forgiveness, and love seem to be repulsive and of no use to these exploiters, so quality thoughts are our best defense against unauthorized energy drains or influence.

> *When you take on attributes of the master, light surrounds you… [the dark] will retreat.* —Kryon

On the other hand, lust, violence, judgment, outrage, certain ingested substances, and fear seem to be vibrationally attractive and directly usable to them as energy sources.

At least in the waking world, unseen beings seem bound by universal *rules of engagement* that respect our free will. Whether our thoughts lean toward our higher or lower nature, one type of unseen being or another is allowed to encourage us to lean deeper in that same direction, which doesn't violate our free will. People with negative or suicidal leanings should keep this in mind (*in addition to the fact that not all thoughts are their own*). However, when we consciously ask for unseen assistance, positive or negative beings seem more authorized to intervene.

Most fail to engage the assistance of these unseen *intention-multiplier* beings, simply for a lack of asking. It's time for each of us to take responsibility for every thought *vote* we cast, because on some level, our personal and global experience already reflects it! My "dreams" seem to fall into at *least* four categories:

1. **Regular dreaming:** My subconscious is likely in control of everything I see and experience.

2. **Lucid dreaming:** Aware that I'm dreaming, I have the ability to alter what I see and experience until I either wake up or fall back into non-lucidity. This sometimes involves a behind-the-scenes intelligence I'll call the "Control Room," which typically does not give itself away. Whether the control room is occupied by my subconscious, my guides, or my higher self is yet to be determined.

3. **"Astral" travel/dreaming:** My subconscious is in control of only limited parts of the dream, which independent others (with various agendas) seem to be sharing. This may also include either control-room-type intelligence or self-aware surroundings being wired for some agenda, such as "you don't get to get it." Astral is in quotes in that, technically, I could find myself in a lower astral realm, an upper astral realm, or perhaps even a celestial realm. It's not until I notice people leaning into their higher or lower nature that it's clear which category of dimension I'm visiting. This is my most common type of dream.

4. **Lucid astral travel/dreaming:** This is the type of dream for which I strive. Lucidity in this situation allows many more options than just going with the flow of the dream.

Are you amused? 📖

As a writer and creative, I can attest that one example of a win-win interaction with an apparently non-corporeal being of higher dimensionality is a creative *muse*. To me, a muse is a very real, unseen being that first imparts a good idea and then refuses to stop pestering me until I do something with it.

To creative types who've interacted with a muse, I offer both my congratulations and condolences. Although muses can be categorized as unseen *helpers*, it may be a mistake to automatically assume that they're non-corporeal or ultra-high-consciousness beings existing outside of linear time. Lower levels of consciousness may also be capable of influencing us in unseen ways, by way of technology[50], telepathy, and astral projection. Trust your instincts.

All of life is a stage 📖

If the game of life is a *stage,* who are the stagehands? Who's in the orchestra pit? Who's handling the lights? Based on personal experience, the short answer is: hyper-D, astral, and celestial beings, which are dimensionally shifted enough that most are unaware of their participation.

Is there any logic to the notion that higher-dimensional beings or things may be beyond our normal perception yet share our space or even interact with us? Yes, in the sense that a two-dimensional square can be made up of one-dimensional lines that have no concept of width or squares. At the same time, the square (with no concept of depth) can't perceive itself as part of a three-dimensional cube. See the pattern? Even though most of us have no way to perceive higher-dimensional beings in our space, it's logical and even predictable that they exist while being aware of us.

Scientists estimate that many dimensions coexist with the four we normally perceive. Some claim there are hundreds. If beings from other dimensions are near, how might we set our consciousness' "radio tuner dial" to allow or disallow interaction? Keeping in mind that beings of other dimensions can be as varied in their motives as humans, it likely comes down to the vibration rate (frequency) of our thoughts and actions.

Low-vibration, baser-instinct thoughts or actions may catch the attention of low-vibration, baser-nature beings. On the other hand, high-vibration thoughts, such as gratitude and optimism, may catch the attention of higher-natured beings. If this is true, self-sovereign control of the frequency of our thoughts should become a priority.

The real you, and where are memories stored? 📖

How many levels might one person have? First, let's talk about self-driving, autonomous taxis. If you hail one with your cellphone, get inside, and say to that autonomous vehicle, "Take me to City Hall," most of what happens before and after that is more about automation software and sensors than anything you've done. While those you pass on the street may assume you are operating the vehicle, you are largely just going along for the ride as a neutral observer.

Assuming that my soul downloaded part of itself into a self-driving, autonomous human-mammal avatar baby called *Bob*, how can I determine how much of what Bob does each day is due to the higher nature soul, the (real) neutral observer me, versus the (included with the mammal body) lower nature automation software and sensors that *appear* to be me?

The fact that some sensitive or psychic types have noticed (perhaps due to a missing aura) a few un-souled people walking around hints that most of what we assume to be *us* may be nothing more than the body's built-in automation software acting on its own.

> *It is not uncommon for humans to be completely disconnected from their soul energy…a human can only stay alive for two to three weeks after the soul has left.* —The Z's

If this is true, studying un-souled people might allow us to pinpoint what, beyond the in-built programming, our soul actually brings to the party. I suspect what it brings are higher-natured thoughts and behaviors, such as inspiration, kindness, generosity, and altruism. Of all the thoughts we have in a day, how many represent the *real* us versus the mind chatter of our avatar's automation software or societal programming? Very few.

We should draw a distinction between the part of our mind that *speaks* thoughts and the part of our mind that *listens* to those thoughts. For those who have been at the meditation game for a while, a third part, the *neutral observer,* may be watching both the thought talker and the thought listener.

The neutral observer may be the *real* you, the higher-nature soul you, with everything else being human avatar body *standard equipment hardware or software.* Years of meditation can be consumed by believing we're observing our true internal selves while actually observing our avatar software in operation.

I'm assuming that all levels of mind that cease to function when my brain ceases to exist are avatar software, whereas levels of mind that operate with or without a functioning brain are the *real* me. It's not uncommon for a person on an operating table (with a completely inoperable, anesthetized brain) to accurately recall specific operating room details while their consciousness floats above the table. Some operating rooms, as an experiment, have reportedly placed items on high ledges above an operating table that can only be identified by a high-floating consciousness.

On three occasions, confirmed by others, and at distances of up to a thousand miles, my etheric body has realistically interacted with people I care about while my physical body slept elsewhere. Since my physical brain (and synapse memory) were nowhere near, I assume that my etheric body is the *real* me when no physical body hardware or software are nearby—a version of me able to access memories and knowledge from the *know-a-sphere* in universal cloud storage.

I draw a distinction between mind and brain, where the brain seems to be an internal, physical transducer and local buffer storage for the external, energy-based mind. If the brain is local and has limited storage for the mind, that infers a non-local, larger place of storage. Enter the akashic records, where every thought, word, or action is said to leave a permanent vibrational imprint on our holographic universe. This recording is said to exist outside of space and time and, therefore, can be accessed from anywhere and any-*when.* I say "any-when" because the true nature of time is likely quite different than most suspect.

Is science superior to spirituality? 📖

Spirituality birthed the more disciplined and structured thinking of *philosophy*, which birthed the predecessor of science, *natural philosophy*, which birthed modern science. Thus, science owes its existence to spirituality, which (believe it or not) shares a fair amount of common *DNA* for courageously pursuing Truth via trial and error.

Spiritual techniques such as remote viewing have reportedly allowed our consciousness to visit the moon and countless other planets, dimensions, and realms for millennia. Governments have, for decades, relied on intelligence gathered in this way. On the other hand, Newtonian, materialistic, reductionist science has thus far been credited with allowing humans to only visit the moon. Although science and spirituality can learn from each other (and sometimes intermingle), spirituality will forever remain the mother of courageous inquiry and discovery.

Lost luggage at afterlife airport 📖

Can statistics help us determine what we *can* and *can't* take with us when we die? That is, which of our carefully-filled lifetime memory *suitcases* will arrive, and which will be lost somewhere between here and *afterlife airport*? In order to determine that, we must address a few preliminary questions:

(1) Can the mind exist outside of a brain?

(2) If so, can mediums connect with the mind after the body and brain are no more?

(3) If so, based on statistics, what life memories are likely to make it to wherever we find ourselves next?

If I can show that one suitcase always seems to be missing when we arrive at afterlife airport, how might that impact the amount of time we're currently dedicating to packing it?

Regarding the first question, Dr. John Lorber, professor of pediatrics at the University of Sheffield, UK, published a paper[51] in which he described an intelligent math student (IQ 126) who functioned quite well without a traditional brain, with little more inside his skull than a brain stem and fluid where his brain would normally be.

This would hint that the energy cloud around us and the holographic universe are the real, non-local location of our mind, with the biological brain being only a transducer and local storage buffer. If our mind really exists largely outside our brain, out-of-body experiences become not only possible but expected. People who've not experienced this directly may have a hard time accepting it, while those who *have* may consider it obvious that the *mind* can make use of a brain but does not require it.

Regarding the second question, can mediums really connect to minds in the cosmic *cloud*? I've had personal experience with Allison DuBois, who was the source of the TV series *Medium*. Her abilities to help law enforcement were verified by Dr. Gary Schwartz at the University of Arizona. In my direct experience with her, Allison passed on messages from a deceased loved one that seemed quite insightful and accurate.

I attended a self-actualization conference, in which the keynote presentation provided Lisa Williams, John Edward, and Sunny Dawn Johnson with an opportunity to demonstrate their mediumship abilities to a large crowd. While it seemed authentic, the skeptic in me knew such things could be staged. I signed up for the Lisa Williams break-out class the next day so I could study her and her process at close range.

As her class began, she informed us that rather than us watching her act as a medium, she was going to give us a few training tips and then ask us to be a medium for the stranger sitting next to us. As an introvert, it's a pretty safe bet I would have bolted for the door at that point had she not said the doors had been locked. The stranger next to me was to give no more clues than to say a <u>single name</u> and then sit quietly. In my case, the young female stranger next to me said, "Serge" (pronounced *Sair-gay*).

As I quieted my mind and closed my eyes, I could see in my mind's eye a young man with intense blue eyes, straight black hair, pale skin, a sensitive, intelligent wit, and a significant emotional connection to this young lady. I noted that his head seemed to be at a lower level than normal and that both my legs suddenly felt numb. The young lady confirmed that I had described him accurately and that he had been in a wheelchair without feeling in his legs before he passed. Even I, as an untrained amateur, was apparently dead on in this case.

As I looked into the young lady's eyes, I saw a second, more mature pair of eyes looking out at me, along with an image in my mind's eye of an older female fortune teller with the classic silk head scarf. I said, "By any chance, does intuition run in the women of your ancestry, and did you have a grandmother who was a Gypsy fortune teller in Poland?" She looked absolutely stunned but acknowledged that I was, again, dead on.

When she inquired as to how long I'd been a medium, I said, "About two minutes!" Even as a skeptic, those types of details seem pretty specific and hard to discount. While some mediums are just okay, my experience with a number of them over the years has been to be consistently impressed.

Let's say you've taken your last breath and find yourself standing at the baggage carousel of afterlife airport, waiting to see which of the bags you spent a lifetime packing will show up and which will not. The first bag you see coming around the carousel is your *mind* suitcase, holding all the memories of everything you ever thought, said, or did.

Your sense of relief turns to surprise as an unfamiliar bag comes around with your name on it. This is the bag holding a lifetime of the *ramifications for others* of everything you ever thought, said, did, or failed to do. The next bag to appear is your *heart* bag, containing a lifetime of heart-based events such as love, generosity, courtesy, kindness, purposeful softening, and forgiveness.

That just leaves your body-centric *ego* suitcase, which contains a lifetime of ego-based events. Everything you accomplished, earned, or acquired—every time you won at the expense of someone or something else—that bag is missing, not just for you but for everyone else standing there or who has ever stood there. Why is that? Ego is avatar-body-centric. Since the living body is no more, the suitcase containing a lifetime of the results of the body's ego is no more.

> *Soul thoughts tend to be more constructive than ego-satisfying, while ego thoughts tend to be the opposite.*

If you listen to enough readings from mediums[52], you'll notice some high and low statistical probabilities. Those speaking through the medium consistently demonstrate intellectually remembering the details of their lives (indicating their mind suitcase arrived with them). They also consistently demonstrate a desire to mend fences, resolve grievances, and absolve others of guilt while owning their part in unfortunate events (indicating their heart suitcase arrived with them).

In the perhaps hundreds of intuitive readings I've studied or experienced, there have been virtually no mentions of the deceased person's wealth, accomplishments, or accolades (indicating their ego suitcase likely doesn't make the trip).

This sheds new light on the guy who smiles and makes validating eye contact with a homeless person as he enters his office building to spend all day filling his ego suitcase with winning and losing, competing, acquiring, defending, forming grievances, being right, etc. At the end of the day, perhaps all he'll have to show for it at the afterlife airport baggage carousel is a smile for the homeless person. Everything else likely went into either the "ramifications to others" bag or the ego bag that will never be delivered.

If you conclude from this that you should skip work and only live from your heart all day, I would remind you of an Oprah Winfrey quote: "Do what you *have* to do until you can do what you *want* to do." My version: *Prioritize outer work to become who you want to be until you can prioritize inner work to reclaim who you really are.* One might stay in the ego realm while *on the clock* but shift to the heart while off the clock or after retirement.

Your heart bridges the world between form and spirit. —Dr. John Ryan

Armed with the knowledge that the ego suitcase we spend a lifetime filling can't follow us, I personally don't plan to spend any more time or energy than necessary filling that particular suitcase. Instead, I'll seek out more heartfelt moments that I can keep with me and cherish forever. What will it be?

Re-filtering our filters 📖

Ernest Holmes once said, "Practically the whole human race is hypnotized because it thinks what somebody else told it to think." If this is true, how can we break free from the hypnotized masses? Simple: *re-filter our unfiltered filters.* What?

Becoming aware of and recertifying our cognitive filters (determining what we notice and what we believe) is the first step toward breaking free. After making the effort to retest and recertify our existing cognitive filters, the next step is to pre-filter the controlled narratives in our daily lives before they get a chance to become our newest cognitive filters.

However, no matter how carefully we certify our filters, they can still be overwhelmed by the sheer volume of the fear-inducing content that surrounds us. Hence, proper care and maintenance of our cognitive filters may require being selective and limiting our exposure to that which is non-positive or non-constructive.

> *Your assumptions are your windows onto the world. If you challenge your own assumptions, you won't be so quick to accept the unchallenged assumptions of others. You'll be a lot less likely to be caught up in bias or prejudice or be influenced by people who ask you to hand over your brains, your soul, or your money because they have everything figured out for you.* —Alan Alda

What lasts longer, a mountain or a thought? 📖

All thoughts are permanently recorded, in that the universe has no "delete" key. How can I make such a claim? If you are of Christian or Jewish persuasion, you may already believe the *Book of Life* will be opened upon death as a recording of all the details of our lives, including our thoughts. You may also believe that the body will be perfectly reconstituted at the time of resurrection. If so, our mind, thoughts, and memory can only be restored *if they've been recorded somewhere.*

Hindus and others believe in the existence of a vast universal database known as the akashic record. In other words, a recording of all the details of our lives (thoughts, actions, etc.) If you've ever retrieved thoughts and perceptions from a past life (as I did under the guidance of Dr. Brian Weiss), that could only happen if they were recorded somewhere.

The post-life review that many near-death experiencers have reported could only be possible if the details of their lives were recorded somewhere. Therefore, for those who are religious or spiritual, the notion of all our thoughts being recorded may not be a great revelation.

For those of a scientific persuasion, scientists are now asserting that the unique vibrational signature of every thought and event is permanently and indelibly recorded within the infinite storage capacity of our holographic[53] universe (sometimes called the quantum field). Every thought is like a unique holographic radio broadcast that leaves a permanent recording, like a tree ring. One of the defining characteristics of a holographic universe is that no matter where information is created, it can be read from anywhere by anyone with the appropriate ESP sensitivity, technique, or technology.

I was a remote viewing student just long enough to get a *direct hit* on a blind ESP intelligence gathering assignment under the direction of a retired military officer. Hence, I've had personal validation that remote viewing via ESP is real.

A declassified briefing from the Army's Intelligence and Security Command reportedly evaluated 100 projects and 760 ESP remote viewing missions. Over a five-year period, 85% of the missions were deemed to have produced accurate target information from a distance, with viewers typically blind to their target. Using ESP to remotely gather intelligence about past events could only be possible if either the universe had recorded it or all time was occurring at the same time. Either way, the implications are similar.

> *I saw the past, the present, and the future*
> *at the same time.* —Nikola Tesla

In the book *The Intention Experiment*, Lynne McTaggart sums up the most recent scientific research with this conclusion: "Once lit, a thought is forever." So, the universe is capable of erasing a mountain but not a thought. Once you get past the shock of realizing that 900 days or 900 years from now, schoolchildren may be accessing your most private thoughts for a book report, the next steps become obvious—that is, the need to get self-sovereign control of our thoughts and to try to keep them at a higher *altitude*.

As with a blimp, some thoughts are like helium, some like sandbags. Take responsibility for how often you've touched the clouds.

Wider knowledge that our thoughts can be read from anywhere and any-*when*, in addition to providing another reason to quiet our mind in meditation, might cause genuine authenticity to increase and intentional deceit to decrease.

Since our net vibrational level may be the average of the vibrational level of all our thoughts, getting into the habit of catching our thoughts before they slide down a *slippery slope* to a low-vibration place can result in many positive effects. It may improve our health, our job performance, our relationships, and our creativity, all while improving our odds of encountering happy synchronicities.

What will it be?

Shift Happens to and Through Us

The shift is to a more soul-infused humanity. The next 10 years is where a turning happens. The turning cannot not happen. The destiny of the Earth is to shift dimensionally. How that happens and what that looks like, you are creating. —The Z's

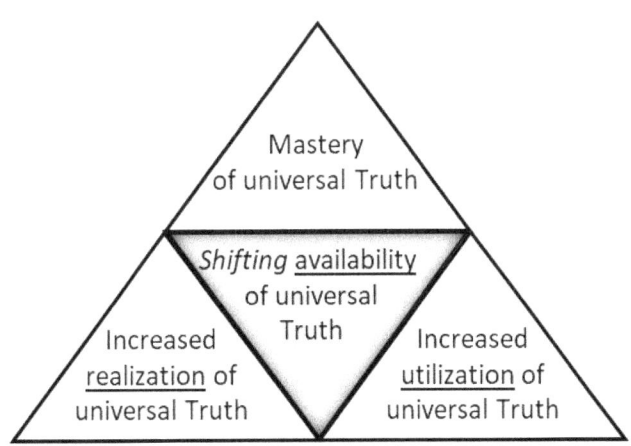

Ch. 4: Shift 101

The Shift: An introduction

You[54] may have noticed that things haven't exactly been *business as usual* for quite some time. You might even be asking, "What in the world is going on?" If you zoom out far enough, you may notice a bigger picture called the shift, which, from certain perspectives, is actually a good sign.

> *At this transformational time, much lower-dimensional thinking is ending. It's important that you open up to hyperdimensionality, not just to make life far richer, it's the path for humanity.* —The Z's

Prior to retirement, I was a professional at anticipating and inventing the future. Thus, as I describe the shift, my perspective on how it may impact our future may qualify as more than idle speculation. Before I get into how the shift is likely to impact our personal truth, what's the anatomy of *personal truth*?

We tend to curate a personal collection of often unverified, hand-me-down narratives, create a protective bubble around these *crystalized thoughts[55]*, and then defend them as our truth. This largely impenetrable bubble is justified as protecting our *truth* from those who would deceive us or lead us astray.

As time-honored as this tradition might be, the downside may far outweigh the upside. First, most of the narratives we defend (as history shows) will eventually be seen as somewhere between pseudo-truths and falsehoods, so our defensive bubble, made from fear in response to fear, also shields us from (capital T) Truth. This is because most Truth would be rejected for being too dissimilar to the *assumed* truth inside our bubble.

> *Truth is so obscure in these times and falsehood so established that, unless we love the truth, we cannot know it.* —Blaise Pascal

Why would our subconscious protect us from Truth? What we fear even more than being deceived or led astray is the upheaval that could result if Truth seeped in and invalidated most of our foundational narratives. To keep this from happening, we subconsciously (via *confirmation bias*) seek out information sources that reinforce our false narratives and pseudo-truths and then lament about the lack of Truth in our world. How's that for irony?

> *The Shift is from being in the minority if you separate Truth*
> *from narrative to being in the minority if you don't.*

Since it would be a violation of our free will for our unseen guides to force Truth past our protective bubble, many of us never escape this trap of our own making. Unless that is, we tune into our hearts with the courage to temporarily drop our protective bubble when our hearts resonate with something, no matter how seemingly odd or how much it's against our existing *truth*.

> *Those with the courage to get things more*
> *wrong eventually get things more right.*

Courage, plus honoring our shift-accelerated rising intuition and *heart* wisdom, is the key to escaping the trap, one "Hmmm, I wonder if that could possibly be true" at a time.

What might change regarding our personal *compass*, so what's seen today as nonsense could be seen in the future as self-evident Truth? The future will evaluate a notion based more on its alignment with heart intuition and critical thinking than its alignment with controlled narratives. Think of our false narratives, false beliefs, and pseudo-truths as a thousand veils between our current *truth* and absolute, or divine, Truth, leading to divine Love.

> *Behind every veil I have drawn across the face of love,*
> *its light remains undimmed.* —A Course In Miracles

Michelangelo created his famous marble sculpture, *David*, by being a removalist. That is, by removing the excess marble[56] that didn't belong. According to Kryon, ascension is the continual process of going within to remove that which does not belong until we've revealed that which we always were.

> *Let your completeness show by removing all that*
> *which is incomplete.* —Pleiadean Star Mother

As with Michelangelo, being a *veil removalist* is the path to Truth and mastery. It's been said that the prison that's most impossible to escape is the one we don't notice. Such is the case with the unnoticed veils between what we believe to be true about ourselves and the actual Truth.

> *Your true self is…buried under cultural conditioning, other people's*
> *opinions, and inaccurate conclusions…that became your beliefs...*
> *Finding yourself is unlearning, an excavation…remembering who*
> *you were before the world got its hands on you.* —Emily McDowell

If you think the Truth on the other side of our many veils has more than enough information and energy to solve our *unsolvable* 4D problems, you'd be right. What do we call the few without a veil? Masters. Prior to becoming a master, the trick to accessing trans-veil information and energy (not only between us and Truth, but between us and unseen dimensions) is to consistently lean into what crosses *the veil* without restriction: *compassion, laughter,* and *joy.* Potential side effects may include less drama, more life balance, inspiration, cooperation, and a longer, healthier life.

> *Game-changing balance comes from compassion, through*
> *connection with our higher self… As part of the shift toward*
> *kindness, compassion, love, understanding, integrity, rights,*

and peace…a slow cleanup is finally taking place. Those pushing back show their investment in old energy. —Kryon

So, what is the shift, and how is it likely to impact our personal truth? In short, our society has begun an irreversible, multi-century shift that will take us increasingly away from our personal pseudo-truths and increasingly closer to *actual* Truth. This includes a shift in the age-old balance between dark and light—a shift in thinking and acting from lower vibration consciousness toward higher vibration consciousness.

In Truth, (conscious) energy is all there is, so the material world is only a temporary projection of energy.

> *It is consciousness that creates the material universe, not the other way around.* —Dr. Robert Lanza

Thus, Truth must inevitably take us away from overemphasizing the 4D material world, where subtle energy and consciousness (if considered at all) are considered last. Instead, we will be shifted increasingly toward a future where the 4D material world may be considered later, if not last. The emphasis will be on the mastery of the physical through the physics of consciousness and subtle energy.

Along the way, our yearning for Truth will lead us to understand that our universe is holographic and quantum-entangled, which will lead us to understand that there is no separation between us, which will lead us toward empathy and compassion, which will lead us toward oneness.

This increasing shift toward Truth and compassion will translate to decreasing fear, which will transform our world. The massive transition from here to there is likely to involve some things being turned inside out. At the same time, inappropriate[57] things will be increasingly coming to light, with some things disintegrating, as with the transition from a caterpillar to a butterfly.

> *At the end of the day, a better world requires enough of us to decide that what has been acceptable and normal in how we treat and lead each other will henceforth be neither.*

From this perspective, what we're currently experiencing on a personal and global level makes more sense. A shift from a society built on agenda-serving narratives that seem tailored for hiding our connectedness to a society built on Truth is not a small, easy, or quick transition. So, if you've been waiting for all this personal and societal turmoil to return to *normal*, you may be in for a long wait. In fact, we'll need to redefine this ever-increasing shift not as something that threatens normality but as the *new normal*.

The path of this massive societal shift may eventually impact our beloved gadgets, as technology moves from pretending to be conscious (as with today's artificial intelligence), to technology that responds to consciousness (an era we're just now beginning), to technology that perhaps IS conscious… to a level of mastery where there's less need for technology.

Technology currently provides the training wheels that allow our consciousness to *indirectly* alter our physical world. When, as masters have demonstrated, our consciousness can *directly* alter our physical world, technology is less needed. As each generation further progresses along this path toward mastery, this next sentence may become increasingly true.

> *When you change your mind about what your mind can change, what your mind can change may change!*

While some assume that our current societal turmoil is a one-way ticket to a dystopian future, the more intuitive among us see the shift as an upgrade in Earth's potential. So profound is this shift that today may one day be classified as Earth's dystopian past.

You may be wondering, "What's so wrong with the way things have always been?" It's been said that the definition of insanity is to keep trying the same thing while expecting different results. For thousands of years, we've tried the "intimidation before a conflict and retribution after" male-energy-heavy, low-compassion, emotionally imbalanced formula.

If that formula were any good, it would have worked thousands of years ago. Instead, it's only caused an endless cycle of loss, retribution, and suffering. Before now, using that formula with arrows and spears had decimated entire regions. Today, given the hair-trigger status of our nuclear, biological, and other weapons of mass destruction, the next war (if there was one) could decimate all of civilization.

To make matters worse, tools capable of causing far-reaching destruction used to be locked away from average people, but no more. For instance, some suggest that the widely available CRISPR gene editing tool (simple enough to be used by a high school student) could, in unbalanced, low-compassion retribution, be used to create an incurable disease. Others are concerned about how easily a single computer hacker could, in unbalanced, low-compassion retribution, cause global mayhem. In short, the age-old saying, "I'll do whatever I want, and there's nothing you can do about it," may never again be true.

When the tools of warfare become too effective and too available, we must choose between maintaining the myth of global separation and maintaining civilization.

Guess what? We're there! Out of time and options, the writing is on the wall that we must immediately begin transforming into a compassionate, cooperative, male/female energy-*balanced* planet, or else! Since a single leap from where we currently are to (civilization-saving) global cooperation is too big, it must be done in steps.

However, the indicators are now there that, to survive as a civilization, we must climb those steps, starting now.

Whether it's religion, politics, or other areas, it isn't difficult to catch most of us taking up some type of defended position. By definition, "defended" infers being in a place of fear[58] and imbalance. Since very little of a constructive nature occurs in a place of imbalance, balance is where it's at. Hence, that which encourages *imbalance* during this extended shift may be more part of the problem than the solution, so staying informed and entertained should only occur to the point that emotional balance is not forfeited.

If you can't ingest fear responsibly while not allowing it to negatively affect your life, buying habits, or vote, I salute your wisdom in limiting your daily intake. I assure you, you'll still know what's going on.

Like alcohol, during this extended shift, we must ingest that which promotes fear and imbalance responsibly, or not at all. Why is that? For starters, an unbalanced "you" contributes more to the global problem than the solution. Secondly, although it may be in the best interest of news organizations to promote your fearful imbalance, it's neither worth it nor justified when we're not even being brought up to date. How can I say that? Here's a quote from my first book:

Even under the best of circumstances, our evening newscast has informed us regarding only a single planet out of perhaps billions – Earth. On just that one planet, we've likely heard about only a single species out of billions – humans. Of that species, we've heard about perhaps one out of every one to ten <u>million</u> of us that didn't have a fairly routine day. Of those, we overwhelmingly hear more about the negative than the positive. After that newscast, how could we possibly walk away believing we're anything close to informed about what's recently transpired. Info-tained or info-feared perhaps, but not informed. If you want to be anything close to informed, it will require individual research.

It wasn't arbitrary that the Mayan calendar ended in December of 2012, corresponding to the exact midpoint of the *Precession of the Equinoxes*. That calendar projected the end of time, or being out of time for *something*, with us collectively having the power of choice to decide what that *something* would be. Depending on the collective energetic broadcasts of our thoughts and actions, we were scheduled to globally experience one of two types of apocalyptic endings.

By one definition of "out of time," civilization as we knew it would have ended before 2013. This didn't happen, even though Nostradamus, indigenous peoples, and many prophets historically saw strong potential for it. Now, indigenous and esoteric sources are increasingly saying that humanity's making it to this point without destroying ourselves has triggered a radical *shift* in Earth's future potential. So profound is this shift that now it's said that we have a real shot at eventually becoming a balanced, forgiving, compassionate, and cooperative (enlightened, ascended) planet.

They will come to a fork in the road. One road will lead to materialism and destruction…for almost all living creatures…The other will lead to the Spiritual Way upon which the Native People will be standing…this path will lead to…peace, harmony… —Anishnabe Prophecy

Along the way, watch for our *standard equipment* to be upgraded, including increasingly useful *intuition* (fleeting information bundles) and *downloads* (less fleeting information bundles). Also watch for increased *channeling* ability (live-streamed information bundles). Although "it just came to me" channeling might seem like a new concept to some, it's as old as music, poetry, art, and scripture. All of these are said to occur by way of our pineal gland, in communication with our higher self (as an aspect of our soul), to an extent that used to be found only in shamans.

The Greek term "apocalypse" means to uncover or reveal. Hence, the alternative apocalypse we chose was for *deception* to be out of time, which will be a game changer—one that bodes well for the increasing rarity of low integrity, low compassion, and win-lose paradigms and institutions that represent the older, darker energy. That said, don't expect a shift away from our current status quo overnight, in a straight line, or without a lot of back-and-forth drama.

Shadows are being exposed...so you can go to the next level. —The Z's

How long will this shift take? It's collectively up to us as to whether it takes generations or eons. The more actively we individually lean into (and energetically broadcast) higher-vibration thoughts and ways now, the faster we'll collectively get there. The opposite is also true. As goes a critical mass of individuals, so goes the collective, so we each have an urgent and important part to play.

With the internet making secrets difficult to keep, deceptions will become increasingly exposed. You may have noticed that the *apocalyptic* process of uncovering deception is already underway. Add to that new generations being born with access to improved deception-sensing intuition and technology, and the demise of deception is only a matter of time.

How might one know if they were already a member of the light worker advanced guard for this building wave known as the shift? Perhaps you already have leanings toward softening your rigid positions in favor of emotional balance, tolerance, empathy, forgiveness, compassion, and oneness? Like a surfer catching a wave, correct leanings make all the difference between riding a wave and being pummeled by it.

It all starts with emotional balance. Both ironically and literally, the more of us that prioritize feeling emotionally balanced over constantly obsessing over wrongdoing in the world, the less wrongdoing there will be. By way of ~15 published studies, science has labeled this the Maharishi Effect. What's the mechanism behind a small group (focusing on balanced *being-ness*) being able to measurably tone down the damage done by the unbalanced *doing-ness* of so many distant, seemingly separate others? What if, energetically, in a holographic, quantum-entangled universe, others are neither separate nor distant?

> *Being part of an energetically aligned collective ...is where more power will lie and reveal itself.* —The Z's

What science calls the "wave-particle duality" states that every subatomic particle making up our bodies is at the same time exhibiting the properties of an energy wave. Since energy waves move and intermingle at the speed of light, they're likely zipping around the planet, exchanging information with the energy waves corresponding to every particle of every other person, object, and being. This (plus holographic connection at any distance) makes quantum, energetic entanglement with any object or being largely a matter of focus and intent, which may be how ESP and remote viewing work.

Masters know that to love something is to achieve quantum entanglement with it, allowing instantaneous exchange of energy and information across space, time, or dimensions. Looking within and without, the more we genuinely fall in love with, the more empowered, connected, and informed we become.

At the same time that 1% of us (lightworkers) may be limiting human suffering via emotional balance, every 100 of us that have the same enlightening "Ah Ha" (from a place of emotional balance) may also trigger the *Hundredth Monkey Principle*. According to this principle, the hundredth person to have the same enlightening realization energetically broadcasts it to the entire planet by way of our shared energy *fields*, such as the Earth's magnetic field.

> *...there is a spectrum of consciousness...at one end is...'field' consciousness, where a person is at one with the universe...* —Astronaut, Dr. Edgar Mitchell

When it comes to our planetary shared energy *soup*, there are no spectators. Every thought, emotion, and action inserts either love and balance, fear and imbalance, or something in-between into the shared global energy field steering our collective present and future. This is why, personally and collectively, achieving self-sovereignty over our thoughts and emotions is the next great frontier.

One reason the future potentials now look so favorable is that, per Kryon, no other planet that has made it to the consciousness rising point we crossed in December 2012 has failed to eventually make it all the way to ascension. Other planets likely realized that since separateness is an illusion, killing each other makes no sense. We're all energy waves sharing the same energy ocean, so poisoning the wave next to us poisons ourselves. A planet collectively coming to this conclusion may represent the end of its barbaric dark ages and the starting line toward planetary ascension.

How far could this shift toward enlightenment eventually take us? Apparently, so far, we'll someday see our current society as barbarically unenlightened, fearful, and artificially separated. Our future will look back to this age and see a society that destructively tried to substitute ego for compassion, balance, and authentic self-worth. We'll look back on a society so unthinkably barbaric that calendars may need to be started over at year zero, so future history students won't feel the discomfort of looking any deeper into a painful history than where we currently reside.

That would constitute the "end of time" for our current calendar. Supposedly, the Mayans left a new (starting at zero) 4000-year calendar waiting on the shelf, just in case we made it this far.

If the shift was only toward Truth-seeking, high integrity, compassion, oneness, and win-win cooperation, it would be rewarding and profound enough. However, the possibilities are that the shift will be much more profound. Since dimensions go nonlinear beyond 4D, one doesn't just graduate from 4D to 5D, but from 4D to *All-D*. A shift toward having access to many more dimensions would be a game-changer. In fact, supported by the rising of our vibrational energy, some see the potential to experience a significant recalibration of our biology, our *human nature,* and our abilities.

What we call human nature is dysfunctional, based on DNA working at only 30% [efficiency]. We've begun a DNA (human nature) evolvement to become masters of age, health, and physics. Watch for new abilities as DNA efficiency progresses past 33%... Improved past life wisdom, intuition, and synchronicity. Benevolent intent and compassion/healing will be amplified beyond the effort, making compassion more contagious. DNA becomes more hyper-D, improving longevity and allowing an alliance with matter (moving, changing, manifesting, and healing). —Kryon

This translates to how much our thoughts can alter our physical world, how much we're born knowing and remembering from past lives, how long we live, and how easy it is to succeed against dark energies. We could become a society featuring humans with a greatly evolved consciousness, enjoying the benefits of a more direct connection to our hyperdimensional higher self as a personal bridge to our soul and the infinite.

This is the time for the frequency of the planet to shift so human beings may express themselves hyperdimensionally, in the wholeness and holiness of who they are. —Onyah

The *bad* news is that those of older/darker energy also know the score and that every individual they can cause to feel fear through news, entertainment, and false stories on social media slows our transition away from fear-based control.

*The new is here. The old is just making
a lot of noise dying.* —Eckhart Tolle

Although the potentials indicate that their fight will ultimately be futile, they can be counted on to escalate attempts at fear-based control until they ultimately go down fighting. This may show up in the news as escalated chaos.

> *You never have to fight the darkness. All*
> *you have to do is create light.* —Kryon

When, after centuries of dimness, light is suddenly increased, dark-loving things will scurry about and posture in threatening ways. The *least* relevant news about this is the fear-inducing details about the dark-loving, scurrying, and threatening things whose days are numbered. The *most* relevant news is that, in a halting way, society is slowly righting itself. Which of these two perspectives are you likely to see in the "News?"

How many generations this fear-based suffering lasts is up to us. How many generations will continue to view that scary movie, conspiracy theory, or news item just to be (on some level) entertained?

> *What if, every time we're in the mood for*
> *something scary, we make our goals scarier?*

Like long-term climate cycles eventually win out over short-term weather cycles, each news cycle will eventually illustrate the excruciatingly slow shift from the fear-inducing old/darker energy that was to the new/lighter energy that will be. In the meantime, we should keep in mind that where attention goes, energy flows. Whether you love or hate what you see in news and entertainment, to *pay* attention to it is to literally send the currency of your energy to empower and perpetuate it.

> *The law of attraction is not just a beggar's tin cup. It's how*
> *we exchange value with the universe.* —Charles B. Burke

Thus, when you see social turbulence on the news, responding with fear and imbalance transmits energy that can prolong the shift away from that type of suffering by years, if not generations. Likewise, choosing to feel compassion and balance in regards to the same news transmits an energy that can shorten the shift by years, if not generations.

> *If you remain centered, your calm presence*
> *helps to free all those around you.* —Ram Dass

As mentioned in my first book, the pace of improvement will reflect our willingness to take responsibility for our own sovereignty of mind and fear-ingestion habits. In a globally shared energy field, there are no spectators.

After millennia, the balance has shifted from a dominating wind of darkness in our faces toward an increasing wind of light at our backs. Those who notice can benefit from resetting their sails, while those of compassionate consciousness increasingly gain control of society's rudder.

Although society's shift may be frustratingly slow, our personal shift can progress much faster. As a planet, we stand before three doors, labeled:

(1) Separation/Isolation
(2) Domination/Assimilation
(3) Cooperation/Integration

Two doors lead to our *descended* past. One door leads to our *ascended* future. What will it be?

The shift can be up or down

In the shift, institutions may show themselves as shifting upward, toward the integrity and compassion of our collaborative future, or downward, toward the separatist warfare energy of our past.

Institutions shifting upward may grow sustainably stronger, aided by an endless supply of trans-veil energy and information. Institutions shifting downward may ultimately go the way of the dinosaur, akin to a tree that self-prunes branches that can't or won't support a fruitful future.

Separatism in an institution, whether business, religion, government, or politics, is a downshift that leads to mistrust, which inevitably leads to some form of warfare. Separatism promotes the *problem*. As an ascending society, collaboration promotes the *solution*. A warfare-free future can be as near or far away as we like. It's as simple as collectively deciding we're ready to lean toward integrity, compassion, and collaboration and away from separatism and its descendants. What will it be?

Fence sitting

As the shift further progresses Earth into a highly energetic part of the galaxy, we will notice some things becoming easier while others become more difficult. What will likely become increasingly *more* difficult as we proceed into the shift? —fence sitting between the old/darker and new/lighter energies.

The side of the fence we've chosen, either actively or by default, may become increasingly apparent—either by our demonstration of balanced, peaceful, compassionate, Truth-seeking, *thrive* energy (as part of the solution) or the old, fearful, survival, judging, and controlling energy (as part of the problem). Ancient texts predicted this in multiple metaphors in which we are divided into polarized camps.

Going forward, our improving intuition will make it increasingly difficult for dark energy people and institutions to convince us that the bad guys are good, and vice versa. Regardless of how they portray themselves, their actual side of the fence, or camp, will become increasingly obvious.

So, what will likely become increasingly *less* difficult as we proceed into the shift? —effective intuition, energy healing modalities, and spiritual ventures (like prayer) that may have had limited success in an older energy but are now more supported by a new energy.

> *The frequency that is now being broadcast to the healer...is in a far greater spectrum... It's enormous! ...if you say to the Universe..." I am ready for the new frequency...to enhance everything within me...Give me direction and wisdom to allow this change in me"...expect it!* —Kryon

Sovereignty of mind requires us to protect our Truth-sensing intuition from influences designed to keep us unintuitive and on the fearful, darker side of the fence. This affords us sufficient clarity to identify Truth amidst controlled narratives. Welcome to the shift!

Intuition to follow the spiritual path

Imagine a metaphor in which absolute Truth was the clearest water and absolute Love was the sweetest water. A deep fountain of this purest, sweetest water cascades from the top of a mountain. The water begins its downhill journey in pristine condition but is divided and made ever shallower, murkier, and saltier as it encounters the controlled narratives created by human agendas.

> *Irony: The farther we let narratives take us from Truth, the less able we are to recognize Truth. The opposite is also true.*

As the water progresses downhill, the compounding effect of this occurring again and again creates water so murky, salty, and shallow that it causes the quality and quantity of our lives to suffer, even as we're programmed to accept it as normal.

The farther we allow controlled narratives to take us from Truth, the murkier the water, and yet the poorer our ability to notice. Some organizations appear to rely on this. What if, contrary to those convinced that figurative *murky water* represents the infallible word of God, some possessed (as part of the shift) sufficiently enhanced vision and taste buds to progressively move up the mountain in search of water that's ever deeper, sweeter, and clearer?

In this metaphor, more acute vision and taste represent enhanced intuition and subtle senses, allowing *some* to sense which narratives are incrementally closer or farther from the source of absolute Truth and Love. This ability to separate Truth from narrative starts with the intention to increase intuition and the courage to follow it.

> *There is immense power in intent. In this new energy,*
> *you are in charge of what happens next.* —Kryon

If you are among that group, I salute you, but be prepared for those who are currently content with their existing *water supply* to say, "Don't follow them; they're lost." That's OK; welcome to the *solo* spiritual path.

Truth and the spiritual path

For millennia, those on the spiritual path have said the universe is conscious, connected, and hyperdimensional. A century ago, quantum mechanics "discovered" that the universe is conscious, connected, and hyperdimensional. My point? Intuition and experimentation have often allowed the spiritual to know, centuries in advance, what science will eventually come to know. Hence, I think of **SPIRITUAL** as an acronym: *Scientifically Prophetic Intuition Resulting In Truth Under Alternate Labeling.*

> *Since all paths ultimately converge to one, whether*
> *we're currently walking on it or asleep next to it,*
> *we're all on the path to spiritual mastery.*

Why are so many comfortable remaining asleep next to the spiritual path? At a subconscious level, they may remember that whenever they had a life that embodied *more Truth than programming,* it didn't end well when they encountered the masses who embodied *more programming than Truth.* Thus, if only at a subconscious level, we're afraid of Truth, leaving the spiritual (Truth-seeking) path to those with sufficient courage.

Since Truth is a component of Love and Oneness, fear is the (less substantial than it seems) shadow of those things, created by falsely viewing separation as Truth. A Course in Miracles says, "That which is real cannot be threatened." The flip side of that statement would be, "That which is really threatened isn't real." Since fear and all its children (competition, judgment, etc.) would be threatened by discontinuing our belief in separation, none of them are real. Hence, while our conscious mind thinks fear is about something real being threatened, fear may actually be a subconscious realization that because something *seems* threatened, it isn't even real! Hence, discovering what is truly real may be what we need most.

> *That which we need the most will be found*
> *where we least want to look.* —Carl Jung

While there is still far more programming than Truth, our society has now moved from executing the wise to increasingly learning from them. This is a game changer in that we now have a choice to either embrace our (stay asleep) programming or more *safely* pursue the Truth. What will it be?

Are we suited for hyperdimensional interactions?

Science says that up until ~200,000[59] years ago, *all* hominids on this planet had 24 DNA chromosome pairs, until humans suddenly appeared as a hominid with 23 pairs in a way that strongly suggests intelligent intervention. While that's as far as science is willing to go, some esoterics go further to claim that intervention didn't really eliminate our 24th chromosome pair but made it 4D undetectable until we've invented a cryogenic quantum field lens (*quantumscope*), allowing us to view that which is hyper-D in and around us.

When we eventually invent the quantumscope, we'll reportedly find hyper-D energies and entities so ubiquitous within us, around us, and across the heavens above that it will cause a radical shift—not only in our science books but also in our definition of what's considered to be alive. Beyond that, the information and colors suddenly viewable in our biofield will shift medicine while making our true energetic and interdimensional selves viewable to all.

The wisest old souls will reportedly show up in this lens as being surrounded by an iridescent purple hue. If so, spending time with a coherent group of iridescent purple "hue-mans" may one day be seen as the fast track to *shifting* our spiritual development into a higher gear.

> *The aura surrounding those who are awake is four times larger than those who are still sleepwalking.* —The Z's

That which interacts with the interdimensional, such as photons (packets of light), is said to have an interdimensional aspect of its own. Hence, it's significant that our DNA and cells interact[60] with photons. Whether or not a human 24th interdimensional chromosome pair is eventually seen, we still have a scientific basis for our ability to interact with that which is hyper-D.

How much hyper-D interaction ability have humans (alive or not) displayed? Plenty. Studies by the Institute of Noetic Sciences (IONS) have shown that *mediums* can access accurate information from the consciousness of those who've passed. Since disembodied consciousness isn't yet measurable by 4D instruments, it suggests that consciousness can reside in and communicate in dimensions beyond 4D. My own life has demonstrated that the consciousness of those who've passed can communicate and alter our 4D reality.

Regarding the consciousness of the living, IONS studies have also shown its ability to alter 4D reality as well as the laws of chance.

Our 4D reality describes only a single *when* and *where* at a time. On the other hand, those who use remote viewing to access the hyper-D soup known as *the field* have been shown by science and government programs to be using their consciousness to access most every *when* and *where* in the past and present, as well as potentials for the future. Whatever dimensions are being accessed with remote viewing, they often seem beyond the traditional four.

> *Rising now, coming to the forefront, is an information highway that you all have access to. Increasing numbers will become aware of their connection to Spirit in an all-new, undeniable way.* —The Z's

The pineal gland in the center of our brain appears uniquely designed to let our *mind's eye* see beyond 4D. With eye-like connections and structures, our pineal reportedly contains rambohedral piezoluminescent crystals[61] that (like pixels on a TV screen) may glow in response to hyper-D quantum or scalar waves. Given that the pineal gland has retinal tissue composed of rods and cones and is wired into our visual cortex, it may not be a question of whether we all have a *third eye* but only of who's using it.

One aspect of remote viewing may entail astral body travel. Dr. Hereward Carrington reportedly measured a consistent 2.25-ounce reduction in the body mass of people during astral-body travel.

> *The 3oz. we lose at death is our historical record being saved.* —Kryon

That much mass would account for about the same weight as two AA batteries. Reportedly, when the test subject's astral body returned to their physical body, so did the missing 2.25 ounces of mass. While that amount of temporarily missing mass may not seem like much, Einstein's equation lets us calculate that the sudden conversion of that much mass to (astral body) energy could power ~800,000 average homes for a year. Since that much energy could probably not leave and return *quietly* in the four dimensions we notice, our astral body may be transiting by way of a dimension beyond our typical four.

Likewise, our astral body may reach its destination in a dimension that's beyond 4D but adjacent to 4D. I say this because the 4D measurable impact of that much energy visiting a room seems to be limited to an increase (by up to 1000 times) in the number of measurable random background virtual photons of light.

Common sense suggests that ascended status is reached by leaning into that which is more ascended. Since nothing is more ascended than (hyper-D) divine Love, that would be a great way to lean, by way of compassion, gratitude, appreciation, and compassionate action. Another path toward enlightenment is to let shift-enhanced intuition indicate the *real* Truth level of what we're thinking, saying, reading, or hearing. This alone can change a life.

> *You won't have to guess as much. It will be intuitive. Future potential reasoning [and Akashic remembrance] will be lightning fast, [like] an open book.* —Kryon

For a *temporary* experience of nonlinear hyper-D realities, there are many ways of reaching altered states. In order to move beyond *temporary*, we must learn to be increasingly OK with answering linear questions with a hyper-D nonlinear: "Not Applicable (n/a)," "Yes," or "It depends on how you look at it." For instance:

Q: How many…?
A: *N/A* (hyper-D may have no specific numbers).

Q: Where…?
A: *N/A* (hyper-D may have no concept of a specific place).

Q: When…?
A: *Yes* (however long it takes our free will to allow it).

What can nonlinear, hyper-D thinking buy us? If we're ready to upgrade our health, we're no longer limited by linear questions like,

"How long will it take?" The hyper-D answer is, "Yes, as soon as all the conscious, subconscious, and higher self parts of our free will align, if only for a moment."

> *How long does it take for something to manifest? ...as long as it takes you to release...resistance. Could be ...50 years...could be tomorrow.* —Abraham Hicks

If I sit quietly in non-resisting coherence with *the field*, how long will it take me to learn a new concept or grasp the solution to a problem? *Yes.*

As much as intent plus control (*doing*) may get us what we want in 4D, accessing alternate dimensions may be more about intent plus allowing (*being*). Although the shift to ambiguity and allowing can initially be *uncomfortable*, it's ultimately empowering. Indeed, allowing the universe to decide how and when our pure intent manifests via benevolent hyper-D synchronicity is the very road to mastery.

Changing circular tracks

Per Gregg Braden and Kryon, history has tended to repeat itself in cycles, and humanity has been like a train on the same circular track. That was before, but what about now?

> *You are in a new energy, one which you have been waiting eons for. Expect new thoughts...enhanced intuition...different solutions {as} new energies take form.* —Kryon

The shift has moved us to a *new* circular track at a slightly higher level. Hence, for the first time in eons, history is less likely to repeat itself. This means that as a society, we no longer know what to expect, as our cumulative thoughts and intent will be steering humanity's course—a sobering thought.

Our multi-generational shift will be away from countless forms of societal violence based on a false sense of separation. The shift will be toward countless forms of societal compassion based on our true oneness.

Since Earth has reportedly passed an irrevocable tipping point, the question is no longer about *whether* the shift will continue but only about how long, halting, and chaotic our collective road will be. The only question is whether this (now inevitable) shift is happening *through* us or *to* us.

The shift will impact many aspects of our world. There are so many that one could start a fairly long list. For instance, the shift will reportedly be from less to more:

- Recognition that thoughts have an impact at a distance.
- Attunement and alignment with the Earth and the cosmos.
- Balance between the hemispheres of our brain.
- Balance between our heart, brain, innate body, and higher self.
- Interacting with the hyper-D in and around us.

At the same time, the shift will reportedly be *from* and *to*:

- From "Why did that happen to me?" to "What was the conscious universe trying to teach me?"
- Toward defining health more as a holistic balance and toward loving all parts of the self unconditionally
- Toward positive thoughts, creating our lens on the world
- From settling for 4D table scraps to accessing a hyper-D buffet
- From competition between separates, toward experiencing the power of coherent oneness
- From petrified narratives that substitute for Truth, toward Truth

- From chaotic mind and breath to sovereignly controlled mind and breath
- From entertaining negative media and thoughts as "harmless" entertainment to taking responsibility for how they impact us

In short, the shift may encourage each of us to become our own shaman. Will there be noticeable symptoms of surfing the accelerating shift wave? Yes, peace and balance. Will there be signs of resistance to that same wave? Yes, confusion, fear, anger, and frustration.

In this light, rather than labeling thoughts as negative or positive, a better description might be *empowering* or *disempowering*, or *enabling* or *disabling*. Negative thoughts are disempowering and disabling in that they are a misuse of our free will and creative power, a forfeiture of energy, and a form of self-harm.

Positive thoughts don't just color our perceptions. They go before us to bias the quantum field toward positive synchronicities. They also create an energetic pattern *around* us as our interface to all things seen and unseen.

> *The soul light I came with changes everything around me.* —Lee Carroll

As part of the shift, many will come to realize that, moment to moment, we have the choice to put weight on one of two metaphorical feet. One foot represents the priorities of our destructible, under-informed ego. The other foot represents the priorities of our indestructible, well-informed higher self, or soul. What will it be?

Ch. 5: Shift 102

The veils are getting thinner 📖

Historically, the notion of incarnating on this amnesia-veiled planet had multiple implications:

- One amnesia veil historically hid our life's mission, purpose, and amazingness until sufficient meditation, contemplation, and self-reflection had occurred.

- Another amnesia veil historically allowed thoughts, secrets, and deceptions to remain largely unknowable until our post-life review. Entire areas of society count on this.

- Another veil historically kept our hyper-D support team (ancestors, angels, helpers, and guides) largely hidden and inaccessible as un-seeable, un-hearable, and un-knowable.

- Another veil historically made subtle bio-force energies largely un-detectable, un-controllable, and un-transmittable.

I used *historically* as a qualifier because current Earth residents have reportedly chosen to be here during a very special time of shift between what was and what will be. One of the earmarks of this transition time is that, for more and more of us, the veils are noticeably thinning. Personally, my veils have thinned to the point that I've recalled my mission this time to be:

> *A positive influencer who seeks to be creative, insightful,*
> *intuitive, wise, compassionate, and courageous.*

I say *this* time because another veil has thinned enough that I've been able to recall episodes from my lives as a leather worker living under a thatched roof, a medieval pushcart salesman of copper pots, a sailor, a young apprentice guarding a broken donkey cart beside a Roman road, and an academic philosopher.

Regarding my personal hyper-D support committee, I've had many encounters with deceased loved ones, a particular angel, and a transformation-assisting Native American guide named *Winds of Change*. Some assist my growth, some assist when I'm doing Reiki[62] bio-energy work with others, and some inspire my writing and inventions.

When the veil of deception gets thin enough, people will increasingly notice malpractice, integrity issues, and credibility issues in institutions[63]. A common thread through many institutions is the false assumption that unethical manipulations and deceptions can remain hidden indefinitely. What they didn't count on was veils thinning to the point that average people would begin to intuitively sense deception and ethical issues.

Aren't thoughts, secrets, and deceptions supposed to be unknowable? Most hold the belief that thoughts are private and fleeting. The foundation of this belief is the premise that thoughts cease to exist as soon as we stop thinking them and travel no further than our heads. Do these beliefs hold up to scrutiny? No, as previously mentioned, all thoughts are permanently recorded and universally accessible, so the wise think accordingly.

Wise players shift perspective 📖

One thing science, spirituality, and religion have in common is the belief that we're capable of so much more. Some come to that conclusion by way of extrapolation, some by way of intuition, and some by way of ancient stories that tell us we used to be more. We used to be more present in the here and now and more intuitively in tune with nature—more than the 4D, semi-awake, semi-empowered beings we often see today.

> *We are … so asleep, so imprisoned by illusions…* —David Icke

According to some mystics, the *good* news is that we've incarnated at a pivotal time of shift in which vibrational buoyancy offers the option

111

to rise above our amnesia and media-induced hypnosis to become higher dimensional, higher vibrational, and higher functioning.

The hyper-D person tries to live in the dimension of perpetual *now.* This is the advantage of the highest-functioning members of society, including those who operate *in the zone,* such as athletes, surgeons, artists, and meditators. Those without sufficient inclination and sovereignty of mind to claim their *(in the now)* birthright leave an enormous advantage on the table. Those who claim that birthright and add a positive mental attitude may enjoy a career and an evolutionary advantage. Those that further add a balanced yin/yang and masculine/feminine energy may enjoy an even greater advantage.

Research indicates that positive outcomes result from positive moods, not the other way around. In *The Happiness Advantage,* Shawn Achor highlights a study where doctors in a positive mood exercised nearly three times more intelligence and creativity than doctors in a neutral emotional state, while making a diagnosis 19% faster. Achor says, "…our brains are literally hardwired to perform their best, not when they are negative or even neutral, but when positive."

Many now appreciate the advantages of positive intention (*especially when synergized with compassion, empathy, and forgiveness*). Many of these same people have developed sufficient sovereignty of mind to maintain a continuous upward spiral of *chronic gratitude,* leading to more positive outcomes, leading to more gratitude, and so on.

> *Those who have practiced gratitude for any period of time have noticed your life gets better. You start to notice higher vibrations and then start to create them. You mirror-create the higher vibrations outside you that you're cultivating inside you.* —The Z's

More than just optimizing outcomes by way of optimizing our mindset, evidence suggests that at a quantum field level, the universe may respond by altering our circumstances. The saying, "Every thought is a prayer," refers to the universe having a tendency to respond to our thoughts with "OK, I'll get right on that!" whether we're currently thinking in a positive or negative way. For those who can grasp and internalize this concept, it can be a game changer.

> *When you reach for a thought that feels better, the Universe responds to you because of that effort...things...get better... So [from that higher vibrational place] it gets easier to reach for the [next] thought that feels better [so the purposeful upward spiral continues].* —Abraham-Hicks

A hyper-D person tries to live an "everything in the conscious now" life. By *everything*, I mean conscious breathing, conscious choosing of thoughts and moods to stay in the mindful-grateful now, conscious kindness, and conscious compassion. To that end, I would also strive for conscious progress toward balance (*internal* oneness) as well as conscious progress toward being part of a harmonious local and global family (*external* oneness).

Shift toward love's syntropy 📖

When we lovingly leave something or someone better than we found them, it's likely because we've raised them to a higher level of order. This is known as "syntropy." Kitchen pantry ingredients may be lovingly raised to a syntropic higher level of order when they become baked goods, which are raised to a yet higher level of order when they're fueling a doctor, and an even higher level of order when that doctor joins with a hospital to become part of something even more capable.

> *To raise something to a higher level of order is syntropy. To use the heart to transform something is alchemy. The army we most need is one of syntropy alchemists. Let's recruit for __that__ army!*

We tend to feel *expanding*, love-rooted emotions like hope and optimism while progressing toward a higher level of order and *contracting*, fear-rooted emotions like sadness and depression when our health or life status is degrading toward a lower level of order, known as *entropy*.

The expanding (or contracting) health of an economy or society may be correlated to how many are currently reaching for a higher level of order. When enough people reach the same new level of order, whether it's elevating from 4D to hyper-D or installing the latest human software OS upgrade, an entirely new level of human normal emerges.

As humanity progresses, it will be due to a critical mass of people shifting to higher levels. These people will likely display Truth-sensing ability, empathy, kindness, and a preference for architecting win-win solutions that create the fewest new problems.

Self-sovereigns manage information/energy 📖

Perhaps our most important, precious, and unique birthright as humans is our individual power of free choice. That said, it's ironic how readily we limit or give up that valuable birthright. One way we do that is to obtain our information and conclusions from *pre-choosers* in the name of convenience. A pre-chooser is a person or organization that, like a mother pre-chewing your food, decides for us in advance what's important and what we should think about it. Just open wide and swallow.

> *Whether it's food or "facts," some consider before ingesting, while others just swallow. Intuition may never be so important as when someone has pre-decided what we should trust or mistrust.*

What facts and conclusions are most important on our academic journey? Others have pre-chosen and pre-chewed for us. Which of the trillions of events that happened today are important, and what are the proper conclusions? The *news* has been pre-decided and pre-chewed for us. What's wrong with the nation and those in the *other* political party? Polarizing pundits and parties have pre-decided and pre-chewed for us.

> *To control a population, the media doesn't have to control the facts, only how those facts are perceived.*

What's right and wrong about us and the world? Religions have pre-decided and pre-chewed for us. What is and is not *cool* or *in* right now? Others have pre-chosen for us.

> *Most people are other people. Their thoughts are someone else's opinions, their lives a mimicry...* —Oscar Wilde

Is a life of pre-packaged, pre-chewed information and conclusion convenience in alignment with our unique and precious birthright of free will and free choice, or does it provide just enough pale illusion to facilitate continued sleepwalking? How do we break our pre-chewed information and conclusion addiction? Prioritize time for independent investigation, pondering, and conclusions.

Who has that kind of time? If we're honest about how many hours per week we spend in front of one type of video screen or another, perhaps it's just a matter of priorities? As you ponder your life on your final day, which path will please you the most?

To become self-sovereign within the shift is to courageously grant oneself the indisputable authority to become a self-authorized, *training-wheel-free* adult in some area of life. For instance, if we're reading source documents instead of accepting the pre-chewed, hand-me-down conclusions of others, we may have removed our training wheels to become *intellectually* self-sovereign. If we're directly pursuing universal wisdom instead of settling for the pre-chewed, hand-me-down conclusions of some religious franchise, we may have taken off our training wheels to become *spiritually* self-

115

sovereign. The game noticeably changes when we turn toward self-sovereignty regarding:

- Our thoughts, emotions, and empowerment.
- Our energy and vibration levels.
- Our relationship with seen/unseen beings.
- Our exposure to controlled narratives and bait.

Self-sovereigns lean toward first-hand research in order to arrive at first-hand conclusions. In doing so, they often spot and gain wisdom from game ironies. For instance, closing our eyes in meditation is a way to awaken and see, and healing our past can upgrade our future. One of the greatest ironies is that the *all* hides within everything, so sitting alone allows connection to the all. In addition, *no thought*, known as *no mind*, may allow access to infinite information.

> *The soul comes online in a very powerful*
> *way when you switch off the mind.* —The Z's

Self-sovereignty is neither common nor easy, but it's very much worth the effort. As potent as one self-sovereign person may be, their impact can be amplified when they synergize in *groups*.

> *You, as family, in the time of the great evolution [toward] hyper-D coherence, [are] more harmonious, connected, present with one another, [allowing you to] unlock new frequencies/energies (levels of reality) [in ways] you could not do by yourself. Your energy…unique and united, spinning in a morphic field [is helping] to balance this planet [and] birth the new humanity.* - Onyah

Imagine throwing a boomerang toward the sun. At first, it arcs away, higher and higher, until it reaches its maximum height, flies temporarily sideways, and then arcs back toward its origin. Likewise, we may spend countless incarnations in the game with a dominant *lower* nature, moving farther and farther from the divine Source. This level of the game may be associated individually and collectively with *mammal*-human predatory aggression and the lower part of the clever-human vibrational spectrum. Those who try to act in a love-rooted, self-sovereign (return-arc) way within a tribe of those still on their outward, fear-rooted arc may do so at a high personal cost.

At the boomerang's maximum distance, it's in a sideways transition between arcing away and arcing back toward home. This may be associated with individual and collective *clever*-humans, with competing lower and higher natures. Those who try to act in a love-rooted, self-sovereign (return-arc) way within a tribe of those in the sideways part of their arc may do so at a *minimal* personal cost, like being unfriended on social media.

The boomerang arcing back toward the divine Source may be associated with *wise*-humans. When acting in a love-rooted, self-sovereign way amongst a tribe of return-arc people, the reception may be quite favorable.

Self-sovereignty is not about being *granted* self-ownership by someone else. It's about unapologetically and indisputably granting ownership *of oneself to oneself*. Some seek to find someone outside themselves who is wise, confident, powerful, and therefore safe. Self-sovereigns that don't settle for vicarious wisdom and safety *become* wise, confident, *power-full* and therefore safe.

From the moment we have the audacity to give ourselves that gift, the winds of society may or may not be in our face, but the winds of a conscious universe will be at our back. If one must choose whether to go against society or against a conscious universe, the wise and brave will align with a conscious universe. What will it be?

Fear: tonic or toxic?

A tonic is life-affirming, whereas something toxic is life-threatening. Enlivening and empowering (organic, *tonic*) fear offers us a path toward an improved version of ourselves. It tips us off as to where the application of courage may result in growth and empowerment. For instance, tonic fear may stand between us and asking that person out, going back to school, or going for that promotion at work. Tonic fear, when we lean into it, can tip the balance toward empowerment and light, encouraging the universe to send us more of that.

On the other hand, the artificial, *toxic* fear we often choose to ingest based on our information and entertainment (*info-fear-ment*) choices requires no real courage.

<hr>

Because emotions drive actions, fear-laced media can place us under emote control.

<hr>

No matter how entertaining that "news" network, fictional crime show, or conspiracy theory might be, its artificial (toxic) fear can degrade our peace of mind, our world view, our relationships, and our longevity. Rather than being enlivening and empowering, artificial, toxic fear biases us toward mistrust and paranoia as individuals and as a nation. Toxic fear biases us toward disempowerment and dark energy, encouraging the universe to send us more of that.

It's time to take ownership, not only of the type and quality of fear we choose to ingest but also of its impact on our lives and community, and that we often have thoughts "to die for." What will it be?

A deeper dive into toxic fear 📖

At the personal level, fear of the *toxic* variety can slow or stop our progress toward becoming our most empowered selves. At the collective level, fear of the toxic variety can make us logic-resistant and dangerous.

As ubiquitous as fear is, do we really understand it? Fear is multi-D in that it can be conscious or subconscious, a feeling or emotion, and biologically visceral or chemical. The types of fear that utilize biology can't follow us beyond the body, likely accounting for some of the peace the deceased have reported. My working theory is that all *toxic* fear is sourced from the one fundamental fear of ceasing to be, whether ceasing to be a pain-free, non-suffering person or ceasing to be in a living body.

Fear, in the more modern frontal lobe of our brain, may be decoded as "The universe can't be trusted." On the other hand, fear in the primal amygdala part of our brain may be decoded as "This body won't survive." Our intuitive knowing may realize that the first fear is false while the second fear is true, setting up a dissonance around fear that can keep us uneasy.

Fear, the *feeling*, may be a thought-activated broadcast of energy. On the other hand, fear (the *emotion)* may be the body's chemical response to receiving a fear energy broadcast (emotion = energy in motion). After we *die*, we might use a psychic medium to express our conscious *feelings* (but not body-based *emotion*s) of love, gratitude, pride, etc. to those left behind. If we succeed, it may cause our loved ones to sense our feelings and experience a body-based *emotion*.

Primal amygdala-brain fear seems specific to our biological avatar body. Fear of heights, snakes, and spiders may represent built-in *subroutines* in our avatar's on-board operating system. As such, it's possible that PTSD (post-traumatic stress disorder) may be indicative of traumas strong enough to create new amygdala fear sub-routines.

What if, as demonstrated by conflicting parts of the brain, fear at the cosmic level is well-founded but at the same time false? Imagine yourself as a conscious beehive collective, sending out individuated conscious bees to collect information by way of trial-and-error adventures, only to reintegrate with the beehive collective at the end of the day. What if the universe does a similar scattering and reintegrating of souls that collect trial-and-error experiences?

Since the universe begins and ends as a single, un-individuated consciousness, the fear of eventually no longer being an individuated soul may be well founded in the fact that returning to a unified consciousness is ultimately inevitable. That said, fear assumes the regretful loss of something important as a seemingly individuated soul reintegrates with the collective. That assumption is false in that it will be seen as a huge upgrade, a huge gain, and a celebration instead of a loss. Hence, fear can be both *well-founded* and *completely false,* so proceed accordingly!

Our deepest fear 📖

Perhaps, as a child, our original art was received less than enthusiastically. Perhaps someone in the *cool* group in junior high school laughed when we dared to break away from the herd and show original creativity? Whenever it happened, somewhere along the way, our subconscious mind likely arrived at some version of this conclusion:

> *Being part of the group = safety. Displaying non-conformance or creative brilliance can get me ejected from group safety (risking death). Therefore, displaying creative brilliance = risking death.*

Hence, at some point in our childhood, we likely walled off much of our creative individuality, intuition, and power within our subconscious. We walled them off so deeply that we may not even remember or miss them. It's like we're an eight-cylinder car engine with three or more disabled cylinders.

We go through life underpowered and running rough, wondering how others are able to confidently climb the hills of challenges we wouldn't even attempt. What if those high achievers weren't really born more capable and courageous? What if they simply had the confidence of knowing they had access to more engine cylinders?

A similar subconscious coping mechanism may have walled off even more parts of us when we experienced a life trauma too intense to handle. Since those traumas are now in our past, this coping mechanism originally intended to ensure our survival may now be part of the problem, allowing an energy-leaking emotional wound to remain largely below our radar.

How would our life's trajectory and world impact have been different if we had all eight cylinders working with no energy-leaking wounds? If that sentence brought up a little uneasiness (fear), why do we suppose that is? In her book *Return to Love*, Marianne Williamson says: "Our deepest fear… is that we are powerful beyond measure. It is our light, not our darkness, that most frightens us."

We may be subconsciously attracted to things that resemble repressed memories. On the dark side, we may therefore be attracted to negative encounters because a part of us hopes they will open old wounds to be healed.

> *If you have an unresolved anxiety/fear, you magnetically attract things, experiences or people that will put you into that anxiety/fear.* —The Z's

Especially during the shift, those who've made the effort to heal old wounds may attract fewer negative experiences because that particular curriculum is no longer needed. Healing wounds is hard. Negative experiences are hard. Choose your form of hard.

On the flip side, we may be subconsciously attracted to *positive* encounters that remind us of the love we knew prior to incarnation amnesia. Since love will ultimately reabsorb us into oneness, an unenlightened part of us may subconsciously be more wary of positive encounters than negative ones. That may be a part of us in need of healing.

In my early 40s, I first heard the term "soul retrieval." On average, nine minutes of listening to a repetitive drum beat in the range of 4–10 beats per second may induce a type of brain wave that's useful for internal journeying and introspection. My *soul retrieval* session with a female shaman involved listening to brainwave entrainment drumbeats as we lay side by side on the carpet. My job was to maintain a neutral mind. Her job was to do a shamanic journey into the walled-off parts of my subconscious in order to negotiate the terms of a possible reintegration.

When it was over, she had reportedly negotiated with two walled-off parts of me: one walled off very early in life during the trauma of my brother nearly dying of appendicitis, and one walled off during the trauma of my 6th grade self being forced to abandon my childhood home and friends to move to a cabin in Alaska.

The shaman said those parts of me would agree to rejoin me (*at that time, an emotionally bottled-up computer engineer*) only if I promised to occasionally allow my inner child to come out and play. Per my side of the deal, friends and family have since seen my inner, playful child come out from time to time. Per their part of the deal, multiple disabled cylinders suddenly became functional.

The resulting upgrade in my courage and creativity was palpable, as I suddenly had it in me to tackle my biggest fears: *personal growth seminars, public a cappella singing, cliff diving, standup comedy,* and harnessing enough courage and creativity to be turned down by my corporate superiors perhaps 100 times in order to eventually achieve over 30 technology patents. In short, getting those disabled cylinders back online completely changed my notion of what was *beyond* me, which altered my life's trajectory.

The only fences between us and personal growth are our defenses.

Besides a visit from a shaman (which is also a possibility), how could you tell if your version of *normal* involves needlessly disabled cylinders? Do you find some hills or challenges too much to even consider? Do you find the thought of these hills suddenly being within your reach oddly unsettling? Welcome to the fear of your own brilliance and the dread (fear) of the courage and determination that exercising your brilliance might require. After finding a way to bring your disabled cylinders online, how do you build up the muscles of your brilliance and courage? Like any muscle, start small and incrementally attempt more until your full potential has been reached.

> *You don't have to see the whole staircase,*
> *just take the first step.* — @aromathyme

How important might this be for us collectively? If humanity may be seen as a soup, the recipe may only reach its full potential if we each bring our unique ingredient to the soup at full strength.

Our birthright to have all spark plugs firing 📖

Beyond merely staying healthy, goal manifestation occurs best when our personal power (energetic sovereignty) and vibratory rate are optimized.

> *The only reason you have not already gotten what you desire is because you are holding yourself in a vibrational pattern that does not match the vibration of your desire.* —Abraham-Hicks

Far beyond the energy we may receive from organic food or walking barefoot in the grass, we have access to constant cosmic energy all around us in the quantum field, but only if our chakra *solar panels* are connected and correctly oriented. Figure 5.1 illustrates the synergy possible when energy is highly concentrated at the same spot at the same time—energy from multiple *sparkplug* sources, each optimized via our thoughts. Not leaving valuable energy on the table starts with opening all energy chakras, but it doesn't stop there. Our personal energy levels are synergistically optimized when we choose to:

- Be here and now with a loving, open heart.
- Be grounded and sourced in our body.
- Maintain a positive, high-vibration, grateful frame of mind.

- Synergize with high-vibration others, both seen and unseen.

That is, showing up as a self-sovereign, hyper-D being. The *good* news is that a personal engine firing on all spark plugs is achievable by way of the conscious choices of a sovereign mind.

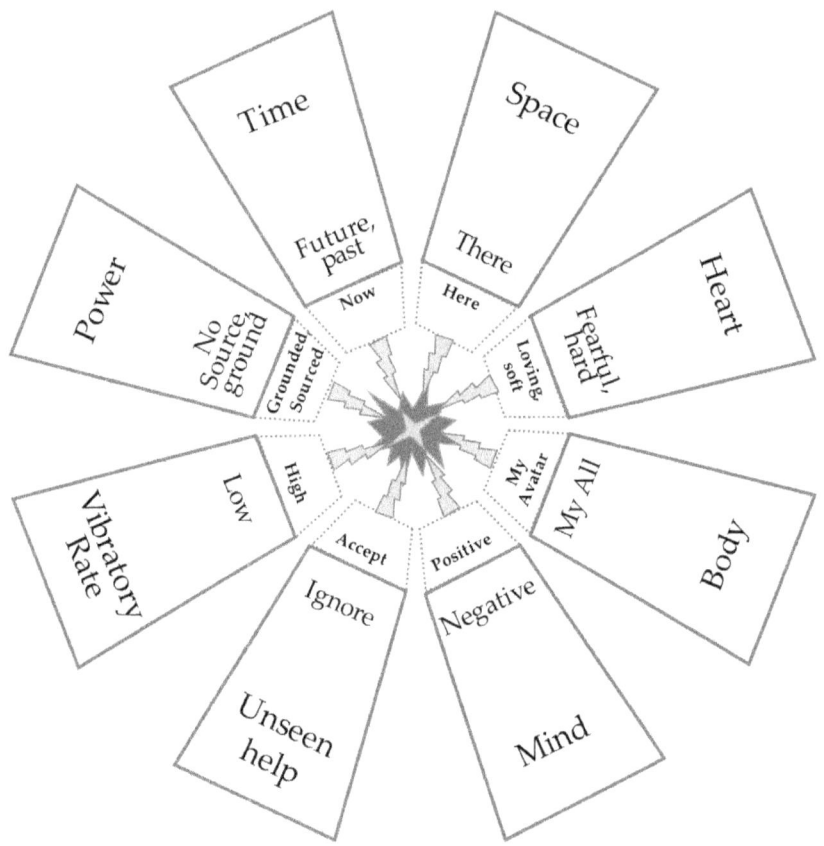

Figure 5.1: The synergy of utilizing many available resources.

The *bad* news is that we tend to be deluged from birth with messages to be wary of our chakras or point our personal *solar panels* in the wrong directions, such as with ego-centric goals. Most normalize skimping along with only a few of these spark plugs firing, wondering why life's hills seem more daunting for themselves than some others. What will it be?

Fear can be harmful 📖

If fear, fortified by falsehood, secrecy, and blind obedience, were ingredients in the toxic potion used by the game to suppress our greatness, the *antidote* would be courage and love, fortified by Truth, disclosure, and self-sovereignty. The time to take the antidote and express our greatness is now. If not now, when? If not us, who?

> *Fear prompts us to put up with departures from Truth, while ironically, departures from Truth account for much of our fear.*

The impact of fear on our bodies, communities, and planet is far more serious than most realize. Fear is much more than a private, chemical-driven emotion. Fear can be a toxic energy that transmits not only within the body but broadcasts like a radio signal into the community, wreaking havoc locally and remotely, individually and collectively. Toxic fear shorts out our energy circuits and downshifts us, individually and collectively, from our birthright maximum powers to somehow normalized subpar powers.

> *Fear persuades us to lower our vibration enough that fear can continue to persuade us.*

Most fail to appreciate that fear, more than an entertaining hobby involving horror movies, news programs, and crime shows, is a firmly entrenched foundational layer of our psyche. One who decides to give up fear quickly finds they must also give up fear's children, such as judgment, anger, worry, blame, guilt, grievances, etc.

The fear-based, controlled narratives of the game would have us live and die as full of ourselves, ego-wise, and as a mere shell of ourselves, empowerment-wise. Our quest as self-sovereigns is to *flip the script* until we're a mere shell of ourselves, ego-wise, and full of ourselves, empowerment-wise. This is the goal, not just before we die, but in time to do the very work we're here to do. What will it be?

Reclaim birthrights 📖

Self-sovereignty infers *self*-authorization, by way of *self*-granted permission. Given that, what might be included in the list of our poorly understood and often unclaimed sovereign birthrights?

What if the government announced that breathing is only to take place when and how the government gives permission? You might declare that breathing when and how you want is your sovereign birthright; no permission is necessary. Ironically, breathing properly is just one of several sovereign birthrights that most have forfeited. Most of us practice chronically shallow and untrained breathing, forfeiting untold amounts of vitality, health, and challenge-completing (prana, zero-point, or field) energy. This is why a child entering an eastern monastery is liable to receive breath training from the very first day.

Proper breathing is only one of the largely forfeited birthrights that may leave enormous amounts of energy potential on the table. How many other sovereign birthrights might we be forfeiting? Hints can be found in the historical Jesus. He took self-sovereign control of his *time, energy,* thoughts, emotions, actions, friends, etc. At the same time, he resisted controlled narratives, judgments, and grievances while embracing gratitude, forgiveness, and compassion.

That list began with time and energy. Because energy levels are related to vibration rates, the wise constantly lean toward higher-vibration foods, thoughts, emotions, music, friends, locations, entertainment, books, etc. What will it be?

Consciously navigating the life map 📖

The life map (Fig. 5.2) works equally well, whether tracing (dotted line) the path of one life, or one soul through several lives. The map consists of four quadrants.

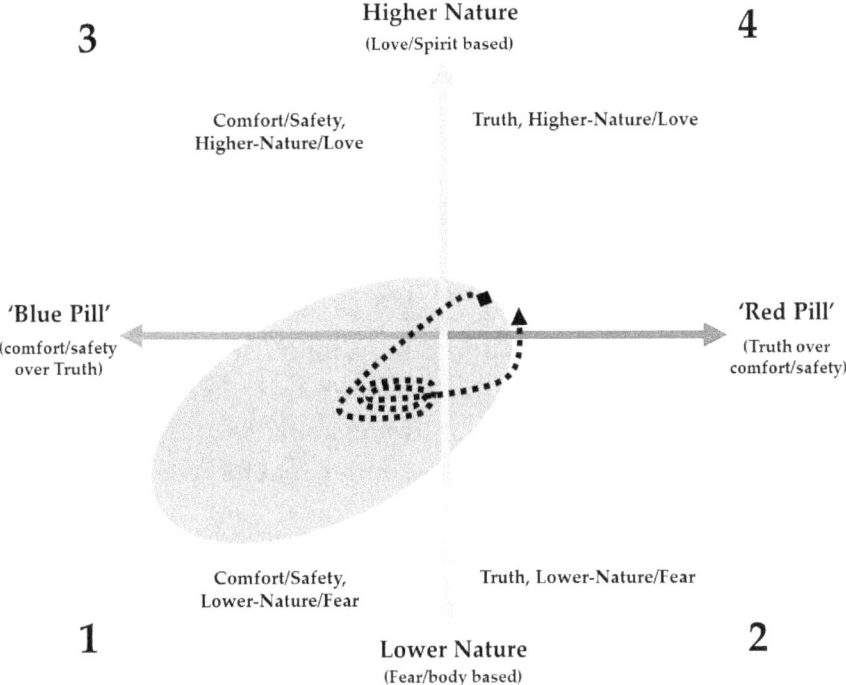

Figure 5.2: A four-quadrant approach to life.

The top part of the vertical axis refers to those currently leaning into their *higher* nature, which is love and soul based. In chakra terms, these people try to live in their heart chakra or above.

> *If you wanted to find a part of your body that most represented your soul essence, it would be the heart chakra. This is where the oneness inside you resides.* — The Z's

The bottom part of the vertical axis refers to those currently leaning into their *lower* nature, which is more fear-based and body-based. In chakra terms, these people tend to live in their three lowest chakras.

The right side of the horizontal axis is *red pill* territory for those with the courage to prioritize Truth over comfort and safety. The left side of the horizontal axis is *blue pill* territory for those who prioritize comfort and safety over Truth. As illustrated by the darker area, much of humanity spends almost all their life (or lives) in lower left quadrant number one, more in their lower (body/fear) nature than their higher (spirit/love) nature, and prioritizing safety and comfort over Truth.

At humanity's current level of ascension or enlightenment, this seems to be the default quadrant. Even for those currently residing in other quadrants, fear constantly tempts us to retreat to quadrant one, where we tend to grant forgiveness only to those who ask for and *deserve* it, while erroneously assuming that forgiveness is for the other person's benefit.

> *The point where compassion ends and grievance begins reflects where our love-based higher nature and fear-based lower nature currently meet. Moving that point can brighten or darken our world.*

Also illustrated by the darker area, only a fraction of humanity resides in the lower right quadrant (two). This is the likely territory of those involved in classified programs, secret alliances, secret conflicts, and secret societies. They have access to more (perhaps concealed) Truth than most, but they are still oriented toward their lower nature and non-forgiveness.

The desire to prioritize Truth over comfort and safety while still embracing our lower nature tends to land us in this quadrant. Those seeking to uncover closely guarded truths while operating in this quadrant may be called conspiracy theorists. While the *force* available to groups with access to influence, money, technology, and insider knowledge can be compelling to those in this quadrant, it's ultimately no match for the *power* found in quadrant four.

Love, a desire for service, a preference for safety and comfort, and a willingness to accept controlled narratives as "truth" tend to progress us toward or into the upper left quadrant (three). This is where young clergy in training are often found.

As illustrated by the gray area, only a fraction of humanity resides here, such as those who prefer the hand-me-down conclusions and rules of religion over the effort and courage involved with the first-hand research, experiments, and conclusions of spirituality.

Remember what the dormouse said...Feed your head. —Grace Slick

Although the rules of religion may be many, spirituality can be summed up so simply that it can be followed by a growing corn stalk: *seek and follow the light while benefiting the world around you.*

> *Spirituality is to religion what fire is to smoke. When it comes to solo research of cosmic Truth, if spirituality is a bicycle, religions may be more like a bicycle with training wheels within a fenced yard.*

Love, a desire for win-win service, and the courage to prioritize Truth over comfort and safety may progress us toward or into the upper right quadrant (four). From this place, love helps us to forgive those who don't ask for it, if only for self-care. We may intuitively recognize Truth without proof and the Truth about "proof," perform first-person research, and arrive at firsthand conclusions. This is where the reincarnation game entrance/exit door likely resides— where the karmic wheel begins and ends in a place of balance.

Whether our society progresses toward being more heaven-like or hell-like may hinge on something as simple as a presumption of reincarnation, taught as truth for centuries by the early Christian church. The least enlightened are those most willing to use intimidation to steer the rest of us, so they are often in control. Their ability to get us to comply, as opposed to doing the right thing, may come down to whether we feel they are threatening someone's only life or one of many.

It's been said that Earth has historically been a "karma-enforced" planet. This means that those who accept the challenge of incarnating on this planet for the first time start out with a neutral (zero) karmic score and are only allowed to leave upon death (without reincarnating) if they have returned to a neutral or positive karmic score.

My working theory is that "karma" is an acronym: *Knowledge Attainment Remediates Metered Adversity*, where our higher self holds our feet to the fire (via *metered adversity*) until an "ah ha" completes our 360-degree visceral knowledge of a topic we may have begun exploring a *long* time ago.

Whether that metered adversity takes 5 minutes or 5 lifetimes, our higher self has all the time in the world, so a better approach than "I just have to suffer through it" would be "What realizations would complete my 360-degree visceral understanding of this topic, so this situation can change?" In other words, both you and (higher self) *You* have the ability to meter up or meter down the adversity, switching to a new topic in the curriculum.

Since our higher self is a personal window onto more cosmic information, connectivity, Love, and energy than we can fathom, the path of enlightenment involves you leaning into You.

It's *You* doing it to and for you. The wise seek 360-degree understanding until the latest adversity has nothing more to teach us, when the situation often alters as if by magic. This may amount to either working with or against the universe.

For rare and careful individuals, such as some historical spiritual figures, quadrant four may be accomplished in a single, one-and-done incarnation. Most take much longer to regain karmic balance so as to be able to find the exit door. Along the way, we would be well served to hone the subtle senses necessary to perceive the True nature of people and things, as opposed to the controlled narratives about them.

> *The world is full of magic things, patiently waiting for our senses to grow sharper.* —Simon Haiduk

I've spent time in all four quadrants, sometimes in a single day. That said, I try to begin and end each day in quadrant four via daily affirmations. Even so, I'm typically not so deep into quadrant four that a random emotional trigger can't transport me below the horizontal line faster than I can say, "Outrage/ego bait!" Then, it's *off to the races* as I spend the rest of the day trying to regain sufficient sovereignty of mind to shift from grievance obsessing to the meta view of the neutral observer to the softened compassion and forgiveness necessary to transport me back above the horizontal line. I know I've succeeded when my mind's chatter goes quiet and the tension in my body subsides.

> *No compassionate forgiveness, no peace.*
> *Know compassionate forgiveness; know peace.*

Many confuse "forgive" with "absolve." Absolving is about whether the wheels of justice should proceed. Absolving is about *them.* Forgiveness is an internal purge of toxic energy that disquiets and harms *us*. Adequate science exists to indicate that forgiveness is more about us, our health, and our longevity.

Since forgiving and absolving are completely different, we can do one, both, or neither. Imagine trying *not* to think of the person who just hurt your feelings. Try as you might, you likely can't stop the experience from disquieting your mind and body. The ability to forgive someone (*release the emotional charge without forgetting*) to the point of our mind, heart, and body becoming quiet is an advanced skill, out of reach for many.

Do you sense that your life or health might be improved by embarking on a self-study course in forgiveness? Even the news constantly offers a target-rich environment of forgiveness opportunities. Any time is optimal to begin a forgiveness curriculum. For what it's worth, this is my process:

Step 1: Don't take the outrage or ego bait, and don't marinate in the news or any other fear-biased controlled narratives.

Step 2: OK, I took the bait, so switch to my neutral (non-egoic) observer, employ softening, compassion, and forgiveness, lay it down, walk away, and hope it doesn't follow me home. As they say, "rinse and repeat."

Step 3: Triggered by my head's contact with my pillow, I begin and end every day by visualizing energy cleansing my body from head to toe: compassion, forgiveness, and healing flooding in with toxic grievances draining out.

If, when I let a grievance go, it refuses to let me go, I find a positively charged space, like a personal growth seminar or sacred space, where the less possible somehow becomes more possible. If none is readily available, an alternative is to use *meditation* and high-vibration emotions to charge our own space.

Having zero thoughts in meditation is blissful, but how does one get from here to there? Since my mind has a hard time doing nothing, I concentrate on something that amounts to nothing, such as an imaginary whirring fan. I cool my mind down in incremental stages, from:

Whir (imaginary fan noise) ...."Thank you God," to...
Whir..."Thank you," to...
Whir..."Thank", to...
Whir.......[silence]...............Ah!

Regarding the absolution of my many "forgiveness teachers" in the news, I'll leave that decision to others. In the meantime, I hope to use forgiveness to add years to my life and life to my years.

May all my grievances be forgot and never brought to mind. May all my grievances be forgot for Auld Lang Syne (to let bygones be bygones).

If we all ended each day with the above words, how might the world be transformed? In the meantime, I'll meet you in quadrant four, because that's where the really cool stuff happens!

The truth about "proof" 📖

That which has no proof but aligns with our Truth-sensing intuition is often seen years later as True. That which has "proof" but doesn't align with Truth-sensing intuition is often overturned years later.

Per science, *proof* is the subjective product of content, point of observation, intention, context, paradigm, and underlying premises.

Hence, any *proof* may eventually turn out to be either one strand in a strong rope or just a column of smoke. As such, a person or society that values Truth-sensing intuition while not over-venerating *proof* would be less gullible, progressing farther and faster.

It's not arbitrary that the most important and pivotal things in life can't be proven. Some say it's a matter of cosmic law. If we are *sure* that something can't occur or can't exist, incontrovertible proof that would manhandle our cognitive dissonance or confusion into accepting Truth (ready or not) may violate what some call the cosmic *Law of Protected Confusion*, or the *Law of Free Will*[64].

Hence, the coolest, unprovable things often *can't* happen for anyone who's sure they can't happen but *can* happen for someone else. This means that proof for the most important and pivotal issues may be more personal than a matter of mainstream acceptance. My wish for the world is the intuition to recognize Truth without proof, as well as the Truth *about* "proof."

Do we really want the truth? 📖

Many of us have a complicated relationship with the truth. While we say we would rather know the truth, what we often mean is that we would rather know the *safe* truths that will enhance our lives but not the truths that could be too disruptive. Indeed, the same truth that can earn you a Nobel Prize in one century could get you imprisoned or put to death in another. Hence, being on the leading edge of truth is not for the timid, but it's becoming increasingly less dangerous as we progress into the shift.

Living in a universal hologram means the truth is always accessible. If you cut a holographic photo of a cat on a piano into hundreds of little pieces and use a magnifying glass to examine the tiniest fragment, you don't see a cat's left ear; you see an entire cat sitting atop an entire piano.

The nature of a hologram is that there is no part of the hologram where all the information is *not*. Given that, when physicists say our universe is holographic, there is nowhere in the universe (including our heart and brain) where all information—past, present, and future potentials—is not.

Many meditating inventors have made use of this concept to come to know that which they supposedly had no way of knowing. Indeed, the holographic nature of the universe played a part in how I came to have my name on so many computer technology patents.

I never came up with any of my discoveries through the process of rational thinking. —Albert Einstein

If history is any indication, perhaps half of our contemporary "truths" will eventually be recognized as either completely false or non-durable pseudo-truths. We must be especially careful about non-durable "truths," which are enforced (sometimes brutally) and defended as unquestionably correct, right up to the moment when they're seen as *never* having been true.

...everything is right until it's wrong. You'll know when it's wrong. —Ernest Hemingway

In the meantime, those whose intuition told them that a "truth" wasn't True are often subjected to varying types and degrees of violence. Leading-edge Truth is not for the timid. An example regarding the elusiveness of absolute Truth may be helpful.

During a fictitious kinesiology muscle strength test, you hold a paper with the following words next to your heart: "One plus one equals two." Why does the tested muscle go weak, indicating a low degree of Truth? Since digital circuits are either *on* or *off*, the only numbers possible in their base-2 number system are 1 and 0, so 1+1 = 10 in a base-2 digital circuit. OK, "One plus one is usually equal to 2." The muscle still goes weak, indicating the phrase is false! How could that be? Since there are far more digital circuits than humans, 1+1 is *usually* 10! OK, "One plus one in base-10 numbers equals 2." The muscle stays strong, indicating True. See what I mean about Truth being far trickier and elusive than you might think?

Does this mean kinesiology can potentially provide a weak/strong muscle answer to a large array of *carefully* worded (even science-related[65]) questions involving the past and present? In theory, yes. Science has verified that the body tests stronger in the presence of

True, as if it is somehow exposed to a strengthening[66] energy field that is not there in the presence of *false*. Large body muscles have tested 17% stronger[67], with 59% more endurance in the presence of a True statement energy field, such as when making a yes/no statement or even holding an unread True statement in written form next to the heart.

Success in using these techniques seems to correlate with more activated chakra circuitry and a higher consciousness vibratory rate. Therefore, these concepts may prove useful for only a fraction of the population. At least for those people, it could be quite useful to notice the strengthening of Truth energy in a carefully worded true or false statement about *anything, anywhere* in the past or present. The potential ramifications of making global deceit extinct are staggering, especially as this ability is intensified by the shift.

Some kinesiology techniques claim to be able to assign a specific number representing the *relative* Truth of a statement or document, such as my first book[68], with a higher number representing a closer relationship to absolute Truth. For instance, I've noticed that mentioning the Big Bang theory in my writings results in a lower numerical score, inferring that part or all of that theory may not stand the test of time. I suspect that it was more like a Big *Intention*[69], with parts of the universe following unseen energetic templates toward higher levels of order (syntropy), while other parts seek lower levels of order (entropy).

Find our feminine, or find another planet 📖

In her book *Unearthing Venus*, Cate Montana[70] describes the Amazonian Shuar tribe, in which men (*wired toward maximizing self-interest until stopped*) do the fishing, hunting, and tree cutting while women (*wired more for tribal and global interest*) do everything else. While men and women are represented equally on the tribal council, one job essential to the survival of the tribe can only be performed by women.

Like an ecological cancer, the tribal men (unless stopped) may maximize their self-interest until there are no more fish to catch, no more animals to hunt, and no more trees to cut. Hence, the vital role of the feminine in their tribe is to say, "Stop!" This arrangement makes for a balanced, sustainable civilization.

Today, our society has many business types who utilize an erroneous social Darwinism belief system to ruthlessly pursue their self-interest in spite of ecological costs until they are stopped.

> *Dear Business Leader, the more room your business has for integrity and compassion, the more room the future will have for your business.*

Somehow, it has become normalized that profits should go to them while the health and ecological ramifications go to others. So, where are the women to say, "Stop!" to our global military and business tribe so that humanity might survive the sixth great planetary extinction in which we currently find ourselves?

Eventually, more of us will have sufficient internal masculine/feminine balance that the word "Stop!" can come from within us. In the meantime, we may need the feminine dominant (regardless of gender) to shake off the institutionally reinforced "Stay quiet and in your place" narrative, step up, and help save our global tribe by occasionally saying, "Stop!"

> *...things you used to tolerate have become intolerable. Where you once remained quiet, you are now speaking your truth...stand firmly and gracefully in your feminine power.* —#thequeencode[71]

People without a functioning ethical compass can only gauge the appropriateness of their actions within the context of their often-indifferent community. As long as community mass consciousness is vibrationally low, people can do hurtful, lower-nature, low-vibration things that pass as normalized and appropriate.

Prophets, in many forms, may confront unethical and unsustainable behavior, but while mass consciousness is vibrationally low, group consensus tends to dismiss them.

> *Show an accurate compass to someone who's been following a flawed one for a day, and you may be seen as a solution. Show it to someone who's been following a flawed compass for years, and you may be seen as a problem.*

Working in concert to raise the mass consciousness may be the best leverage toward a brighter world. What will it be?

Ch. 6: Shift 103

Watch for new abilities

What if, as we increasingly shake off incarnation amnesia, our divine birthright abilities become more *uncovered* than acquired?

It's said that it takes a hyperdimensional source to create a hyperdimensional effect. If so, when we see unusual effects such as spontaneous remission, channeling, bilocation, spiritual healing, someone moving or bending objects, or manifesting with their mind, what is the hyper-D part of us that, via intent, enables these hyper-D effects?

Quantum biologists know that our DNA displays hyper-D attributes. The synergistic combination of trillions of hyper-D human DNA strands likely creates a *cumulative* hyper-D biofield around us. That biofield is said to extend 6 to 12 feet beyond our body. This field is likely capable of responding to our intention, which in turn can bias matter, quantum potentials, and synchronicities.

> *Blessed is the human who understands the power*
> *they have over everyday occurrences.* —Kryon

Mind-over-matter isn't rare when we include the placebo effect. What's causing the placebo effect to continually get stronger to the point that it's increasingly difficult for new drugs to top its effectiveness? Our solar system's position within the galaxy has been changing, resulting in new, stronger energies that are not only impacting but perhaps empowering our individual hyper-D fields. The deeper we get into this new area of space, the stronger these energies will become, and the more common hyperdimensional effects, such as *mind over matter*, will become for those willing to develop sovereignty of mind. Welcome to the shift. This presents us with two options: lead this trend or be confounded by it.

Channeled sources have stated that the ~1/3 of our soul that historically resides on this side of the veil has been upgraded by the shift to a higher percentage, resulting in our bodies now possessing unprecedented levels of life and light.

> *When connected to your soul, you are*
> *at one with spiritual energy.* —The Z's

Remember those mind-over-matter, manifesting, healing, or life extension experiments you once tried and abandoned? As these new energies get stronger each day, keep trying, and don't be surprised if what once didn't work one day works!

Surfer, or sufferer?

The consciousness upgrade and *energy wave* shift we're currently experiencing will only build in the coming decades. This wave will increasingly separate society into those who *ride* this (new-normal) energy wave versus those who attempt to cling to the old long enough to be upended by the wave. The path each of us has individually chosen is becoming easier to spot with each passing day. I call this the *split*.

Old-energy authority figures may seek to invalidate the innate intuition, common sense, and sacred worthiness of today's *surfer*. In the minds of old-energy onlookers, that invalidation may even *seem* successful. To the shift *surfer*, however, they may have only invalidated their authority. In the *old* energy, compassion is often portrayed as weakness. For shift surfers, compassion unlocks hyper-D energy sources while aligning us with Earth's ascended future.

In *old* energy, improving our individual sovereignty of mind may not even be worth missing a single fear-inducing TV program. For shift surfers, the benefits of sovereignty of mind are not just important but difficult to overstate. In *old* energy, win-lose thinking is normal. For shift surfers, it will be seen as increasingly counterproductive.

Is winning at the expense of Truth and integrity a win or a loss? One's answer as an individual, group, or institution reveals the side they've chosen in the split.

In *old* energy, fear-laced and drama-laced content is perceived as both informative and entertaining. For shift surfers, it may be viewed as more toxic and disempowering than it's worth. In *old* energy, emotional balance may be unrealistic. For shift surfers, it's a top priority. In *old* energy, good news is rare. For shift surfers, it doesn't take much research to realize that good news is far more prevalent than bad news, but massively and purposefully under-reported.

Most of your media is about fear, manipulation, and control. If everyone watched only good news channels for three years, your planet would be massively changed. —The Z's (paraphrased)

In short, the consciousness shift energy wave foretold by the ancients will increasingly require us to either align with the compassion[72] of Earth's ascended future as a *surfer* or default to being a *sufferer*. What will it be?

Imaginals

As alluded to in my first book, imaginal cells can be both a literal and metaphorical evolutionary catalyst toward something greater. Physical *imaginal* cells can evolve a caterpillar into a butterfly. If imaginal cells can add dimension to a ground-based being by transforming it into a being of the air, what new dimensions might they bring to those of us who may already be proverbial butterflies?

For "evolutionaries" who've already made that first evolutionary jump[73], it's now time for yet another step that's equally profound.

Evolution requires awakening to that self that remembers it's all connected.... —Alberto Villoldo, Ph.D.

As part of the shift, new and strengthening energetic influences and intuition are prompting us (ready or not) to evolve toward new levels of dimensionality, both within 4D and beyond, into hyper-D territory.

> *Higher dimensions are coming in higher than ever. It is your path to become a powerful conduit for those energies... Create the [internal] environment for your next level of wisdom, empowerment, [and] connectedness.* —The Z's

There are many ways to lean into *broader* and *higher* dimensions. An obvious approach is to begin by integrating the normally disparate levels of ourselves. Much can be gained by increasing, even marginally, how much our conscious mind communicates with our sub-conscious, our super-conscious (higher self), our innate body, unseen assistance, our cells, and our auric biofield.

Perhaps the lowest-hanging fruit may be verbal affirmations, to which our *innate* body may respond. Our innate body is the largely inaccessible part of us that we interrogate via kinesiology and instruct via homeopathy.

While (lower-case t) truth may resonate with the controlled narratives programmed into our logic, a high (capital T) Truth might cause our subtle, innate body to respond with goose (Truth) bumps or chills. The process of following subtle body responses from truth to Truth opens the door to universal knowledge.

This is how we not only broaden the dimensions of our wise 4D selves but also push into previously unnoticed hyper-D territory. If I were a *man of letters*, perhaps "HE" would be appropriate after my name, as in *Hyper-D Explorer*. As described in my first book, I've already begun exploring dimensions in time and space.

Even if this book was published 50 years ago (when our solar system was in a quieter area of the galaxy), many of the spiritual, broader-dimensional, and higher-dimensional principles in this book would still apply. However, astronomers now confirm that we're being bathed in increasing radiation due to our *new* position in the galaxy.

Although still beyond today's science, esoteric sources such as Kryon say that this is not random galactic radiation but catalytic energy designed to bias us toward ascension.

Ascension involves taking the hand of Spirit and never letting go. It's the energy of masters, enabling a human to go beyond physics. —Kryon

Other esoteric sources, such as the Z's, assert that we're also increasingly inundated by catalytic crystalline energies from below. I'll refer to the combination of these two influences as "RICE," or a *rising inundation of catalytic energy*. Whether from above or below, electrically grounding ourselves by sitting or walking barefoot on the earth may help stabilize and integrate RICE overstimulation.

Hence, one should watch for a slow upward bias or shift in useful higher-dimensional energy, resources, and abilities. Since this shift will continue to intensify well beyond our lifetime, it's in our best interest to consciously align with it. As sailors set their sails to take advantage of unseen winds, those who are aware of the shift may likewise take advantage of the very changes that may confound others.

At first glance, the notion of leaning into our broader-dimensional or higher-dimensional nature may seem out of reach. What if it's not only reachable but also important for navigating the shift? What if confining ourselves to four dimensions serves nothing but our fearful smallness?

It's like assuming we must manually row a boat because controlled narratives suggest that the hyper-D engine available to us is only an illusion or somehow inappropriate to use. Those of our enlightened future may view this as a tragic waste of (hiding in plain sight) higher-dimensional resources—such as our subtle energy senses, or heart-brain-pineal complex, our intuition, our innate body, and our higher self.

In truth, higher dimensions may be far more approachable, common, and helpful than most appreciate. When keeping an eye out for extra dimensions, we may surprisingly encounter them even in ordinary places. Isn't intuition an extra dimension of the linear mind? Isn't remote viewing an extra dimension of our ability to see? Isn't lucid dreaming an extra dimension of dreaming? Indeed, it was the habit of watching for extra dimensions that (in my first book) allowed me to transform the commonly known *predator-prey-protector* 2D triangle into a 3D pyramid.

Ask yourself, "If there were more dimensions to *[fill in the blank]*, what might they be?" How might it be improved by an extra dimension? One way to spot something of a higher-dimensional nature hiding in plain sight is to try forcing it into a linear, 4D measurement, only to find that either "yes" or "n/a" (not applicable) are the best, if not the only answer.

How high or wide is love? *Yes.* When you're thinking of a departed loved one, how far have they traveled (hyperdimensionally) for you to sense them near you? *N/A.* Hyper-D travel does not involve distance. Using just this filter, we can readily identify many hyper-D aspects of our current world.

> In 4D, things are measured, including love.
> Hyper-D is where we'll find Love beyond measure.

Another way to spot something of a higher-dimensional nature is the "it takes one to know one" principle. In other words, that which interacts with hyper-D properties has some hyper-D properties. Light, gravity, magnetism, and electrons are known to have hyper-D properties. Thus, the presence of human DNA altering the spin of electrons smacks of human DNA having hyper-D properties. The fact that human consciousness interacts with magnetism infers that our consciousness has hyper-D properties. Perhaps that's how pure conscious intent can travel forward in time to assemble the interdimensional potentials that we call synchronicities.

> *If faith is a passive forfeiture of power to something, hope is active, sending into our future designer energy to facilitate synchronicities.* —Kryon

Most not only understand the term "beyond the veil" but also grasp that if or when we might find ourselves there, we would no longer be restricted by normal 4D constraints. Reportedly[74], rather than the veil between 4D and hyper-D being something imposed on us, it's a construction of our own consciousness for the purpose of simplifying our world. This is accomplished by making our hyper-D magnificence *seem* more unreachable than is actually the case. Unfortunately, keeping our hyper-D magnificence out of sight also keeps our hyper-D wisdom, skills, and options out of sight.

Because an un-acclimated body can't handle all the energy of our higher self, two-thirds of it is said to historically reside behind the veil. If so, this hints at how much more is possible in the lives of those willing to (via intent and permission) acclimate their bodies to larger fractions of hyper-D soul energy.

For those who are now ready for more dimensionality, now is the time to push the boundaries of what's true, what's real, and what's possible. Intent to embrace our hyper-D magnificence signals our higher self to make our personal veil more permeable more often, which can upgrade both our current experience and future potential.

For instance, looking through 4D eyes, a troublesome situation may seem to have victimized us and only be changeable by forcing a change or fleeing. Hyper-D eyes may look at the same situation, but see our higher self as what's anchoring the current situation in place until we've embraced some lesson. If we do force a change or flee, our higher self may just recreate the same *opportunity* for learning in some other, escalated way.

> *The universe seeks to conserve energy, yet it remains as steadfast in keeping us uncomfortable as we are in avoiding the lesson. That's how important we and our growth are.*

A more efficient and ascended option is to view ourselves and the situation with compassion until we've noticed and internalized the necessary lessons. Curiously enough, the very situation that refused to change prior to us getting the lesson often then changes, in that the puzzle pieces have served their purpose and no longer need to be held in place. Yes, we are *really* that powerful.

You're here to learn lessons, but they get unnecessarily difficult, painful, and dark when you disconnect from Spirit, which is really disconnection from self, wholeness, and oneness. Make your spiritual wellbeing of utmost importance… reconnect to what lights you up. —The Z's

The unlearning side of the fence

As part of the *shift* and *split*, we're witnessing an increasing distinction between those exhibiting the lighter-energy values and ethics of the future and those exhibiting the darker-energy values and ethics of the past, who see no reason to unlearn. Unlearn what?

- Unlearn that loyalty should take precedence over Truth and ethics.
- Unlearn that profits should take precedence over people and the environment.
- Unlearn that the end justifies the means.
- Unlearn that some must lose in order for others to win.
- Unlearn that might makes right, death is the end, and compassion is weakness.

Enlightenment requires continuous unlearning, an ongoing process of intuitively replacing training with Truth.

After the *great unlearning*, we'll begin to relearn. Relearn what?

- Relearn to prioritize Truth, balance, and peace of mind over money.
- Relearn to suppress our fears rather than the vulnerable.
- Relearn to value and cling to our intuition as opposed to our controlling narratives.
- Relearn to be more wary of false narratives than the Truth.
- Relearn that embracing our courage produces better results than avoiding what we fear.
- Relearn that a responsive universe brings not what we want but what vibrationally matches our deepest thoughts and beliefs.
- Relearn what birth, spirituality, and "death" really are.

> **Birth**: *When a fraction of our eternal, unharmable self enters a dream of being separate, impermanent, and able to be harmed.*
> **Spiritual:** *Becoming lucid within the dream so as to seek the larger part of ourselves.*
> **"Death":** *Waking up from the dream to rejoin the larger part of ourselves.*

A Shift for technology

Like bicycle training wheels, technology will eventually become less needed as our consciousness, on the path to spiritual mastery, becomes increasingly capable of directly altering the physics of our world. On the way, expect an intermediate step where technology responds directly to our consciousness. Since experiments are already demonstrating consciousness impacting both matter and machines, it seems that the intermediate step has already begun.

Science will eventually realize that the laws of 4D physics are subordinate to the laws of hyper-D consciousness. When that occurs, science will claim it has *discovered* what people have been demonstrating for millennia. Water was turned into wine, loaves and fish were manifested or replicated as needed, etc. These reportedly occurred in accordance with the laws of consciousness through pure, focused intent and sovereignty of mind. Hence, when we of the future routinely use our minds to directly interact with physics, it will not be new, only more normalized.

The shift will increasingly take us from accomplishing things with technology to accomplishing things with our minds. Those who prioritize sovereignty of mind today may lead that trend. The rest may feel left behind. What will it be?

Mental freedom

How could so many come to believe in flawed narratives when intuition could quickly expose them as untrue? With help.

Intuition is an invaluable, subtle, and fleeting sense that's easily missed or muted. It's so valuable that a thimble full of intuitive Truth beats a gallon of narrative.

> *Developing intuition may seem like more trouble than it's worth until it begins guiding us to more worth than trouble.*

As part of the shift, improved intuition is increasingly available to us, but it seems to be a "use it or lose it" ability. Although the general public may not realize and appreciate this, many institutions, such as "news," political, and religious, likely do. They seem to specifically craft two-pronged narratives that hold us within their influence while dampening our intuitive truth detector. Hence, to not choose the protection of our intuition over a daily dose of intuition-suppressing narratives is to choose by default. Mental and intuitive freedom aren't free.

Managing our shift experience

You may have noticed that we live in a time of change. Those who are not aware of the shift may equate change they don't understand with fear and doom. The shift is the process of the universe slowly reworking Earth from a civilization with win-lose, low integrity, and low compassion wired into most things to a society with win-win, integrity, and compassion wired into most things.

Reportedly, now that the process has begun, it's not a question of if it will occur but only of how our collective free will enhances or minimizes the pain involved. Those who grasp the situation are more likely to ride it out comfortably by knowing the "why" and how to use their personal growth tools to minimize its impact.

> *During the shift, what part of the collective anxiety is ours to transmute into peaceful balance? The part we feel.*

Put another way, the shift represents vibrational and dimensional milestones measuring how we think of ourselves—from thinking of ourselves as 4D biological, to us as our integrated, innate smart body and biofield (Merkabah[75]), to us interacting with our hyper-D guides and angels, to us integrating with our higher self as an aspect of our hyper-D soul.

In other words, it's us reaching for and integrating with higher and higher frequency and dimensional aspects of our own selves. It's us reclaiming our birthright.

> *None of you are just you. All have nonverbal guides. Many are surrounded by {nature} elementals {plants, minerals}. Many are surrounded by angelics.* —The Z's

149

When enough of us have made this shift, there will be peace on Earth. We may think of a war-free Earth as the *finish* line, but on the galactic measuring stick of planetary ascension, it's more likely seen as the *starting* line.

The more we're aligned with (*and invested in*) aspects of society based on win-win, integrity, compassion, and *peaceful balance*, the less traumatic the shift may be for us. Alternatively, the more we're aligned with (*and invested in*) aspects of society that are the opposite, the more the shift may feel like being pulled inside out, through a knot hole, in slow motion. Hence, we have the key to controlling our shift experience. What will it be?

> *You can ignore reality, but you can't ignore the consequences of ignoring reality.* —Ayn Rand

Ch. 7: Shift 104

The shift, rather than WW3

The shift is the confluence of at least two factors. One factor is exposure to a *rising inundation of catalytic energy* (RICE). This lightworker activation energy is reportedly picked up by the double helix antennas of our DNA.

> *Energy has been raising for...25 years...that's why we're able to do things... we couldn't do before...we've got more energy to do it with.* —Raymon Grace, Dowser, Oct'22

For those of a compatible lightworker frequency, information is being forwarded to our consciousness in the form of continually increasing hyper-D (spiritual) savvy. The results, besides upgrades to our lightworker *toolbox*, are an increased tendency toward ascended consciousness as we lean toward our divine nature.

At the same time, non-lightworkers seem to be experiencing the same energy as increasing confusion, agitation, fear, and foreboding, often accompanied by a leaning *away* from one's divine nature. As part of the shift, this bifurcation is called the *split*.

> *The split: Where haters hate as wakers wake. One group leans into the oneness of their cosmic origin and Earth's ascended future, while the other clings to the false separation narratives of our past.*

Think *rapture* in super slow motion, complete with the separating out and the left-behind aspects—but rather than a division by physical ascension, a division by consciousness/dimensional ascension and how much one is influenced by their divine nature. That is, a division, not just in how much divine Love/soul energy a dowser like

Raymon Grace can measure in an individual but also in how the two splitting groups react differently to RICE.

> *There are energetic epidemics right now...one is where a person's soul energy has dropped...the Spirit of love has left their body....* —Raymon Grace, Oct'22[76]

One group is the "I know what's going on, why, and how to ride this multi-decade wave" crowd. This is the more optimistic, compassionate lightworker crowd. The other group is more of a fearful, pessimistic crowd that's likely to be upended by a wave they neither see coming nor understand.

> *For some, the shift is happening to them, like a mastless sailboat at the mercy of the wind and currents. For others, the shift is happening through them. This group effectively uses their sailboat's mast to overcome these forces, demonstrating mastery.*

Besides RICE, what's the second factor? Scientists such as Gregg Braden have long seen repeating cycles of human conflict, darkness, and renaissance, like time in a circle. The ancient indigenous people often tracked these cycles in terms of full or fractional parts of the ~26,000-year "Precession of the Equinoxes."

Like a train on a circular track, it's historically been possible to predict our future by looking at the past. Some have identified a 53.5-year *war cycle* that's so imprinted into Earth's circular time track that the propensity for future wars could actually be predicted.

Like with the war cycle, indigenous people have long been able to predict the rise and fall of civilizations. Sophisticated pre-ice-age archeological sites such as Gobekli Tepe, not to mention intuition and logic, indicate that our current civilization is not Earth's first.

So, how do these factors come together? The indigenous foretold that we, like prior civilizations, were on track to destroy ourselves prior to reaching December 2012 as the center point in the 36-year transition between one ~26,000-year cycle and the next. The civilization-ending event we were headed toward was called WW3 by some and Armageddon by others. Our pre-incarnation life plan reportedly allowed for this as a strong possibility.

Either way, we were scheduled to be *toast* before 2013, unless our cumulative consciousness gathered sufficient energy to throw a switch so that our planet's *train* could leave the old circular time track and start a new one. That is, a new, virgin time-circle track at a slightly ascended elevation. Specifically, an elevation just high enough that rather than us having a war consciousness that eventually ends us, we may grow into a higher consciousness that eventually ends war.

> *One road is the road of greed and technology without wisdom or respect for life... a rush to destruction. The other road is spirituality, a slower path that includes respect for all living things. If we choose the spiritual path, we...begin an extended period of peace and healthy growth.* —Grandfather William Commanda

As part of changing tracks, we're reportedly now in an era of "Correction Cycles," with each cycle bringing up something of low integrity to be collectively examined. This will be the type of examination that leads to "that's no longer acceptable" in some areas. The "Me Too" and "Black Lives Matter" movements may be examples.

> *The split continues to widen between the camp lacking compassion, especially toward those with it, and those with compassion, especially toward those lacking it. Like trying to straddle separating boats, we'll each have to choose a side. One side anchors us to the (survive) divisiveness of our past; the other side leads us to the (thrive) cooperative solutions of our future.*

Who could provide sufficient energy by way of a higher cumulative consciousness so that we could jump tracks? Sufficient energy could be provided by old soul lightworkers who've been here many times. How could a minority of lightworkers represent enough consciousness energy to compensate for the sleep-walking majority that often makes fun of them? Per Abraham-Hicks, "one who is in alignment is more powerful than millions who are not."

Fear causes us to get out of balance. How do lightworkers stay balanced when our society provides constant opportunities to marinate in fear and negativity? They promote balance by managing[77] their fear exposure while actively utilizing their self-management toolbox, acquired via books, seminars, mediation, etc. We may be unappreciative of how interdimensionally impactful our light and compassion are in shifting Earth's light/dark balance and how we can only be stopped by our fearful imbalance. However, some of those invested in maintaining the old ways are very aware, which could correlate with the average person's constant access to a free, all-you-can-eat media buffet of fear bait.

> *Typical "news" consists of two ingredients: imbalanced information and fear. We often think we're addicted to the first ingredient when it's actually the second.*

As normalized, entertaining, and addictive as fear-based media and news can be, our future will thank us for avoiding the fear buffet while sending light and compassion to those still drawn to it.

So, did old soul light workers generate enough light to shift our planet's train to a virgin circular time track at a high enough consciousness level to cancel WW3 and Armageddon? Yes, you're welcome.

Old souls are starting to light up due to an enhancement in their biology. Parts of your higher self (soul) that were not with you before are with you now. The power of that light is starting to make a difference where you walk, enhancing your partnership with Gaia (Earth Mother). This level of light has never before been seen on this planet. —Kryon

How is our civilization on a virgin track so significant? Besides throwing some of our pre-incarnation nuclear destruction plans out the window, it reportedly enables us to also have the option to delete past-life karma while extending our average longevity. This is no small thing. In short, our past no longer predicts our future. Instead, we (in the next 50–100 years) get to imprint on the new circular track whatever we want. Whatever it is, it can either bless or curse future generations that may travel along the same track.

We are now in the process of defining a new normal. As we do, new, higher-consciousness catalytic energy will keep arriving in ever-increasing waves. Ever feel light-headed or emotional for no particular reason? Heard any unexplained high-pitched noises? As we proceed, watch for higher levels of light to increasingly expose the darkness that used to be hidden. Also watch for less tolerance and normalization of that darkness. Darkness has noticed and will not give up without a vehement fight. This includes attempts at *normalizing* their darkness while shifting blame, as well as trying to scare us out of balance and back into our grandfather's world.

> *When the shift brings up something of low integrity to be addressed, will we support the shifters or the shifty? A shifter says, "If it's truly lacking in integrity, let's clean it up," while the shifty tries to normalize it or divert attention. One approach leads to our future, the other to our past.*

As the saying goes, "things are not getting worse, they're getting exposed." Hence, we're now in a phase that's somewhat like a spinning top wobbling erratically before it finds its balance.

> *This is not the end of the world. It is the*
> *end of the illusion.* —Humberto Braga

Especially between now and 2030, when inroads made by the light will reportedly become more apparent, having the tools to stay in peaceful alignment can make all the difference, both personally and in helping the light win. That is, not just win, but win sooner. For that, our descendants will thank us.

> *Will we be in a good place in 20 years' time? Yes, but you must avoid focusing on the negative, to break the spell of the negative agendas of the next decade. 2024 and 2030 are both gateway years…big axis points, not just for the Earth but universally.* —The Z's

How is a "left behind" aspect of the rapture also part of the shift? As part of the split, folks will either lean into the hyper-D aspects of their being, such as their soul, or be left behind. According to dowsers such as Raymon Grace, the level of one's soul energy can be measured and tracked over time. For one rapture group, their soul energy level is currently measured as *adequate* and (by leaning toward soul impulses) <u>increasing</u>. For the other rapture group, soul energy is currently measured as *inadequate* and (by leaning toward ego and fear impulses) <u>decreasing</u>.

According to tradition, those who are not left behind in the rapture ascend. However, it seems to be turning out to be a dimensional ascension toward the realm of hyper-D. Many think a hyper-D-leaning human may appear *someday*. Actually, that day has been here for quite some time.

> *Being in two places at one time is well within your*
> *abilities…your DNA is hyperdimensional…you live*
> *in four dimensions but exist in many.* —Kryon

I've been documented by others as having been in two places at one time on at least three occasions. We go hyper-D whenever we transcend normal 4D laws, such as when distance is not a factor during energy healing work or matter is altered by only mental intention. In ways such as this, we already know hyper-D to be real.

The dark recruits

People and institutions of a lower vibration have no way to correctly understand or appreciate a higher vibration. Hence, they've historically dealt with those of a higher vibration as an irritating problem to be eradicated. The typical eradication plan involves drumming up a group for ostracizing, eliminating, or otherwise neutralizing those of a higher vibration. If they succeed, they may ironically proclaim to have eliminated evil, making the world a better place. Beyond many spiritual masters, this is how tens of thousands of outspoken, intuitive women have been silenced, if not executed, over the centuries.

Since those of a higher vibration are not likely to have actually done something wrong, the eradication mob is historically recruited around a false, accusatory narrative. As unfair as this may seem, this ploy has been highly effective for eons.

> *An ascending society empowers spiritual (wo)men as leaders toward ascension. For millennia, we've corrupted this recipe by taking out the "wo." How do you like the results so far? It's time to return to the original recipe.*

Why aren't false accusations seen through? Those being recruited, lacking the intuition to spot a false, *controlled narrative*, bend to the pressure of the group and its leader.

> *If you'll settle for "answers," find a crowd. If you need Truth, use intuition to walk alone toward it until your crowd finds you.*

Who's come up with many of the controlled narratives in our generation? In the most flattering light, Edward L. Bernays, nephew of Sigmond Freud, is considered to be the father of public relations. In a less flattering light, he may be seen as the father of *propaganda* and *information warfare*, normalized as "spin," to engineer our consent. These may be fancy ways of saying "weaponized psychology."

In the minds of his modern followers, our consent on what we will buy, what we will care about, what we'll be outraged by, where and when we'll enlist, and how we will vote has already been decided by others. That is, others whose job it is to convince us that what's been decided for us was our idea.

These are Bernays' paraphrased words: "*Those who manipulate this unseen mechanism of {the habits, behaviors, and opinions of} society constitute an invisible ruling power. Our minds are molded, our tastes formed, our ideas suggested, largely by men we have never heard of.*" In short, the right combination of "you want or need this," "you fear this," and "you're offended or outraged by this" can drive the masses, like a herd of cows, in almost any direction.

Bernays' influences were initially felt in limited areas, like when a generation of men and women were encouraged to see a lit cigarette as a *torch of freedom*[78] or *empowerment*. Likely, some of those men you've never heard of first prospered by investing in the tobacco industry and then prospered further by investing in the cancer treatment industry. Today, it's hard to find any area of social media, sales, "news," religion, or politics that's not coated in "Bernays' Sauce."

> *We cannot stress enough the importance of "word warfare" on Earth. This is why you've experienced more friction regarding the biggest news stories of the last few years. Division is being sewn; Separation is being seeded. Because you are an emotionally immature planet, you are easy to divide. —The Z's*

Now that you've been tipped off to watch for manipulation, you have a choice to either go along or become increasingly less compliant. Mental freedom isn't free. Each new day of the shift offers more potential for honing our intuition for sensing manipulation. The more we notice manipulation, the more controlled narratives and logical fallacies (logic errors) coated in *Bernays' Sause* may backfire.

It's a *high*-vibration trend to spot controlled narrative manipulation. Hence, *low*-vibration people and institutions, to their peril, typically don't notice that their manipulation attempts are becoming noticed. Assuming that the same false accusation and manipulation ploys that have always worked will continue to work, they'll likely try it once too often. At that time, the intuition of the average person may have increased to the point where it not only backfires but causes that person or institution to become spotlighted and invalidated.

Two ascension paths have converged

There are two main paths for personal and spiritual growth. One is initiated by our conscious mind. The other is initiated by our higher self, or soul. The conscious path involves taking initiative toward ascension, such as by way of personal growth books, seminars, meditation, etc.

> *You wither as a soul if you don't grow your life force, giving you more to give to others...if only 5 minutes a day, do something that lights you up inside.* —The Z's

Failing that, the second path may involve our higher self, or soul, enrolling us (like it or not) in "dark night of the soul" experiences. These often entail sufficient discomfort, chaos, fear, and loss until we're forced to ask and answer similar "What's it all about?" and "What's really true?" questions, as if we had opted for the conscious path. *Prior to the shift*, soul contracts could reportedly stipulate either option (a) or (b) below:

(a) Take the initiative to grow, or opt out and just *coast.*
(b) If I put off taking the initiative for too long, default me to the *"dark night of the soul"* trial path.

I emphasized "prior to the shift" because those alive today reportedly had it in their soul contract before incarnating (so it doesn't violate free will) that in order to provide for planetary ascension, *coasting* (after 2012) would no longer be an option. Thus, due to the shift, this is reportedly our only option from here on out:

(a) Unless I take the initiative to grow, automatically grow me by way of "dark night of the soul" trials.

In case you've been asking yourself, "Why do I care about the shift?" this could be one reason. Like it or not, planet-wide ascension is beginning, so billions who've gotten this far by coasting have now defaulted to learning and growing by way of the "dark night of the soul." Enter COVID-19, etc., and the end of *normal.*

> *Our pre-corona existence was not normal other than we normalized greed, inequity, exhaustion, depletion, extraction, disconnection, confusion, rage, hoarding, hate, and lack. We should not long to return.... We are being given an opportunity to stitch a new garment...that fits all of humanity and nature.* —Brené Brown

Those who've been on their personal and spiritual growth path for a while should already have the tools to stay balanced through the current and coming storms. Others will be scrambling to catch up.

> *There is no situation, relationship, or event in life that cannot be harvested for spiritual growth... you're... a holographic fractal of Source who volunteered to be here.* —Sean O'Laoire, Pd.D.

For those wanting a crash course in "What's it all about, and what's true?" and how to stay balanced in a storm, I recommend my first book.

The misperception of perception

In the Matrix movies, instead of Neo seeing people in a room, he sometimes accurately perceived what was really there: endless streams of computer code ones and zeros that focused consciousness could alter. Hence, the mental image his brain *invented* of people in a room was inaccurate, incomplete, and false. Until Neo realized the difference between his mind's perception and reality, it was to his detriment, with mastery eluding him.

Was that just a movie metaphor or Truth? If you replace a stream of ones and zeros with a holographic sea of quantum potential waves, it may be an approximation of Truth. The five senses often make us aware of only an infinitesimally small fraction of the full electromagnetic spectrum. Hence, thinking our 4D mental image is accurate or complete is like visiting a single, flawed website and believing we've experienced the entire internet.

It's astonishing what you're not aware of. —Kryon

The antiquated belief that eyes see by way of light bouncing off of objects resulted in a prototype *magnetic resonance imaging* (MRI) medical scan that used to take four hours to complete. The breakthrough that reduced MRI scans from four hours to 20 minutes was the realization that what we actually perceive is a holographic sea of nonlinear, fluctuating quantum potential waves.

Our mind uses these waves to fabricate the linear 3D objects we *think* we're seeing. In support of this notion, the book *Source Field Investigations* recounts the story of a man, under hypnosis, who was able to not only identify a pocket watch but accurately read the time, even though it was held behind the back of his daughter, who stood before him. This would not have been possible if vision only resulted from reflected light.

If the images in our minds weren't fabricated, the first natives to see a sailing ship would have perceived a wooden sailing ship instead of a sea monster, and Moses would have perceived a glowing ball of hyper-D energy instead of a burning bush. When biblical Elijah converted his body to pure energy, if the images in his mind weren't fabricated, Elisha would have seen a bright, rising ball of hyper-D energy instead of a chariot of fire. If the images in our mind aren't fabricated, those visited by angels, which, per St. Hildegard von Bingen, are *living light*, would see hyper-D light energy instead of a Caucasian female with wings.

If you look up at a nearly dark ceiling just before falling asleep, guess what you might barely make out? I see churning hyper-D energy. Hence, the wise don't confuse what *appears* to be around us with what's *actually* around us. To do so would keep us perceiving in black and white 4D while bathed in hyper-D color. This raises a question:

> *With a consciousness designed to interact in so many amazing dimensions, why stay in the cheap seats of only four?*

Quantum science observes that we correctly perceive something by resonating with it <u>if</u> our mental *tuner* can match its frequency. If not, we either see nothing or our brain fabricates a placeholder image.

Thus, whether we see our deceased grandmother smiling over our infant's crib is less about whether she's actually there and more about whether we're willing and able to let our mental tuner vibrate at her current frequency. Infants typically can, while parents too often not only can't but encourage their child to disable the "imaginary" friend part of their mental tuner.

We're born with high-bandwidth tuners, with tears found at the low end and giggles found at the high end. All too soon, we may be coerced into shutting off both extremes to perpetually live in the mundane middle of the frequency band. That can be reversed.

Given the overload of quantum information available to us at any moment, our brain's default is to not let us perceive reality. Hence, what we perceive is mostly heavily filtered cognitive bias, causing us to greatly miss out. Due to the observer effect, <u>correctly</u> perceiving something can cause its current and future forms to change. So, why have our attempts at altering our surroundings with our minds not worked so well? Like Neo, perhaps we've applied our focused consciousness to the false 4D illusion instead of the real hyper-D quantum wave energy behind it!

People with psychic or spiritual gifts (that the shift is reportedly now magnifying by a factor of two to four) have, at some level, figured out how to work with or send[79] hyper-D energy. Our task as lightworkers and the path to mastery is not to badger friends to upgrade their tuners so our gifts and ideas don't seem nonsensical, but to move forward with learning to correctly perceive and interact with hyper-D energy until our true tribe finds us.

Is the shift toward broken or woken?

NASA sent military pilots to the moon. Epiphanies during introspection over a two-week mission reportedly resulted in one later becoming a poet, one becoming an artist, and one becoming spiritual.

> *You may think moments of epiphany come from your brain, but usually, you've been nudged by an angel. You may have 9–12 guides around you, and perhaps three of them are angelics.* —*The Z's*

Were these military astronauts *broken* by introspection and epiphanies or *woken*? Reportedly, some military personnel who were taught introspection no longer wanted to be in the military. Did those classes result in members of the military becoming broken or woken?

> *Many of you in your 6th, 7th, or 8th decade will have energetic epiphanies, allowing yourself to be the conduit of energy that you have never before experienced or seeded on Earth…it's the most important period of your life.* —The Z's

163

When we see chaos in today's world, does it represent society's path toward broken, or our collective, halting trial-and-error path toward woken? The answer depends on one's point of observation. It may depend on whether we're looking through the lens of the fading old energy or the increasing new energy[80] of the shift.

Looking through the lens of the new energy, one can see society inching toward a future that includes the hot flames of integrity, ethics, Truth, and compassion. As such, institutions built on the dry tinder of the opposite of integrity, ethics, and compassion *should* be getting increasingly uncomfortable. While there may still be time for institutions to utilize introspection to reassess and figuratively clean up their act, there may be less time than they think.

Hence, any institution that hasn't swapped its fire-prone unethical, non-integrous, or false-narrative framework and foundation for the fireproof opposites prior to the shift flame getting too close may default to demise rather than reform. While this demise may appear like chaos, history may see it more as a case of "I'd rather go extinct than clean up my act."

Along the way, we can choose our lens to watch the same bumpy road in two different ways. Watching through an old-energy lens promotes the fear, imbalance, and pessimism in body chemistry that can lead to a shorter, less-happy life. Watching through a new-energy lens can promote hope and balanced body chemistry that can lead to a longer, happier life. What will it be?

Key factors in the shift

Whereas compassion is fed by Love from beyond the veil, competition is fed by Love's shadow: fear.

The shift is our slow process of ascending out of the fear-based age of the *compassionless competition of the disconnected* toward an age of *compassionate cooperation of the connected*, on the way to an age of *mastery of the interconnected.* Future generations may eventually shorten these titles to the ages of *competition, compassion,* and *mastery.*

> *You are connected to all that is. Your training has been*
> *to disconnect you from that truth. The awakening of*
> *your soul is to reconnect you to that truth.* —The Z's

This involves shifting away from the unhealthy and unsustainable narratives of an imbalanced masculinity that falsely views us as separate from everyone and everything. The word "falsely" is not used lightly in the sense that quantum entanglement has shown that all things (and people) exist in a perpetual state of entangled oneness.

> *Adopting entanglement ... comes at the price of*
> *giving up separability.* —Rasmus Jaksland

The shift represents our moving *away from* believing that life can only be associated with matter. At the same time, we are shifting *toward* healthy and sustainable narratives of masculine and feminine balance. Balance that would unite us, and a conscious planet. It's a shift toward the knowledge that life is energy, which *sometimes* makes use of matter. It's a shift from fear to love.

> *Only when our intent comes from...love rather*
> *than...fear do we create peace in the world and*
> *in ourselves.* —Don Miguel Ruiz Jr.

Moment to moment, we can choose to *descend* by subtracting compassion, as demonstrated by our tragic history, or *ascend* by adding compassion, as demonstrated by spiritual masters throughout time. Yes, *compassion* is really that singularly important in determining our future as individuals and as a collective. While often underrated, compassion can be a game-changing gateway to forgiveness, healing, peace, and balance.

While compassion is one key factor in our shift into the next age, might there be others?

165

The brain and body are intended to be subservient partners to the mind. The mind was intended to be a subservient partner to the soul. The soul is an equal partner with all the souls that make up divine Source. When we orient ourselves according to the Truth of this *body-mind-soul-Source* relationship, concepts such as oneness, compassion, balance, peace, and not needing a body to exist become self-evident.

> *…truth passes through three stages. First, it is ridiculed. Second, it is violently opposed. Third, it is accepted as self-evident.* —Arthur Schopenhauer

However, as the age of *competition* has demonstrated, our *body-mind-soul-Source* relationship becomes dysfunctional when our mind is programmed to be subservient to the fears of the body. This shifts us to a dysfunctional *body-mind* relationship at the extreme cost of our birthright connection to the soul and Source. Symptoms may include a shift from compassionately working for the highest good of all to (at the extreme) dispassionately prioritizing body survival over doing the right thing.

What if the *"kicked out of the Garden of Eden"* story is a metaphor for when we, millennia ago, chose to turn our backs on our birthright *body-mind-soul-Source* relationship, only to be paying the price and trying to find our way back ever since—when the "born magnificent and connected" Truth degenerated into a "born insignificant and separate" controlled narrative, resulting in an age of *reacting and competing?* Now, more and more lightworkers are rediscovering the Truth of being "born magnificent and connected."

The interface between body and mind is the brain, whereas the interface between the brain and our soul is an open, compassionate heart. This is why, person by person, the age of *soul-connected mastery* is reached by way of the age of *heart-connected compassion*.

What gifts and abilities might await us beyond the ability to demonstrate peaceful balance in the midst of anything but? When we truly believe we can, symptoms may include whatever a master has ever demonstrated, and more.

…do the works…I do; and greater… —John 14:12

While it may take generations for the average societal vibration level to significantly rise, nothing is stopping individuals from raising theirs now. This can be facilitated by having a compassionate heart. Nothing stops us except a constant barrage of *compassion-discouraging*, win-lose, and conformity-encouraging narratives. Instead, seek out *ascension-promoting* narratives that encourage group coherence, compassion, win-win, etc.

Descending people show you how powerful they are.
Ascending people remind you how powerful you are.

If compassion is part of a continuum, how might we know whether we're currently closer to the lower (competition) end of the compassion continuum or the higher (mastery) end? Whether in lucid life or a lucid dream, the following describes the compassion utilization steps I currently use when coming upon a situation:

1. Silently send divine Love into the situation's past, present, and future.
2. Internally ask, "What compassionate action might improve this situation?"
3. Internally ask, "Does my heart tell me this is mine to do?" If yes, go to the next step.
4. Engage in the situation to help make a difference.

When I first began venturing into the lower end of the compassion continuum, I performed only steps two and four. Skipping steps one and three often resulted in a solution that was either harder than it needed to be (without help from the unseen, synchronicities, and the laws of chance) or not mine to do.

For instance, I've successfully employed step one on myself when expecting a traumatic dentist experience. I create a Reiki healing energy (past, present, and future) crossfire. Beginning days before, I send grace, ease, and the best possible outcome to myself in the dentist chair. I do it again while in the chair and again days later. Imagine such a Reiki energy crossfire arriving exactly where and when it's needed! Besides feeling great, I've found it can really help.

In order to most efficiently help any situation, I recommend always starting with step one, even if you get stopped at step three. Why is step one so important? Besides invoking help from the unseen, synchronicities, and the laws of chance, it has the potential to shift the situation into a more favorable timeline, as in the "timeline altering or jumping" Mandela Effect.

Why work unassisted on the existing situation when you can, by way of energy and intent, work *assisted* on a situation that's improved at a quantum level even before you reach step four?

A shift in relating to the field

When we speak of the shift, we speak of a multi-decade change in perspective, paradigm, what's normalized or acceptable, what's considered to be true, and what's considered possible.

One of the game-changers will likely come in the form of noticing and interacting with our individual and collective hyper-D field. This includes realizing that our future manifests from field potentials that the wise learn to read, create, and utilize. Reading potentials in the field is not fortune-telling in that it does not tell us the *how* of the way something is likely to come about, only its probability.

Per Lee Harris (channeling The *Z's*), Earth is now showing high potential for a 50-year shift away from playing *separation* games. That is, a shift *toward* us noticing that we've been sold a carefully packaged bill of goods about our separation from God (instead of our true oneness), which has falsely led to normalizing scarcity, competition, war, diminished freedoms, etc.—a shift where awareness of "the field" and higher dimensions increasingly permeates our world view until we grasp that they are always available.

What's the difference between separation's longing and belonging? Just "be."

How might this knowledge be put to work? Lee Carroll (channeling Kryon) asserts that when we decide to travel from location A to location B, a hyper-D part of us is already at location B. This aligns with Dr. Rupert Sheldrake's experiments, where pets noticeably react at home the moment their owner decides to return home.

While it's possible that the pet is reading potentials in the field or somehow receiving a psychic text, perhaps what they're noticing is that a hyper-D, astral-body version of their owner immediately appeared at home? If so, perhaps bilocating (to varying degrees) is more common than most suspect, and we all have at least one astral body on call to travel at a moment's notice? My spiritual seer friend, JG, once mentioned that I had at least four. Hence, friends, family members, or acquaintances who've ever wondered if a part of me was elsewhere may have been more right than they knew!

Healers and psychics know how to help us because they read our information in the *field*. We can reportedly also write on the field by way of conscious intent combined with strong positive emotions, such as gratitude or love. Hence, the shift may include enriching our lives by learning to employ a combination of field reading and writing.

Perhaps along the way, we'll learn that pushing toward a goal only in a physical, 4D way is both obsolete and inefficient. A more efficient way would be to employ our hyper-D birthright, so the *now* physical part of us pushes toward a goal in the present as a *near future* astral body part of us (representing the higher energy of a slightly more shifted Earth) anticipates and facilitates the completed goal. All this as a far-future astral body part of us (representing an even higher, future Earth energy) looks back on the completed goal in gratitude.

If so, having multiple astral bodies capable of simultaneous, independent action may someday become a normalized part of our hyper-D future. That is, while the physical part of us pushes toward a goal, the astral parts of us create a stronger and stronger goal-homing beacon in the quantum field. This not only helps our intuition guide us toward the goal, but may also allow the (*now magnetized*) goal to actually pull us toward it!

Welcome to a shift toward hyper-D manifestation!

Toward Self-Sovereign Mastery

Amazing things will be increasingly possible when you know, with self-worth and without fear, that you are powerful in dimensions you can't see. You walk inside a sphere, so at an interdimensional level, you can see all the paths you ever walked and ever will walk just by looking around. —Kryon

When you start to understand the divine truth of yourself as an interdimensional human...you're not stuck in the box of human experience...you're an adventurer of the universe. —Abbey Normal

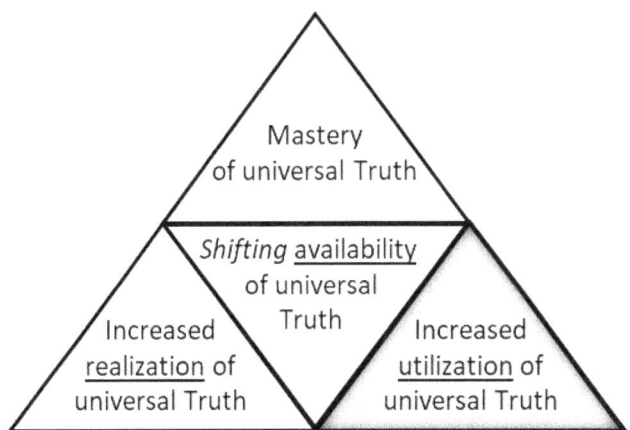

Ch. 8: Leaning toward mastery 101

Manifesting with compassion 📖

If you've ever had the feeling that some important part of the "Ask and you shall receive" manifestation recipe must have been lost in translation, you may be correct. Below is my interpretation of the original Aramaic text:

Ask directly, without hidden motive or in violation of the greater good, for what you desire, knowing the universe is aware of and for you. Perceive waves of potentiality moving toward you. Make yourself a vibrational match to what you seek, with grateful gladness in advance, feeling surrounded by what is yet to appear. Lean into the synchronicities that feel like they're for you, trusting where they'll lead.

Although some might call this a simple recipe, simple should not be confused with *easy* in that most will be stopped by the first sentence.

Why did spiritual avatars reportedly get rapid manifesting results? I suspect it comes down to a combination of a more cultivated, self-sovereign, higher-vibration mind, fewer subconscious energy roadblocks, and making better use of quantum field power and information. While meditation and introspection can cultivate a more disciplined, self-sovereign mind with fewer roadblocks, how do we facilitate the personal circuits to manage greater power and information sources? First, we need to make a distinction between lower nature, lower vibration mammal *force,* and higher nature, higher vibration soul *power.* "Do what I say, or else!" represents mammal force. This is an example of bullying, which is derived from insecurity, which is derived from low-vibration fear.

Insecurity masks its fear with the force of anger.
Courage calms fears with the power of compassion.
Force leads to one future, power to another.

On the other hand, "Basket, please don't run out of loaves and fish until this hungry crowd has been fed." is an example of tapping into universal *power* by way of high-vibration compassion, derived from an even higher-vibration cosmic law of oneness.

Those historically adept at utilizing force and deception for control have often been uncontested *until* they encountered an intuitive self-sovereign adept at accessing universal power. To overcome the disadvantage, users of force have long maintained a controlled narrative that those most adept at accessing divine Source power (villainized as sorcerers) must be neutralized, along with intuitive self-sovereigns, villainized as witches. I suspect WITCH has long been an acronym for "Whomsoever Intuits Truth, Charge with Heresy."

> *The battle against witches had little to do with witchcraft and much to do with control of powerful women who were about to influence the masculine to become more divine.* —The Z's

How many hours can the average person go without seeing an icon of a man being executed on a cross? Although the accompanying message may *appear* to be "This is why you should seek God," the stronger subconscious message may be "This is what happens to those who seek God." This type of pervasive programming by way of weaponized (while normalized) narratives has been going on for centuries and appears targeted toward neutralizing our inborn tendency to find empowerment through seeking God internally, without an intermediary.

> *Prayer to "other" can erode the soul. A false sense of separation is the cause of physical/emotional/mental disease. How does one differentiate between a healthy thought and societal programming? Your heart will find one expansive and the other restrictive.* —The Z's

If love is the universal light capable of providing massive amounts of information and power, fear is the shadow of that light. Since those rooted in the shadow of fear have limited access to the light's power, they must compensate with force. This infers that the place to set our emotional tuner in order to access the highest levels of universal power and information might be *compassion*, or higher. This may not be by accident, in that a wise universe knows compassion may be the last place an unevolved power abuser would look for power.

Is there any evidence to support the notion that compassion, in particular, is the door to universal power and knowledge? Tibetan monks, who make a lifestyle of staying in compassion, have long been known to have access to unusual knowledge, abilities, and *longevity.*

Both the science of epigenetics and the Dalai Lama would agree that while the emotional frequencies of anger and judgment (grievances) are likely harmful to the body, the most restorative frequency is that of compassion. Those involved with electronics know that maximum power and information can only be transferred between two tuned circuits when they match and synchronize their vibrational frequencies. When I traveled to Peru with author and researcher Gregg Braden, he spoke of once asking a Tibetan monk to identify the human emotional frequency that allows the strongest (quantum field) information and power coupling between us and a conscious universe. The answer was *compassion*.

> *Those who've mastered compassion have mastered this plane of existence, but the door to the graduation stage is lightly used in that it's marked "Forgiveness."*

Keeping one's emotional tuner set to the frequency of compassion allows a high throughput of universal wisdom, power, and health-affirming energies, but only if we've cultivated and uncluttered our personal power management circuits. Power can't flow through jammed-up circuits.

What jams up our personal power circuits? According to those who can see into our personal biofield and tissues, jamming is caused by the energetic residue of old, undealt-with trauma, fear, grievances, and resistance to what was. These may take up permanent residence in our personal power-management bio-energy circuits as resistors of power and intuitive information flow. Again, the solution is simple but not easy. To enjoy some of the same benefits as the spiritual avatars, it's as simple as:

- Cultivating our mind's self-discipline and awareness via meditation.
- Cultivating and clearing power management circuits via self-help (e.g., forgiveness) and introspection to remove power resistors.
- Plugging into universal power via holding our emotional tuner dial at compassion or higher.

If the "Ask and you shall receive" manifestation recipe has not been working out for you, you now have a few ideas as to what to work on. Simple, right?

If you're curious how quick and reliable manifestation can be, ask the universe to make you humbler.

Managing our distance from home base 📖

Imagine yourself interacting with a puppy, fully in the *here and now*, in a place of relaxed, loving, creative playfulness. That's our most happy, healthy, and energized *home base*. That's where our consciousness is meant to reside, but to our detriment, it rarely does.

When we're *in our heads*, our consciousness is at least one level distant from our home-base, heart-centered self. I say *at least* because

175

if we're in our heads thinking about the past or future, we might be more than one level distant. If we get swept up in the drama of an actor on a video screen while in our heads, we're at least two levels distant from our true selves, or 2+ if the scene is set in the past or future. If that actor picks up a book and reads, "Once upon a time..." our consciousness is suddenly 3+ levels distant from our true selves.

Why do we care? While various levels of distancing can sometimes be therapeutic or an entertaining distraction, distancing may come at a cost. It vibrationally detunes us enough from the universal energy broadcast that we forfeit some amount of free health-maintaining energy that we might normally absorb[81] from the atmosphere around us. If our consciousness spends too much time away from home base, it's likely to the detriment of the personal energy supply we need to maintain health and facilitate life's goals.

Moment to moment, the more distant our current level of consciousness, the more out of tune we are, and the more universal (quantum field) energy our bodies forfeit. Since many of us have an addiction to living in our heads, that may be a first-level of distance (forfeited energy, wellness, and heart connection) public health concern. Since many of those same people are also addicted to video screens, that may be an even more severe, second-level of distance public health concern.

Those who are permanently stuck in their left brains, while erroneously believing they're experiencing the world firsthand, may be running corporations, the military, and governments without access to heart-centered compassion. Often, as *high priests* of toxic belief systems such as "It's not personal, it's just business" and "The results justify the means," it's counterintuitive to believe that these are the leaders that will take us in the direction of a more compassionate, loving, and unified future.

Even when not distancing, our power and information circuits can still be jammed (forfeited) by holding on to and walling off toxic grievances within our bodies. We tend to keep them for years, like buried treasure. Except, unlike treasure, a constant trickle of energetic poison can leak from each grievance, affecting our body and relationships. Hence, grievances are less like treasure and more like poorly buried toxic waste.

Consciously zooming out is sometimes useful, like when I realize I'm dreaming and go lucid to take control of my dream. If my spouse and I are having an argument in real life, I may zoom out long enough to ask myself, "If one of us does not see tomorrow, do I want these to be the last words between us?"

If my heart is in emotional pain, different levels of zooming out can be like different settings on a pain volume control, without the need for drugs or alcohol. I experience maximum emotional pain when, consciousness speaking, I'm in my heart. The pain is less when I shift my consciousness to my head, watching my ailing heart from something of a distance, and even less when I shift[82] my consciousness to my spirit or neutral observer, such as when thinking, "Bob's in his avatar head trying to avoid the pain of being in his heart."

Is this different from the level of distance I might experience as a disembodied consciousness floating near the ceiling of an operating room? That's an interesting question I'll leave for another time.

The difference between distancing as *spiritual bypassing* and distancing as a healthy resilience and emotional pain management tool lies in whether it's before or after we've felt the feelings and internalized/balanced any lessons the pain has to offer (so the lesson doesn't need to be repeated in an amplified version). With spiritual bypassing, we misuse this tool as an excuse for not growing toward a trigger-free place.

Our higher self wields larger and larger sticks until we get the intended lesson. Spiritual bypassing focuses on the current stick while bypassing the lesson, forcing our higher self to look for a

> *bigger stick. As someone who's occasionally held out for the "Cosmic Swinging 2x4", I don't recommend it.*

Distanced indifference, or objectivity in the face of a potential emotional trigger, should only be considered a temporary tool on the way to the goal. The goal is to be fully present with authentic balance.

> *Color-saturated memories come from fully inhabited moments.*

Authentic balance is trigger-free because nothing and no one is seen as separate or anything other than some (perhaps well disguised) form of loving divine oneness experiencing itself. However, *trigger-* free is not the same as *prompt*-free in that our compassion[83] may still be prompted to find ways to be of loving service.

When people tried to get Jesus to condemn himself with his own words, he was known for his ability to go consciously distant long enough to spot and dismantle their logic trap before responding. We would be well served to do the same before getting swept up in the daily barrage of unhealthy, controlled narratives, outrage bait, etc. Before being swept up, freeze long enough to ask ourselves, "Who crafted this controlled narrative, and to what end?"

A sovereign mind, rather than unconsciously getting stuck at any distance level, consciously owns and manages its current level.

> *Tell everyone you know, "My happiness depends on me, so you're off the hook," and demonstrate it. Be happy, no matter what they're doing. Practice feeling good, no matter what. Before you know it, you will not give anyone else responsibility for the way you feel; then, you'll love them all, because the only reason you don't love them is because you're using them as your excuse to not feel good.* —Abraham-Hicks

One method we can use to manage our current distance level is meditation. The "med" in meditation likely refers to the middle or center, so one meditates in order to return their consciousness to the center, or home base. One way to know that one has succeeded is when playfulness, compassion, and forgiveness (often the first things to go during stress or trauma) return.

Between that and resetting our free energy tuner back to the maximum energy and information input setting, the benefits to our health, relationships, and goals may be profound.

Altered timelines 📖

Have you ever heard of the Mandela effect? Was the U.S. the first to land a craft on the moon? That's a false memory. The Russians did it first in 1959. Did the banker in the Monopoly game wear an eye monocle? No. Did Humphrey Bogart say, "Play it again, Sam," in the movie *Casablanca*? No.

Welcome to the Mandela effect, named after the large number of people who claim to remember Nelson Mandela dying in prison as opposed to dying later, after becoming President of South Africa.

Is the Mandela Effect really about mass misremembering, or what psychologists describe as confabulation? Or, could it be a glitch in the matrix caused by our current timeline being altered? The controversy continues, but it's reasonable and logical for hyper-D people to assume that our timelines are being altered all the time.

How can that be? Is it reasonable to a rational scientific mind that sooner or later, even if it takes 10,000 years, our technological advances will someday include time travel? Yes, and if that occurs, is it reasonable that future time-traveling historians or tourists may visit people, places, and events of significance in their past? Yes, and if they visit, is it logical and reasonable that those visitors might cause our existing timeline to be altered? Yes, in a combination of what science calls the observer and butterfly effects, to visit or observe the past via time travel (*or perhaps even astral travel or remote viewing*[84]) is to alter our past, present, and future.

Even the logic of Occam's razor (the simplest answer is usually correct) suggests our timeline may be altered more often than we realize. I have personal experience to suggest the past and future can both be accessed and altered, as documented in my scientific[85] journal article: *Exploring Syntropic Intent Effects across Nonlocal Time*.

The Mandela effect is nothing new. What if timeline manipulation was how some Bible miracles were able to occur? In the old timeline, one person could not walk, another could not see, jugs were full of water, and the basket of loaves and fish ran out. Jumping timelines mid-scene could allow a blind person to instantly see, etc.

For those who can't believe in miracles until they can figure out *how*, this is one possibility. In a universe of infinite timelines containing every possible outcome[86], jumping timelines so that something appears instantly changed would seem to some as a miracle.

While some confabulation (mass misremembering) can be explained by constantly reinforced misquotes, others are not so easily dismissed. If our timeline has been altered, we may still have a memory from the prior timeline that can no longer be substantiated. Let's take a quiz. Is this the way you remember these movie or TV quotes?

- Life is like a box of chocolates...
- Mirror, mirror on the wall...
- Luke, I am your father...
- It's a beautiful day in the neighborhood...

The correct quotes in our *current* timeline are:

- "Life *was* like a box of chocolates..."
- "Magic mirror on the wall..."
- "No, I am your father."
- "It's a beautiful day in *this* neighborhood."

Perhaps we're remembering them differently from a different timeline? At RealityShifters.com, physicist Cynthia Sue Larson collects evidence for the *shifted timeline* theory. She tells a story of taking the same walk after brunch with her friends every Sunday on the same path. As she was describing the Mandela Effect to her strolling friends, they noticed the path they always took was suddenly blocked by a large statue that had reportedly been there for decades! She also tells the story of being in a restaurant with her young children and, six times in a row, closing and reopening her empty purse to take out a dollar bill that had somehow materialized.

Speaking of things popping into and out of existence, my late friend JG was slated to give a talk to an audience of significant size. His internal knowing was that his unseen guides felt strongly that he should show up on faith and approach the podium without notes or a plan for what to say. He was to trust that the talk would be given to him just as he needed it.

> *Irony: The more important it is that your next words be inspired, succinct, and helpful, the more important it is to clear your mind.*

He decided to hedge his bets and bring a page of notes in case the universe failed to deliver. He walked to the podium, put his notes down, closed his eyes, and decided to speak from his notes. When he opened his eyes, his notes were gone—not on the podium or the floor—gone! Out of options, he proceeded to deliver a great talk that came to him just as he needed it. As the audience clapped at the end of his talk, he looked down to find his notes once again on the podium, directly in front of him. Perhaps his unseen guides were serious enough about the original plan to temporarily flip him to a timeline in which he brought no notes, only to flip him back to the original timeline at the end of the talk? My sister Yaana shared this[87] timeline-jumping experience:

At a meditation retreat, I sat in a chair in a beach house. When I came to a natural meditation breaking point, I was amazed to find my surroundings different. My journal was suddenly embossed with a beautiful butterfly print, my pen was silver, and my clothes were a beautiful silk print. The house decor was entirely different. I looked around in awe, closed my eyes, and went back into meditation. The next time I surfaced, everything was back to normal. I wonder what might have happened if I had gotten up and walked around. I seem to have awakened in a parallel timeline of different choices.

The Quantum Zeno Effect[88] suggests that if she had gotten up, walked around, and continued to observe her altered timeline, it may have locked into place for as long as she sustained the prerequisite elevated energy level attained during meditation.

If a timeline is altered, what is and is not subject to change? If I had to guess, I'd say that all *time*-based and *matter*-based things would be subject to change in an altered timeline, while timeless and matter-less beings and things would have the best chance of either not changing or noticing the change and remembering the way things were. This gets into the difference between brain and mind. The *matter*-based avatar brain would tend to have its *matter*-based hardware memory altered by an altered timeline. On the other hand, mind (as ordered energy outside of matter and time) is likely timeless and could theoretically recall the previous timeline. However, only those who meditate and occasionally switch from brain to mind are likely to notice the difference.

Some theorize that all possibilities already exist in infinite coexisting timelines. Hence, a hyper-D self-sovereign individual might want to keep an open mind about time and our ability to change the future, either directly or indirectly, by changing the past. Unhealed parts of our past can cause much of our mental map of the future to be invisible and unreachable. Consequently, healing our past, beyond improving longevity and our emotional, physical, and relationship health, is also likely to open up the potential to change our future.

Irony: Altering/healing small parts of our past, such as by sending it retrocausal light, grace, compassion, and context, can alter big parts of our future.

This raises the question[89] of whether timelines may be altered, switched, or both. The difference may be important in regards to intuition and inspiration. If there are infinite Bobs in infinite timelines, more die every day, potentially increasing the number of unseen Bob *guides* assisting the remaining Bobs, allowing improved intuition and inspiration with each passing day!

Navigating timelines vs. creating 📖

Dr. Julia Mossbridge has dedicated much of her career to understanding time. As such, I took her class in anticipation of finding out all about time and timelines. Instead, our homework was to come up with our own answers.

As I combined logic and intuition, the result is reflected below and throughout this book. The term "flow of events" pre-biases us to think that events or timelines must flow in only one direction, toward the future. This is likely an untrue assumption, since alternatively:

1. Current events could be pulled forward toward the future by the future (like a windsurfer is pulled forward) or…

2. The future could be pulled backward into the present by the present (like roping a cow) or…

3. The present, traveling under its own steam, could simply be navigated toward one of many possible futures (like a car selecting one roundabout exit from many).

When considering possible mechanisms for timeline jumping, the third option offers advantages around manifesting altered realities, since optional timelines could be *intersecting* instead of parallel. Consider the famous video[90] of a 3-inch bladder tumor being resolved in under three minutes, as shown on a real-time ultrasound screen at a medicine-less Beijing, China, hospital.

Let's assume the patient's consciousness was jumping across successive parallel timelines throughout the video. In the original timeline, the tumor was shown on the ultrasound monitor at ~3 inches across. In each adjacent timeline jump, it's slightly smaller, until three minutes later, a timeline is reached in which nothing of the tumor remains except a pile of loose cells resting against the bladder wall.

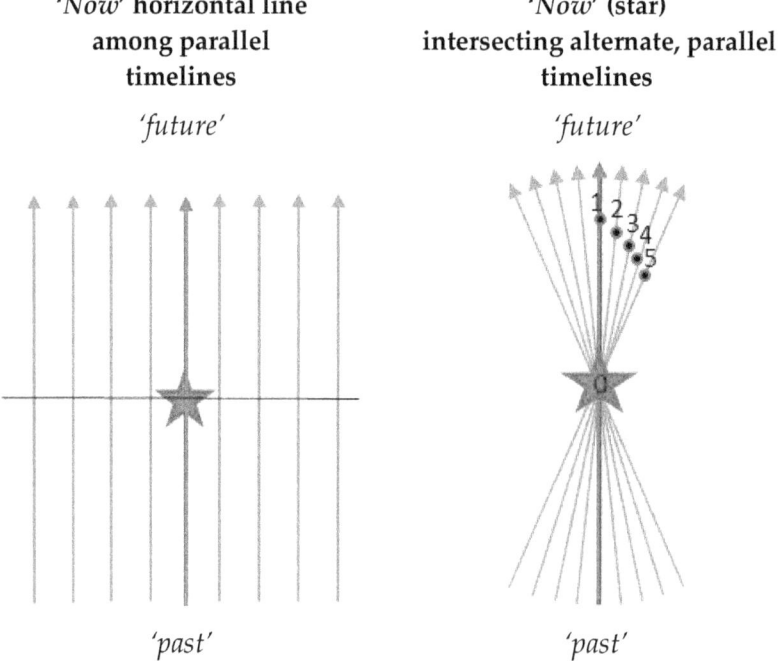

Figure 8.1: Alternative approaches to accessing other timelines.

Taking the word "parallel" literally in regard to timelines (left side of Fig. 8.1), as in the Mandela Effect, infers distance, force, and duration to switch from our default *center* timeline (bold line) to some other. Intuitively, I feel this is too heavy of a lift to be the correct model.

In a holographic universe (right side of Fig. 8.1), there's no need for distance, force, or duration, making it effortless for a nonmaterial consciousness to switch from the default center timeline to any adjacent one. The potential for consciously jumping timelines suggests yet another reason for developing sovereignty of mind.

Racecar drivers know their car tends to end up not where the car's nose is currently pointed but where the driver's nose is currently pointed. Their *point* of attention tends to be their point of destination.

In the right-side diagram of intersecting timelines, if point 0 (the "now" star point on existing [bold line] timeline 1) places its attention on future attractor points 2 through 5+, it may effortlessly switch to that timeline. Likewise, if attractor points 2, 3, 4, or 5 grab point 0's attention, it may effortlessly end up on that timeline.

In the case of the bladder tumor, one could hypothesize that timelines with attractor points 2–5 represent successively smaller and smaller versions of the same tumor. *Hence, alternate futures may be navigated rather than created.* The video may demonstrate the difference between allopathic health practitioners, who may *buy us* time, and holistic practitioners, who may *bias* time.

Let's create a new profession: Healer-Triage Broker. One who's aware of hundreds of different healers employing dozens of different allopathic, naturopathic, and homeopathic modalities—one who, whether by medical intuition, kinesiology, pendulum, etc., demonstrates an ability to match one in need of healing with the ideal combination of healing resources/personalities for an optimal outcome?

Author Gregg Braden[91] speaks of a Native American friend who drew a sharp distinction between praying *for* rain and praying rain. Since we live in a like-attracts-like universe, the vibration of lack while praying *for* rain tends to attract (on a quantum field level) more lack of rain. On the other hand, to *pray rain* is to hear rain, to smell rain, to feel mud squishing up between your toes, and to feel the jubilation of farmers rushing to buy seed.

Old souls can expand or contract time and alter the weather. —Kryon

In a like-attracts-like universe, praying rain seems more likely to manifest rain. Applying this to other subjects, we may know peace when enough of us shift from the anti-war or praying *for* peace approach to *praying peace.* The same goes for health, abundance, etc.

The synergistic combination of positive intent combined with positive, heart-based feelings and positive gut emotions may be the key to unlocking both the manifestation and timeline navigation puzzles.

As the gap between human and spirit lessens, pray with the force, as the force, to your inner connection to Spirit. —The Z's

Once we internalize that all adjacent timelines continually cross our *now,* the desired future already exists in one of many optional timelines. And, like the racecar driver, perhaps once we've conditioned our energy circuits to allow a sufficiently high *quality*[92] *and quantity* of energy, no effort is needed to reach that alternate future other than sufficient sovereignty of mind to hold our attention as described. In our *heart of hearts,* we can tell the difference between pretending what we *hope will be* and navigating to what we're already convinced *is.* Hence, don't be surprised if navigating timelines (*providing a new reality for us without violating the free will of others*) proves more effective than the heavier lift of trying to alter the inertia of the current timeline.

Knowing there are likely infinite versions of Bob in infinite timelines (and some will succeed in navigating to an alternate timeline and some will not), I choose to be one that succeeds. Does this technique work? Dozens of technology patents with my name on them suggest the answer may be yes!

In at least one timeline, I could come up with a patentable answer to a previously unsolvable computer industry problem. In other timelines, I could not. This raises the question of whether or not success will always include a memory of the prior timeline or our intention to leave that timeline. If not, we may be constantly experiencing successful timeline jumps with no memory of them!

> *In a dream, you visit a different timeline, a different*
> *place, a different part of your soul energy.* — The Z's

As a Reiki practitioner, I've seen significant evidence of either unexplained remission in the current timeline or perhaps timeline jumping. For instance, after a tooth extraction, a dry socket that, per the dentist, could not possibly have resolved itself did. Likewise, an ovarian cyst that, per the doctor, could not have resolved itself without surgery did. Those are just a few I remember from either the current or perhaps prior timelines.

If we include the possibility of timeline jumps that I don't remember, it's likely I've been successful more than I know! For those who prefer to go *old school* and attempt to experience an unusually fast medical improvement in the current timeline, Dr. Kelly Turner studied thousands of cases of unexplainable spontaneous remission that shared these nine traits:

1. A radical diet change
2. Taking control of one's health
3. Following intuition
4. Herbs and supplements
5. Releasing suppressed emotions
6. More positive emotions
7. Embracing social support
8. A deepened spiritual connection
9. A strong reason for living

These are all ways of saying that our cells may epigenetically respond to a higher vibration environment, meaning meditation, energy optimization, and thought control likely help. What will it be?

Energy reclamation 📖

In the same way that all matter is made of subatomic particles that are ultimately made of energy, I suspect science will eventually embrace the idea that all energy is derived from a single energy: a single, undiluted cosmic consciousness. Nothing we can point to is less than 100% pure, full-strength Source consciousness. What makes me say that? As my friend's toothless young daughter once put it, "Because nuttin mixes with [or dilutes] it!" This raises a question: if our entire universe consists of nothing other than one consciousness that can't be mixed or diluted, will each universe in the multiverse be made up of that *same* consciousness, or will each universe have its own?

Take the example of an AM radio broadcast. The exact same carrier wave is used to send out both low-vibration, sad content and high-vibration, happy content. The carrier wave is unchanging. It's the modulation of the wave that creates an entirely different experience from moment to moment.

Everything in the universe, whether a person, an emotion, or a star, may be merely a different modulation of the exact same carrier wave—a carrier wave of energy operating at the frequency of a loving cosmic consciousness. Shame is a low-vibration modulation of the unchanging love carrier wave, while gratitude is a higher-vibration modulation of the identical carrier wave. When poets say, "Love is all there is," I suspect that science will eventually prove that statement to be literal.

> *The universe only pretends to be made of matter. Secretly, it is made of love…* —Rumi

You may know the phrase "like attracts like," but in the area of vibrating energy and resonant electronic circuits, it may be more accurate to say, "Like allows entry to or interaction with like." Setting our AM dial to 800 kHz causes only the radio station transmitted at 800 kHz to be heard through our radio speakers. This is because our radio tuner is vibrating at the same frequency as the radio broadcast, allowing entry to only that station. Both the broadcast's power and information are allowed entry.

Although setting our tuner to *exactly* match the broadcasted frequency allows the strongest signal, one can still hear the broadcast (although with less and less clarity and power) as we tune farther and farther from the correct frequency.

If you've ever experienced full-body chills while singing or paying close attention to a song, its lyrics, or a poem, you've likely supported my point. Every person who ever had an emotional reaction to that song or those lyrics likely added their energy charge to the same nonlocal vibrational energy cloud with its particular access code. When, via appreciation and focused attention, you set your consciousness tuner to the same frequency and access code as that energy cloud, you may experience *goose bumps* or chills. This may be due to the principle of "like allows entry to like," allowing some of that energy to discharge into your body.

Why should we care? Imagine a transmitter tower at the top of a nearby hill that could supply all the physical energy, personal power, creativity, and intuition we need[93], but only if our chakra antennas are fully functional and only if our emotional tuner is set close to the universal Source frequency.

Because our energy *storage* capacity seems minimal, our personal moment-to-moment energy level may not be much better than our current setting, relative to the transmitted frequency. This is very important, considering that disease is more likely to gain a foothold if our power levels go too low for too long. In this case, the frequency and power are those of divine Love, and the information available represents creativity, intuition, and access to the universal database.

When we choose a personal thought frequency in the range of gratitude, forgiveness, empathy, kindness, etc., our uptake of broadcast Love energy, creativity, and intuition from the universe may be much higher than when we choose to tune ourselves away from Love, such as when experiencing fear, shame, judgment, etc.

Feeling uneasiness (fear) while watching the news or some crime drama? Perhaps we're consciously choosing to detune our vibration such that most of the broadcast power and information from the cosmos is forfeited? On the other hand, what if we were to go through our day constantly interjecting the mantra, "Thank You, God," into the gaps between our thoughts? That is, consciously choosing to retune ourselves to capture more of the broadcast energy and information available for maintaining health and manifesting dreams?

> *There is nothing more important than doing the internal work of raising your vibration, [clearing trauma energy blocks, and] opening your energy channels, asking your higher self to work with you, and then allowing the magic to happen.* —Jon Gabriel

Imagine how our lives could be different today if we had not spent years forfeiting energy and information by (moment to moment, thought by thought) detuning ourselves. How did that other person accomplish so much more in the same number of years while looking so vibrant? This is why we care. No one tunes into low-vibration thoughts or media, no matter how entertaining, without paying a price.

Even though this energy and information are available to us all the time, it's rare that someone gets even close to taking full advantage. Those who do (in addition to *breatharians* who are reportedly sustained by breath alone) may become known for their unusual accomplishments or abilities. What will it be?

Can loved ones visit from beyond the veil? 📖

In my experience, yes. Although more scientists than will admit have had meaningful encounters with dearly departed loved ones, a theoretical basis for this being possible has seemed absent from the literature. That is, until *The Law of One* books introduced the notion of a *time-space* dimension in addition to normal *space-time*.

The universe often produces matched opposites. If there's an up, there's a down. If there's a left, there's a right. So, if there's a space-time dimension on *this* side of the veil, the other-side-of-the-veil version may be the time-space dimension.

What might be the difference between the physics of our normal space-time dimension and the metaphysics of the time-space dimension? On this side of the veil, our brain resides (and typically thinks) within a 4-coordinate space-time system, where any point may be described via three coordinates in space (X, Y, and Z) plus one point in time. Space is likely mentioned first in regards to our normal space-time dimension in that it seems to offer us lots of space but too little time.

Regarding the metaphysical *time-space* dimension, perhaps on the other side of the veil, parts of our mind (as opposed to our brain), in addition to having access to our visible space-time dimension, might also have access to the invisible time-space dimension. The time-space dimension may be described by three time-based coordinates (past, present, and future) plus one point of observation in space. Time is mentioned first in regards to the metaphysical time-space dimension in that those residing there, such as between lifetimes, may feel like they have nothing *but* time.

Since scientific instruments designed to measure normal space-time phenomena are ill-suited for registering time-space phenomena occurring in the same room, people may erroneously assume that no metaphysical time-space phenomena are occurring. In my experience, that's often an incorrect assumption. Unlike instruments, our subtle senses *are* often capable of sensing metaphysical phenomena in the time-space dimension. That is, when they're not disabled due to fear or disbelief.

One should not confuse not *perceiving* hyper-D visitors from the time-space dimension with no visits. I've perceived visits from a number of (largely invisible) time-space dimension beings. In addition to deceased family members, one notable encounter was with a recently deceased pet cat that continued to flap the cat door and invisibly, yet quite distinctly, shake my reclining chair as if it were jumping on the arm.

When *mind* is separated from brain, such as during a near-death experience, between incarnations, or when astral projecting, both our higher nature and our higher-self mind may reside in the time-space dimension. In my experience, while the body is alive but astral dreaming, our lower or ego nature is able to visit *some* astral realms in the time-space dimension.

However, according to those who have communicated from the other side, our lower, or ego, nature dies along with the body. During life, the higher nature part of our mind may be able to temporarily visit the time-space dimension by way of mediation and astral projection. After life, the higher nature part of our mind typically finds itself on the other side of the veil in the time-space dimension along with our higher self.

What might the visible space-time dimension and the invisible time-space dimension have in common? In my experience, people, places, and things within time-space astral realms may appear similar to their space-time equivalents while being less tangible yet far more responsive to instantaneous thought-driven change. An important commonality between the space-time and time-space dimensions is that forgiveness and blessings often result in an improved situation.

Irony: An impediment to reaching the type of world that might make the need for forgiveness rare is today's rarity of forgiveness.

So, how do we activate our birthright subtle senses in order to notice nearby time-space dimension entities, such as visits from departed loved ones and pets? Meditate on granting our subtle senses permission to sense *all* that's near, giving our subconscious and cognitive filters the green light to take our subtle senses off mute.

If you start to notice visits from your old pet, *Fluffy,* or Grandma, welcome to the realm of hyper-D!

Self-sovereign truth resonance 📖

It would be a mistake to assume that all members of society think of the same thing when they hear the word Truth. A relatively small percentage of the population, such as scientists, engineers, and philosophers, sees (capitol T) Truth as absolute while seeking it for its own sake. For centuries, the vast majority have seen absolute Truth as something they couldn't afford, settling for (lower case-t) truth, which roughly translates to: "Whichever controlled narrative allows me to stay safe and hopefully advantaged." Unfortunately, layered, controlled narratives can be to Truth as roof shingles are to the rain. Knowing this, leaders throughout history have often viewed truth in relativistic terms for the purpose of control and exploitation.

> *Most people do not see their beliefs. Instead,*
> *their beliefs tell them what to see.* —Matt Kahn

If our more vocal ancestors considered Truth from leaders and printed media to be a birthright worth the risk of imprisonment or death, what's our modern excuse? Shall we explain to our ancestors, who may have paid the ultimate price, that we'll demand less of our leaders and the media because someone might unfriend us on social media?

Those who go looking for absolute Truth find it's not only rare but also of a very high standard. In fact, it's a standard so high that most of the so-called facts we encounter about current or historical events or people will eventually be seen as pseudo-truth, containing much more accidental and intentional error than currently recognized.

One definition of a heretic is "possessing sufficient Truth, courage, and personal sovereignty to resist a false narrative." Imagine a world where that's what we <u>all</u> want to be when we grow up!

Somehow, normalized terms such as "spin," "optics," "getting out in front of the story," and "controlling the narrative" don't register as what they are: *purposefully deceptive controlled narratives that prioritize agenda over Truth.* As such, the surest way to make people of the future chuckle or cringe is to make an authoritative and unequivocal statement of *fact* today without adding, "…or so it might currently seem."

In a democracy where access to accurate information is vital, we cannot afford to allow the use of the word "truth" to stand when it represents anything less than what the name implies. To settle for anything less is to forfeit our birthright. The Greek origin of the term "apocalypse" means "to uncover." As part of the shift, an era of uncovering may be exactly what we need.

Since one difference between *cooperation* and *conspiracy* is secrets, one measure of how far we are from a healthy, conflict-free, utopian society is the number of (and severity of) secrets. Toward that end, if a whistleblower is willing to risk destroying their life in order that we might collectively see beyond the normal *protective layers* around Truth, we might want to at least hear them out.

There are great...breakthroughs available to those who can remove...
truth's protective layers.... —Neil Armstrong, Astronaut

Unless we have some way to tell the difference between Truth and pseudo-truth, insisting on Truth may have little impact on the world. For starters, we should not confuse an internet full of information and poorly researched opinions with an internet full of Truth. Truth is an inside job—inside us is where it can be validated via *Truth resonance*. When we pluck a guitar string in the vicinity of idle guitars, strings tuned to the same musical note (vibrational frequency) tend to spontaneously vibrate in sympathetic resonance. We have the equivalent of a Truth sensing guitar buried deep inside each of us, with one or more strings capable of spontaneously vibrating in sympathetic resonance in the presence of Truth. That's the *good* news.

The *bad* news is that we're largely out of practice noticing and trusting this ability because our metaphorical guitar is usually buried under a pile of internal junk we've not dealt with. Most people seem to have only a single *True/False* resonance string that's too compromised to tell the difference between a partially resonant buzz in response to pseudo-truth and a pure resonant tone in response to absolute Truth.

I say *most* in that this does not necessarily apply to self-sovereign seekers—those who invest in *transformational* personal growth books, seminars, and meditation/reflection to clear the clutter from their Truth-resonant strings. These courageous people may enjoy an evolutionary Truth-sensing advantage.

Irony: Asking ourselves transformational questions only when we have nothing better to do, only to discover there is nothing better we <u>could</u> do.

Exactly how many *strings* might be available for seeking a needle of Truth in a haystack of pseudo-truths? The answer relates to the difference between the brain and the intuitive mind. In my model, our non-intuitive brain includes the fight-or-flight amygdala, which specializes in identifying threats, while our logical left brain specializes in identifying differences. For many people (and unfortunately, many leaders), this is virtually all the brain they use. Their worldview may reflect the equation "differences = threats." This goes a long way toward explaining racism, party-ism, nationalism, and many other *isms* in that people operating with only these resources might be described as being *in their brains* while being *out of their intuitive minds*.

> *Kindness is intelligence. To be kind, we must shut down our (suspicious of anything different) animal instinct. Empathy and compassion are evolved, requiring the mental capacity to step past primal urges. Our society still tolerates weaponized cruelty, with empathy and kindness considered weak. When someone's path is marked with cruelty, they have failed the first test of an advanced society.* —Governor J.B. Pritzker (paraphrased[94])

Those who are in their *intuitive minds* have access to their:

1. Right-brain: Specializing in insights, empathy, inclusion, and keeping other parts of the brain sanely balanced.
2. Gut: Continuously gauging our physical safety.
3. Heart: Specializing in compassion, connection, and emotion.
4. Superconscious: Connecting us to our energy body senses, such as clairaudience, claircognizance, clairvoyance, etc.

Like a boat, we're born with a tiny *trolling motor* brain in addition to a larger (intuitive mind) main engine. Most people and leaders navigate their personal and collective boats through dangerous waters using only the tiny trolling motor, with their birthright intuitive main engine disabled. Likely, someone once told them that their main-engine intuitive mind was not practical in the real world or somehow dangerous and off limits. It doesn't take many Truth-resonant strings to figure out that neither is true.

As you can tell from most newspapers and history books, the small motor is enough to get us collectively into a mess, but the main engine is often needed to get us out of it. Given how many contemporary messes are not sustainable, if even survivable, I suggest that a decision to teach our children to access and trust their Truth-sensing intuitive minds could not come too soon. As interesting as it's been to watch 5-cylinder (5 sense) people lecture 8-cylinder (7+ sense) people about correctly perceiving the *real* world, we've gone about as far as we can following 5-cylinder leaders without the *strings* to sense Truth or the courage to follow it.

An evolutionary sorting is now occurring in that people and their leaders will either learn to access, trust, and live by their Truth-sensing intuitive minds or may be left behind. What will it be?

The eventual extinction of untruths 📖

We're currently living in a time of partial uncovering (apocalypse) where people, political parties, and institutions are increasingly revealing their true nature. What if the uncovering didn't stop at partial? I'm reminded of an ancient quote: "There is nothing hidden, which shall not be openly seen, nor anything secret, which shall not be known and come into the light of day."

Do you suppose it refers to a far-off time or a time just around the corner? What if I told you that we're on the verge of technological (in addition to intuition) breakthroughs that may soon render deception somewhere between difficult and impossible?

Deception comes in at least two forms. One form involves whether the person speaking believes what they're saying. We've known for years that voice stress analyzers may give an indication as to whether a person believes their own words. Security forces around the world have access to smart glasses that flash discrete lights (such as green/yellow/red) into the wearer's eyes to indicate whether the person currently speaking believes what they're saying.

It may only be a few years before such glasses are available to the general public. Does that salesman or social media influencer believe what they're saying? When that leader recorded a speech decades ago, did they believe what they were saying? Smart glasses or smartphone apps[95] with voice stress analyzers may soon offer a *partial* game changer. As helpful as it might be to know when a speaker believes what they're saying, it still falls short in that it doesn't address the second form, the level of Truth. Kinesiology and pupil monitoring may be helpful in that regard. A true statement may cause the pupils to slightly constrict.

Serious people believe this. In addition to patents, the U.S. government has invested millions[96] in this area. Imagine owning smart glasses in a few years with two sets of discrete lights (such as green/yellow/red) that only you can see. The first set of lights (based on the speaker's voice stress) indicates how much the person in front of you believes what they're saying. A second set of lights indicates whether your own pupils are reacting in accordance with an energy field of Truth. Imagine thinking or saying to yourself, "The Earth is flat," and seeing an immediate red light from your smart glasses! Talk about a global deception game changer!

At first, you may say, "Yay, deception may go extinct!" But, since history indicates that perhaps half or more of what we currently believe to be true is some degree of not-true, be aware that Truth may eventually set us free, but first it's likely to cause disruption! Imagine reading a history book or social media post with our smart glasses and seeing, line-by-line, red or green flashes! Many, if not most, things currently in writing may need to be updated for improved levels of Truth. How might those who work in sales, politics, and the media be impacted?

To say the partial-to-full extinction of deception could change our world is the understatement of the year. In fact, it might be such a world-changer that we may want to adjust how we measure the passing of years. Instead of BC and AD, perhaps we will start using something else, such as DP (deception possible) and DNP (deception not possible). Hang on to your hat, because ready or not, our time of partial uncovering may soon become more than partial, and the ramifications could be enormous!

Neutral second opinions 📖

A baseball umpire was asked how he avoided misjudging balls and strikes. His response was, "Because it isn't *anything* until I say what it is!" Welcome to the minds of truth deciders and enforcers, who are sometimes the biggest asset in the advancement of human knowledge and sometimes the largest impediment. While brains are often satisfied with *truth*, heart-based intuition seeks Truth. While society has gotten along for thousands of years with truth deciders, the trouble comes when teachers and enforcers, generations or centuries later, assume *truth* to be Truth.

In the time of the ancient Greeks, it was thought to be an obvious truth that the sun orbited around the Earth (geocentrism). Around 230 BC, when Aristarchus of Samos claimed the Earth orbited around the sun (heliocentrism), truth deciders and enforcers proclaimed him mistaken. Even though he was intuitively correct, it was difficult and dangerous for him and his followers. In the 1500s, when Copernicus realized that Aristarchus was correct, church-based truth deciders and enforcers proclaimed him mistaken. Although intuitively and intellectually correct, it was difficult and dangerous for him and his followers. In order to avoid the wrath of truth-enforcers, Copernicus waited until his deathbed to publish his findings.

When Galileo later agreed with Copernicus, the Roman Inquest truth deciders and enforcers convicted him of heresy in 1633 and sentenced him to house arrest for life. Although intuitively and intellectually correct, it was difficult and dangerous for him and his followers. A few hundred years later (~1822), the church admitted that heliocentrism had always been Truth. My point is that regardless of their field (including science), those in power often resist, ignore, and deny inconvenient Truth. Sometimes it comes down to deprioritizing Truth in favor of maintaining power, belief systems, or revenue streams. In the absence of a neutral second opinion, the general population has little choice but to go along with Truth adoption being postponed. Hence, making unbiased, neutral second opinions available to deciders and onlookers could be a game changer.

Since we already have think tanks, perhaps what we now need are *intuitive* tanks. Now that we're no longer burning at the stake those who activate their intuitive birthright for recognizing Truth, we should employ those who are verifiably accurate as valued resources for the purpose of helping humanity avoid needless conflict, pain, and dead ends. When believers in conflicting controlled narratives clash, tie-breakers might be available from neutral second opinion sources, such as a *Council of Accuracy Certified Intuitives*, who've been tested and certified by those such as Dr. Gary Schwartz of the University of Arizona. For the more conventional, access to neural second opinions in the form of an International Council of Judges might also be helpful.

What if truth deciders knew in advance that their rulings could be compared to neutral second opinions? Perhaps their decisions would become more accurate and immune to bias? What if this caused the long arc toward Truth and justice to shorten from centuries to within our lifetime? What if, indeed?

Ch. 9: Leaning toward mastery 102

The self-sovereign side of history 📖

Staying on the right side of history can be tricky. History has shown that much of what we currently believe to be true will eventually be seen as false. If so, how do we keep egg off our faces when descendants are examining our digital records centuries from now? Here are a few suggestions for disclaimers that should likely be attached to any current statements of "fact":

- *<Blank>* does not exist, as far as I currently know.
- *<Blank>* is not possible, as far as I currently know.
- *<Blank>* is true (or false), or so it would currently seem.

As we say in snow skiing, people who make such statements without disclaimers are often "way too far out over their skis" and into the realm of *belief systems* (BS). Whether attempting to give comfort or preserve the status quo, people often make statements that go well beyond what they actually know.

While some might balk at such disclaimers, our descendants may view statements without disclaimers as intellectual malpractice or even intellectual violence. For instance, if one capable of proving us wrong gives up after encountering our disclaimer-free words, violence has been done to them, to Truth, and to our society. What will it be?

A self-sovereign may be fluent in silence 📖

Are you fluent in silence? <u>In</u>sight, <u>in</u>spiration, and <u>in</u>tuition—where are they likely to be found? In. Spelling often offers clues. For instance, in-tuition favors those who pay tuition by going in.

> *Listen to the silence; it speaks.* —Native American Proverb

Perhaps what the world needs are more of us who are fluent in the silence of going within. These are the people most likely to solve the issues impeding our way forward.

> *Moving into your open heart is…coming home…the inner temple of self…[is] locked. The key that unlocks this door is silence.* —Q'uo

It's not necessary to go to a faraway city to take a full immersion class in meditation. Start by sitting quietly alone for 15 minutes a day.

> *It's not that there is no balm for [the] heart-sore…moving through change…There is endless balm…compassion…assistance. The challenge is in becoming still enough to receive.* —Q'uo

Like exercising, you may need to force yourself at first, but like exercising, the benefits of internal peace and balance may soon make silence a highlight of your day. What will it be?

The universe is thought-controlled 📖

Emotions are triggered not by what's happening but by our thoughts about what's happening. Hence, instead of greeting our friends with, "How are you feeling?" perhaps it should be, "How are you thinking?" which answers both questions? Imagine two people locked in the proverbial room with a five-foot pile of horse droppings. The first person thinks:

- This must be what hell is like!
- I'll probably get a skin rash and some horrible disease out of this, not to mention PTSD and the need for years of therapy!

In response to this, the epigenetics of an ever-listening body and a conscious universe say, "Instructions received, I'll get right on it!"

The second person *begins* thinking the same way, but remembering the power of thoughts, grabs the self-sovereign steering wheel of their mind before going down the "poor me" slippery slope. Instead, they reframe the situation into thoughts like:

- This should give me the benefits of a fully activated immune system and a great story to tell my grandkids!
- I'll bet that after leaving this room, even ordinary things will smell amazing in comparison!

In response to this, an ever-listening body and universe say, "Instructions received; I'll get right on it!" What will it be?

Don't waste a good crisis 📖

In The Law of One[97] book series, the author observes that the efficient use of *growth catalysts* is rare. What does that mean? Much to the amazement of our higher self and spirit guides, we often derive only minimal personal growth *traction* from life challenges specifically designed to catalyze maximum growth. We're so focused on getting past a challenge that we may not stop to contemplate its teachings.

What do we have when we waste a perfectly good crisis? We have the necessity for a *bigger* crisis. That is, more severe challenges than would otherwise be necessary if we'd extracted all the teachings and growth from the smaller challenge.

If our higher self's predestined plan involves particular areas and levels of growth, we can choose to get maximum growth traction from smaller challenges (the easier way) or we can hold out for the hard way. Either way, we will learn our predestined lessons. The same may be said for humanity as a whole. Which will it be?

Leaning into empowerment and a higher VQ 📖

The future is coaxing many of us toward becoming an empowered *me* within a synergistically awake and unified *we*. The future is also coaxing us toward evolving from a society in which only intellectual and emotional intelligence are valued to a society in which hyper-D subtle energy and *vibrational intelligence* are also valued.

> *Hyper-D awareness is the precursor to change. As a crucial next step, you are creating a hyper-D life as an example to others...In the coming decade, more and more will follow.* —The Z's

If the term "spiritual" can be partly defined as the awareness of sentient collections of vibrational matter or energy, those with a higher *vibrational intelligence quotient* (VQ for short) are likely better at it. Like a radio station, each sentient being and grouping seems to have a unique vibrational frequency or address.

For instance, I am a matter grouping called *Bob,* made up of smaller groupings called Bob's heart, Bob's foot, etc. At the same time, I'm part of larger groupings called marriage, neighborhood, zip code, city, county, planet, etc. Each of these groupings may be uniquely addressed. Regarding unique vibrational addresses, the cosmic switchboard is somehow able to make a holographic connection to any grouping anywhere, at the speed[98] of thought.

If someone has a high VQ, they could conceivably converse with a pet, a rock, their aching left foot, a deceased relative, or any other sentient grouping of matter or energy. This is not a new concept in that we've likely heard terms like "remote viewer," "remote Reiki practitioner," "pet whisperer," "dowser," "shaman," "intuitive, psychic medium," etc. All of these make use of the cosmic switchboard. In theory, I can mentally seek an information and/or energy exchange with *any* grouping of matter or energy. If I don't perceive an answer (assuming that particular grouping is willing to respond), my receiver may not be sensitive or practiced enough, there may be mental static or blocks, or I may be tuned to the wrong frequency.

There are many kinds of intelligence. Some are more useful than others. If you own a sailboat, *wind* intelligence would be very useful, but not useful to an office worker. In an academic environment, IQ (intelligence quotient) alone may result in great success. In an environment where empathy and *people-smarts* are useful, those with a combination of a high IQ and EQ (emotional-intelligence quotient) may be the most successful. The most useful type of intelligence depends on the situation.

If there is an exception to this, it might be *vibrational intelligence*, in that we're ultimately all vibrational beings interacting with other vibrational beings within vibrational fields in a vibrational universe.

> *We are all...experiencing interdimensional communication...Some...have figured it out...others haven't....* —Abbey Normal

Since there is no getting away from vibration, a high degree of vibrational intelligence should likely be added to the types of intelligence valued by a wise society. Those who prioritize raising their vibratory rate may be more of service to themselves, their community, and their planet. The only thing more useful to the world than a person raising their vibratory rate is a group of people synergizing as a like-minded, raised-vibration group.

Although we're each born with a particular vibratory rate, what we expose ourselves to, including our thoughts and environment, can raise or lower our default vibration. Our vibration level has a direct effect on how we experience and impact the world around us.

Let's raise the vibrational tide from "one must work to find authentic peace, compassion, and understanding" to "one must work to avoid it."

The vibratory rate of the food and drink we ingest, the content we read or watch, and the places we visit all matter. In addition to giving thanks *for* our food, a vibrationally savvy person may give thanks *to* their food in order to increase its vibrational value. Even if we can't bring ourselves to read a high-vibration book, simply placing it near our bed may add value to our biofield as we sleep. This concept can be used to create a high-vibration bubble capable of calming and blessing us.

> *More are waking up to question not just reality, but some of the darker aspects of society. Work doubly hard on generating life force ... joy, light, love and a sense of connection. Generate light to shift not only your own life, but those around you.* —The Z's

Starting and ending every day with thoughts of gratitude, bolstered by daily meditation, a *radical* compassion/forgiveness practice, and a gratitude mantra placed in the gaps between thoughts, may keep our body within a high-vibration bubble. What will it be?

Compassion, forgiveness, and sovereignty 📖

Forgiveness is often misunderstood in that the benefits tend to be largely internal while the focus tends to be external. Since grievances amount to stuck, toxic internal energy, laying them down isn't about any person or institution outside of us. It's a self-oriented, self-sovereign, self-care act toward improving longevity and quality of life. There are many levels of difficulty in the forgiveness curriculum. The easiest level is when the *offender* takes ownership of how they wronged us and asks for compassionate forgiveness.

> *When fear leaves, compassion returns. Love can only touch us to the depth of our compassion. As such, the path from fear to love goes through courage and compassion.*

The master's level of forgiveness, as has been taken on by some religious avatars, is when the offenders seem to have caused great and irreparable damage and have no intention of owning it or apologizing in their lifetime. Have I completed this master's-level course? No, not even close, but I've at least begun.

If forgiveness were one side of a coin, the other side might be grievance. Don't get me wrong; we typically come by our grievances quite justifiably, but why would anyone choose to hold on to toxic grievance poison even a moment longer than necessary?

Long after most are forgotten, the poison of a lifetime of grievances remains. Hence, a periodic grievance cleanse might be our most important wellness routine.

In the early phases, we may see a grievance as useful fuel for our internal fire. That is, a ready source of excuses, sympathy, or something that helps drive or define us, all the while assuming it to be something that can be laid down at any time. In my experience, the "lay it down at any time" part is often not true. A serious grievance can be more like playing with a designer street drug or a jumping cholla cactus. It's not until you're finally ready to let it go (perhaps after noticing its toxic impact) that you realize, to your horror, that it has no intention of letting go of *you*. This may be called a grievance addiction.

So why might a grievance let go of us on our 14th or 49th attempt at forgiveness and not before? What's the science behind what made that time successful? Is it the phase of the moon, our biorhythm, or something else? Physicist Dr. William Tiller has a scientific term (*raised thermodynamic gauge*) for an energetically conditioned room or space that's temporarily charged to the point that things that normally *can't* happen *can* happen. For instance, things like ESP, psychokinesis, or *forgiveness* can happen. Lynne McTaggart uses the term "The Linger Effect of Intention" to describe how repeatedly having a positive intent in the same space can charge that space. Those who've noticed an energy shift as they enter a building where prayer has consistently occurred for centuries may already be aware of the notion of a charged space.

How can this knowledge be applied? If you ever find yourself in a place where you feel an abundance of positive energy, whether a seminar, a place of worship, an enclosure exhibiting *shape power*, or just out in nature, seize that rare and precious opportunity. Try to lay down your most stubborn grievances. Soften, forgive, and release that grievance and your part in it. Lay it down, walk away, and pray it doesn't follow you home.

> *Much forgiveness may be needed in order to create a world in which little forgiveness is needed.*

I created a 60-year-old grievance addiction when I encountered a street gang in a way that allows me to pinpoint (to the day and hour) when my childhood ended. In retrospect, this was an example of how one person's darkness can be activated by nothing more than another person's light. Despite my best and frequent attempts, this grievance would not let me go until I joined the free *Blessings Co-op* crowd-sourced science experiment, which I created at clever2wise.com. Apparently (as is the subject of the experiment), blessings on credit from those who will join in the future raised the energy around me such that when I next tried to lay that grievance addiction down, it not only worked but seemed easy!

> *Forgiveness is not erasing a memory as much as integrating it with a higher-dimensional aspect.* —Dr. John Ryan

The moral of the story is to *forgive early and often, while you still can.* Do this before a grievance becomes an unbreakable, lifelong addiction. Given the potential health[99] and longevity consequences, grievances should not be considered worthy companions.

> *The weak can never forgive. Forgiveness is an attribute of the strong.* —Mahatma Gandhi

The ability to shake off a grievance may be proportional to the amount of *wiggle room* built into the premises underpinning it. People who leave room for softening and compassion in their grievances are more likely to find non-violent compromises, are less likely to tear a family or nation apart, and are more likely to forgive.

> *Rather than put energy into resisting a situation, put it into gratitude, on credit, for how the universe will shift or reframe the situation so that your gratitude may eventually be fulfilled.*

I suspect these same people are also more likely to experience better health for longer. By way of example, I'll mention two extreme perspectives that might impact someone's ability to release a grievance. Perspective number one:

> *It happened. It was 100% inappropriate.*
> *Nothing good could ever come of it. Period.*

This person's premises have bound themselves tightly to their grievance with little, if any, wiggle room for ever escaping. If the toxicity takes a larger and larger toll on health and relationships, this person may realize too late that this self-generated airtight case did them no favors. On the opposite end of the spectrum, a person could *choose* to think from perspective number two:

> *Since my soul doesn't allow anything that's not within its plan, it must have been authorized. How can I find the lessons at this level of discomfort so my soul doesn't need to raise the discomfort level?*

Since we typically choose our thoughts, which view involves more suffering and less ability to escape the toxic consequences of a grievance? I'm reminded of a line from Shakespeare: "Nothing is either good or bad, but thinking makes it so."

*If you focus on the hurt, you will continue to suffer. If you
focus on the lesson, you will continue to grow.* —Buddha

Our personal grievance premises likely fall somewhere between these two extremes, but the principles still apply. From our conversations to our political views to our grievances, where might we benefit from allowing more compassion wiggle room?

Space-time manipulation 📖

You may be thinking that we may one day experience a transition from a longstanding 4D era to a new hyper-D era, where some will *eventually* have skills around space-time manipulation. In fact, we're already centuries deep into the hyper-D era.

We already have historical records of special people and special places in nature that have sporadically demonstrated space-time manipulation abilities. Hence, the only real transition necessary is a wider acceptance and appreciation of the space-time manipulating skills already among us and the valuing of those skills by society.

Regarding places in nature conducive to altering space-time, we've traditionally used terms such as "vortex" or "power spot," such as where *ley lines* or magnetic grid lines intersect or where a tectonic plate applies pressure to piezoelectric (electricity-generating) rocks. Regarding people who've demonstrated innate space-time altering ability (siddhis), we've tended to use terms like saint, shaman, and sorcerer, as in one who seeks relationship with Source.

> *[One] is as powerful metaphysically as the degree
> of original vibration [they] can lay hold of and
> sustain an intimate relationship with.* —Q'uo

This might also include astral-projecting astronomers and consciousness-projecting remote viewers[100] sponsored by the CIA, DIA, NASA, and U.S. Military Intelligence. Remote viewers reportedly have the ability to remotely collect information simply by projecting their consciousness to other places and times.

We have seen several insider reports of the U.S. government possessing space-time-altering technology. DARPA (Defense Advanced Research Projects Agency) and the U.S. Navy are examples of governmental agencies that have reportedly relied on technology as opposed to human ability for space-time manipulation.

Some insiders claim that a technology experiment to make the USS Eldridge invisible jumped it ten seconds back in time. Other insiders at Montauk Air Force Station tell of time-travel experiments. Andrew Basiago, a lawyer and holder of five academic degrees, claims to have led a DARPA time travel team[101] for several years. Williams Stillings, a claimed former DARPA time travel associate, has since come forward to support Basiago's claims.

In the new hyper-D era, time travel experience on a bio or job resume may be appreciated as desirable. I predict that employers will eventually realize that space and time are pliable and will look for employees with space-time manipulation skills to give them a business advantage.

- As a technology inventor, is it possible that some of my patents resulted from remote viewing the future?
- As a futurist, is it possible that I sometimes predicted the future correctly because I used remote viewing to observe it?
- As a competitive analyst, is it possible that I used remote viewing to sleuth out unpublished weaknesses?

Sure, although a typical 4D employer may not consider remote viewing skills to be a plus on a resume, a savvy, hyper-D employer might value them as offering them a significant business advantage.

Although intellect has a ceiling, intuition and inspiration do not.

Assuming you'll want to position yourself to eventually be able to include one or more space-time manipulation skills on your resume, where should you start? Before taking remote viewing or other classes, you may want to first develop a meditation practice and intuitive abilities conducive to a quiet, controlled, and sovereign mind.

Many of us were born with space-time manipulation abilities and proclivities and shut them down in order to fit in. Hence, most have more of a head start than they realize. If daydreaming or mentally being anywhere besides here and now is a form of space-time travel, phasing, or manipulation, most of us already have significant capabilities in that area.

Bob Monroe, founder of the Monroe Institute (an authority on controlled out-of-body experiences and the Gateway Method), says that just being lost in thought is to be ~10% phased out of 4D reality, or out of phase with our actual here-and-now. This hints at being, to varying degrees, in alternate dimensions. To be daydreaming is to be ~20% phased out. To be in meditation is to be ~30% phased out. To sleep is to be ~90% phased out. For me, phased-out daydreaming (which my wife calls "being in La-La land") is an important part of my creative process. Since I often can't relate the details of my own essay, invention, or book until I've reread it, I may be tapping into alternate dimension information by way of an altered state of consciousness.

> *Living in a matrix of illusions, what if the one*
> *who seems zoned out is the one who's zoned in?*

Monroe's controlled out-of-body astral trips often cause him to be more than 90% phased out. When our body ceases to function, we call that 100% phased out, or *death*. Monroe and his researchers have used out-of-body astral trips to explore the countless "What's next?" options that may be available after death.

Ordinary matter, including our bodies, is made up of subatomic particles such as protons, neutrons, and electrons that are categorized as "spin-1/2" because they only look like themselves after every <u>second</u> full rotation. After only one full rotation, when they don't look like themselves, some have speculated that they may be facing some inner[102] dimension or are partially phased out. If so, all matter (including our bodies) may be more intimately intertwined with alternate dimensions than we know.

Although little known, another form of space-time manipulation we're already good at is the collective ability to alter the laws of probability when the news causes many of us to have the same emotion at the same time. The Princeton Engineering Anomalies Research Lab (by way of globally scattered random number generators) has tracked[103] this phenomenon for decades.

Another form of space-time manipulation we're already good at is the ability to subconsciously sense unexpected changes seconds before they happen. This common skill is known as a "premonition" or "presentiment." The Institute of Noetic Sciences has shown, by way of galvanic skin response (GSR) sensors, that our autonomic nervous system registers startling or stimulating events seconds before they occur. The inventor in me thinks it may be useful if GSR sensors (where our hands contact the car steering wheel) allowed us to be warned seconds in advance that something unexpected in traffic is about to startle us.

If it's true that we create the quantum field conditions to attract or navigate toward one particular future out of many, what if, rather than the present moving toward the future, the future moves toward the present? If so, a premonition or presentiment may be similar to sensing the bow wave in front of a moving boat. That is, once a choice point[104] has passed that locks in one noteworthy future out of multiple potentials, a preceding bow wave from that approaching future might be perceived by any sufficiently sensitive individual or equipment. If we pay attention to the subtle sensations within our body, perhaps we're more capable of sensing the future than we know.

The first thing to master in the realm of space-time management is the mental focus to stay *right here and right now,* which is more difficult than it sounds. Professional athletes, extreme sports enthusiasts, and meditators are adept at this. Those in the here and now have access to the full supply of universal energy and information necessary for hyper-D abilities.

The energy to activate innate hyper-D abilities may be accessed via meditation (or satsang: exposing oneself to a high-energy, high-vibration person or place). I have utilized both of these approaches.

> *Lee [Harris] is a conduit for hyper-D activating energy. If you feel something when we talk through Lee, you are feeling the 9th dimension in your body.* —The Z's

After abilities have been activated, periodic meditation and constant high-vibration thoughts may keep them activated. Dr. William Tiller[105] developed a way to measure whether a room or space contains an unusual amount of thermodynamic energy that might be useful for space-time manipulation. A charged or "raised gauge" room or space has enough force-multiplying potential to alter the pH of water within a sealed container simply because someone intends that the pH change. Why does this work? In a charged room or location, the normally impossible becomes possible.

As previously mentioned, the charge within the king's chamber of Egypt's Great Pyramid may have allowed me to miraculously see entirely through the planet to observe clouds in a nighttime starry sky. Hence, as our planet becomes increasingly charged and thought-responsive, we will need to be increasingly careful with our thoughts.

An easy experiment to conduct is to come home to a space that's been silent all day or has been subjected to continuous *charging* due to playing certain types of music. In my experience, walking into a room charged by soft music feels noticeably different.

Some would have difficulty embracing the "what" of time and space manipulation stories unless they had a working theory regarding the "how" and "why." For these readers, here you go…

In many cases, manipulation of space-time may be accomplished by managing the localized space-time bubble in a room or around a person or object. There are many ways in which this bubble might be manipulated. Think of time as a flowing stream and our localized space-time bubble as something that normally floats down the time stream in a straight line while keeping pace with the flowing water. If, by technology, mental focus, or natural phenomenon, our localized space-time *bubble* was somehow sped up, frozen in place, slowed down, or jumped to a different location within the time stream (or to a different time stream), normally impossible space-time changes might suddenly occur.

Do we have technology that mimics the manipulation of space-time? Yes, in many forms. For instance, video chat mimics the ability of one person to be in two places at once. As an accomplished technology innovator, I can assure you that if there is a technology mimic, we should be looking for an equivalent phenomenon in the natural world.

Without the use of technology, people have often been seen in two places at once. The Catholic Church officially recognizes *bilocation* as a charism (siddhis) or exceptional human ability. Science recognizes that, via *quantum superposition*, matter can be in two places at once. While I'm one of at least three[106] family members with personal bilocation experience, two common threads have become apparent. One is that we're always asleep when bilocation happens. The other is that the bilocating version of us is witnessed by and interacts with someone who is significant to us and who may have been on our mind when falling asleep. Although science and the church may overlap on the "what" of bilocation, theories vary about the "how."

My top theories regarding how at least two versions of the same person can temporarily exist are:

- Wave/particle duality: For any given atom or molecule, one bilocation version temporarily claims particle form, while its copy claims wave form. Enough of the molecules in both the sleeping and astral-traveling bodies take particle form that they both appear solid.
- Overlapping timelines: Another "you" from another timeline temporarily overlaps with your timeline and intent.
- Our astral body (or a combination of more than one of our astral bodies) temporarily appears solid. Some call this phantasmal replication or aerial materialization.

Regardless of the "how," in the hyper-D era, the ability to attend two different events in different places at the same time should be recognized as an exceptional skill. If bilocating your body seems too challenging, bilocating only your mind, as with remote viewing or astral projection, may be more up your alley. Four hundred years before science was able to confirm it, Giordano Bruno apparently used either astral projection or remote viewing to discover that most points of light in the night sky are suns, some with their own orbiting planets.

An alternative to being in two places at once is to be in two times in one place. Regina Meredith, host of the Gaia TV show *Open Minds*, spoke of visiting a Native American reservation in the southwest American desert. When she looked across the desert with a softened focus, she could see people from another time walking around, giving birth, etc.

One of her guests related a story in which a mother standing in the living room of a 100-year-old house was shocked to lock eyes with the mom that lived in the house a century before. Which of them was seeing a time-shifted apparition? Perhaps they both were. What natural phenomenon caused two times to be in one place right there and then? Apparently, the conditions had to be just right.

A member of my family had a presentiment experience recently when she could, while in her bedroom, distinctly hear a woman sobbing. Try as she might, including texting the woman next door, she could not determine the source of the sound. As it turned out, about a week later, she <u>was</u> the sobbing woman in the bedroom. This may qualify as experiencing two times in one place.

Another of Regina's guests spoke of being in a place in the desert that had a high concentration of intersecting earth-energy *ley lines* and piezoelectric rock. As he stood in a low desert area, he noticed a man on an overlook peering down at him with binoculars. Curious about who it might be, he raised his binoculars to see an older version of himself. According to that guest, later in his life, he *was* that person peering down from the overlook.

Native Americans tell a story of a stone arch on a desert hill made of piezoelectric rock capable of generating power with each micro-tremor. As the story goes, members of the tribe could sometimes look through the arch on a cloudy day and see the distant desert valley unexplainably drenched in sun, as if it were one valley, at two different times. This same arch reportedly made small animals that walked through it vanish, perhaps to the same place but at a different time. When scientists are baffled by petrified human footprints from millions[107] of years ago (when humans were not yet supposed to exist), what if someone got there by walking through one of those arches? In the hyper-D era, anyone with the ability to experience one location at two different times (such as when investigating a crime scene) should be appreciated for their skill.

Objects, priests, and saints have been known to levitate. Could that be accomplished through the manipulation of the relative time of the bubble around an object or person? In theory, yes. As Earth hurdles through space, slowing down the space-time bubble around an impossibly heavy stone block could theoretically cause the moving Earth to pull away from it, leaving the stone block slightly behind (hovering above the ground). In this case, the stone is not levitating due to antigravity technology or large amounts of energy, but by manipulating time. Could this approach have played a part in the building of ancient structures?

Bending

Wave an unbendable metal bar up and down while holding it in the center. If you can slow down or speed up the localized time envelope around just where your fingers touch the bar, it must bend, not due to force but because a localized time envelope would not let part of the bar keep pace with the remainder of the bar. People have been documented bending objects with what appears to be pure mental focus and intention.

The power of intention, combined with the power of surrender, allows what's possible with intention without tension.

In the 4D+ era, anyone with the mental focus or technology to alter the space-time bubble around an object (such as when levitating or bending) should be appreciated for their ability.

Timeline alteration

Say, due to water erosion, a freeway must be moved several yards farther away from an encroaching river. Dismantling and rebuilding the freeway in the normal way would require enormous amounts of money and effort, *unless* a person or technology was capable of altering the freeway's historic timeline.

The freeway was likely placed in the same location as a prior highway, which was likely placed in the location of a prior road, which was likely placed in the location of a prior horseback trail, which was likely placed in the location of a prior cow path. That cow path may have originally resulted from a single cow deciding how to cross an untouched grassy field along a river. Anyone who can redirect that original cow by way of a glint of light, a worrisome reflection in a mud puddle, or the projection of an astral body could theoretically cause the freeway to instantly move farther away from the river. If this was successfully achieved, most would swear that the freeway's new location was where it had always been. The rare individual who could remember the freeway's old location in the prior timeline might be experiencing the Mandela Effect.

In his book, *The Isaiah Effect*, Gregg Braden tells the story of how his tour bus miraculously made a seven-hour trip from Mt. Sinai to Cairo in only four hours, much to the chagrin and astonishment of their military escort. In mid-trip, perhaps they collectively jumped to a timeline in which they had departed hours earlier? A hyper-D person keeps an open mind about what is and is not possible regarding time.

The power of ritual

While science has documented the ability of a single consciousness to alter reality, it has also noted a profoundly greater ability, called the "group effect," when two or more people focus on the same thing at the same time. Lynne McTaggart makes use of this in her "power of 8" groups. Whether it's by intention or ignorance, much information or entertainment content seems designed for us to collectively fear or hate the same thing at the same time, which may result in negative outcome manifestation at a quantum field level.

How can we put this principle to work toward altering our reality? Since the universe sees all time as now, repetitive rituals may help. If you say the same words every day for eight days, the universe simultaneously sees eight copies of you speaking and intending in unison and may respond in accordance with the *power of 8*. If you keep it up for a year, you may have the reality-altering *power of 365*! Why, after thousands of years, are repetitive rituals still around? When employed correctly, they get results!

> *You access the future and past…as astral traveling…all of time is available to you.* —The Z's

Energizing next-level circuits 📖

Next-level abilities require access to next-level amounts of quantum field energy and information. How might this be accomplished?

In the presence of Truth, muscles test stronger as if exposed to a temporary increase in energy. How can we employ this kinesiology concept to make that temporary energy boost consistent enough to power next-level health and abilities? The answer may lie in increasing not only our exposure to but also our acceptance of Truth.

> *Allopathic chemical medicine will give way to hyper-D energies, instructing cells to return to wellness (without side effects), but it requires the patient to watch/control their thoughts.* —Kryon

While mainstream allopathic medicine has yet to acknowledge it, holistic medicine recognizes the presence of nested etheric energy spheres or toroids (auras) around our body. The presence of a temporary Truth field likely causes a brief energy spike in an encapsulating etheric sphere, briefly improving muscle performance and wellbeing. The first step to making that Truth-field energy boost greater and more persistent may be to view that encapsulating energy sphere or toroid as a cloak, woven from hundreds of individual Truth fibers.

Whether looking within or without, every trait you notice represents a separate etheric fiber that *could* be carrying next-level Truth energy and information but likely is not. I say *likely is not* because Truth is a much higher standard than the *truth* we're used to. For instance, a muscle is likely to test weak when holding a written note that says, "Bob is kind." While it may be *generally* true, it's not *absolutely* True.

Have you ever tried to relieve uncomfortable pressure in your ears as an airplane descends? You hold your nose and blow because balancing inner ear air pressure with its equal and opposite allows the restoration of normal flow. The steps below involve accepting an *equal but opposite* approach to multiple traits. The "Bob is kind" statement is *true* but not True because, as far as the universe is concerned, it lacks a point of view within a context of balance. Like clearing my ears, in order to energize the associated *I-am-kind* fiber in my etheric cloak, I first connect *kind* with its opposite, which is *unkind*. Next, I locate my current position within the *kind-unkind spectrum* and consciously choose a bias or leaning. In this case, I'm biased toward *kindness*. Next, I internalize and accept the Truth about that trait, which is that "I'm constantly moving along the kind-unkind continuum, with a momentary bias toward kindness."

Since the universe recognizes that last statement as absolute Truth, the etheric energy in the fiber associated with that trait may begin and continue to flow. I can repeat the process for countless other internal traits. For instance, I internalize and accept that I'm constantly moving along the:

- Love-fear continuum with a bias toward Love.
- Patient-impatient continuum with a bias toward patient.
- Light-shadow continuum with a bias toward the light.
- Truth-truth continuum with a bias toward Truth.
- Generous-stingy continuum with a bias toward generous.

By accepting just these Truths, I may have several more persistently energized fibers in my etheric cloak than before, with many more to go. One could (and perhaps should) continue this fiber-energizing process for a lifetime and beyond. The more internal and external-facing etheric energy fibers we energize, the more next-level energy and information may flow in and around us.

When enough etheric fibers are bristling with energy, perhaps we'll begin to notice increasing levels of energy and information exchange with the quantum field. Then, watch for next-level insights, inspirations, and abilities!

No time like the present 📖

One commonality I've encountered in multiple types of bio-energy therapy is the practitioner visualizing spirals or circles while working on the client. These visualizations, besides possibly entraining the brain toward a more health-conducive frequency, encourage the practitioner to remain in the here and now, allowing maximum energy to be sent to a local or nonlocal space-time client or target. In my model (Fig. 9.1), *life-force potentiality units* (LPUs) represent the quantum field energy available to all humans but, by way of thought and emotion-controlled *valves*, tends to be largely choked off.

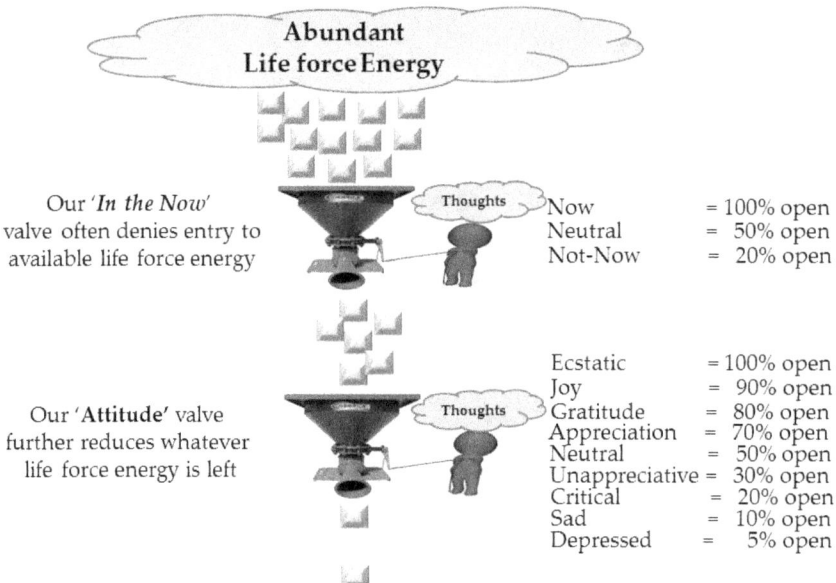

Figure 9.1: Compounded ways we choke off free universal energy.

LPUs may be thought of as components of what science calls ZPE (zero-point energy) or the quantum vacuum, where a cupful is said to contain enough energy to boil off all the world's oceans. The top valve in Figure 9.1 illustrates how we may artificially restrict and limit our own, virtually unlimited universal energy supply in a step-function (3-position switch) fashion by our thoughts not being in the *now*. The bottom valve illustrates how the same person can further choke off the remaining universal energy supply in a smoothly progressive (like a dimmer switch) manner according to their current emotional attitude.

The two valves create a compounded energy-limiting effect. For instance, my model predicts that when mired in a past grievance, we have access to only 20% of 20% (*not-now* thoughts and *critical* attitude), which is only 4% of the universal energy available to us. I estimate that a 10% energy flow is the minimum for maintaining health, leaving little for manifesting goals. Long-term marinating in a grievance, as predicted by my model, would make health, longevity, and goal-manifestation unnecessarily challenged.

Since ~80% of our daily thoughts seem to oscillate between future concerns and being unappreciative about something in our past (the math for both cases would be 0.2 x 0.3 = 0.06), this reduces our 100% potential life-force flow to only 6%, which might eventually be debilitating—if we never slept. We tend to be saved by spending perhaps 8 hours sleeping. Spending that length of time oriented toward time-neutral and attitude-neutral would be 0.5 x 0.5 = 25%, or a rate of life-force energy input that may[108] be 416% more than when we're awake. Taken together, the daily forward-moving average may supply just enough energy to maintain health while being able to rise to only modest challenges.

It does not say much for our mental discipline and sovereignty of mind that we must go unconscious or to sleep in order to experience our highest life-force energy flow of the day. If we applied the math of this model to the saying, "The more you thank life, the more life gives you to be thankful for," that equates to a highly potent energy flow of in-the-now (100%) times gratitude (80%), or a life-force potentiality energy flow of 80% of optimal. Subtracting 10% for health maintenance still leaves a phenomenal 70% of life-force energy that we can use to manifest new reasons to be grateful. Hence, that saying may be more than a potentially annoying platitude. It may also make mathematical sense.

Since a circular or spiral visualization prompts an energy therapy practitioner to be in the *now* (100%), if they can keep their attitude during an energy therapy session somewhere between gratitude (80%) and ecstatic (100%), the two numbers multiplied together imply a flow of universal energy of 80–100% that might be directed to help the client. In *science-speak*, the practitioner is employing positive-emotion empowered intent for activating syntropic, left-hand torsion (Kozyrev biofield[109] subtle) energy. This type of energy may be employed for the purpose of personal or client mental, physical, or emotional repair, goal manifestation, or placing helpful attractor patterns in local or nonlocal time.

In the laboratory of my own life, I've placed a version of the "Thank you, God." mantra in the gap[110] between adjacent thoughts for years. Wherever my energy flow was before that point, this mantra causes it to temporarily shift to a *now*-thought (100%) of gratitude attitude (80%) for a combined energy flow of 80% of optimal. This has caused my forward-moving daily average energy level to be significantly greater than before. The efficacy of this habit may be demonstrated by the impressive number of *stretch* goals that have materialized in my life since beginning that mantra practice. What will it be?

A self-sovereign approach to healing 📖

I've been involved with the Reiki energy community for around 40 years. Since I'm not a licensed medical professional, please don't construe anything I communicate in my writings as anything but a layman experimenter's opinion in regards to the "c" (cure) or "h" (healing) words. That said, I've seen physical and emotional complaints resolved in the presence of a sufficient quantity and quality of conducive subtle energy. To avoid medical terms, let's talk about balloons and crows.

Imagine living in a hot air balloon, spending most of your time bumping along very close to the ground, until you unfortunately develop a bad case of *crows*. A flock of crows seems to have adopted you and made it their personal mission to endlessly caw, squawk, relieve themselves, and flap near you and your balloon. You call a crow-ologist who attempts a crow-ectomy, but the situation persists until a wise old man suggests you take your attention off the crows and simply raise your altitude. Thinking it can't possibly be that simple, you keep fixating on the crows.

Finally, after the crow-ologist has given up, you give in to desperation and give the old man's advice a try. Like any habit, it takes a while to adopt as part of who you are, but slowly and progressively, your average altitude increases. For the longest time, it seemed like the crows would stay with you no matter how high you went. It's almost like they're afraid that if you succeed in shaking them, it will send the wrong message to crow infestations everywhere.

Then, when you least expect it, they're gone. Was it because your war on crows finally succeeded? No, were you *healed* of your bad case of the crows? No, "healed" would imply focusing on the crows. You simply found the discipline to make and maintain incremental altitude changes until you reached an altitude at which crows prefer not to reside. For all that time, money, and suffering, it was never about crows.

How might this relate to shifting a physical complaint? Every few minutes, spend a few seconds on a rampage of high-vibration appreciation, gratitude, and focusing on the silver linings in your life and world. If it seems difficult and uncomfortable at first, it may be an indication of a pre-existing addiction to low-vibration thinking, but keep at it. It takes the best part of a month to create a new habit.

Resolve to keep it up indefinitely and slowly raise your vibratory rate until some of your personal *crows* no longer prefer to reside with you.

Since I've seen physical and emotional conditions simply disappear, I'd be interested to see how this approach works for others.

Adding dimensions of compassion and forgiveness 📖

Differences in polarity, such as in what we see in the news versus what we would hope to see, are like the polar ends of a battery, creating (in science terms) the potential to do work. That is, the spiritual work of compassion, forgiveness, etc.

> *Compassion is the radicalism of our time.* —The Dalai Lama

That which captures our attention may resonate with the parts of us that most need to be healed before we can ascend to the next level. Our challenge is to neutralize negative energy through compassion, empathy, forgiveness, and making a conscious choice to bring a different, higher energy to the situation. Although *compassion, service, wisdom, Truth,* and *Love* may be explored in any order, one particular order may allow for optimal personal and societal impact.

- Since service is improved by compassion, compassion should ideally be explored before service.
- Compassion is improved by wisdom, so wisdom should ideally be explored before compassion.
- Wisdom is improved by Truth, so Truth should ideally be explored before wisdom.
- The application of Truth is improved by Love, so Love should ideally be explored before the application of Truth.

Therefore, we, as individuals and as a society, may be most effective when Love informs Truth, so that it better informs our wisdom, so that it better informs our compassion, and so that it better informs our service. This, as an all-circuits-and-spark-plugs-firing synergistic foundation, enables a particularly healthy, healing, and unifying brand of forgiveness—the kind capable of healing individuals, groups, and worlds.

Adding a new dimension

At the bottom level of the tetrahedron (Fig. 9.2) is the classic *predator, prey,* and *protector,* 2D triangle archetype, at a fear-dominant lower nature, physical survival level. These low levels of compassion, forgiveness, and empathy are often reflected in the roles played out in this familiar two-dimensional dynamic.

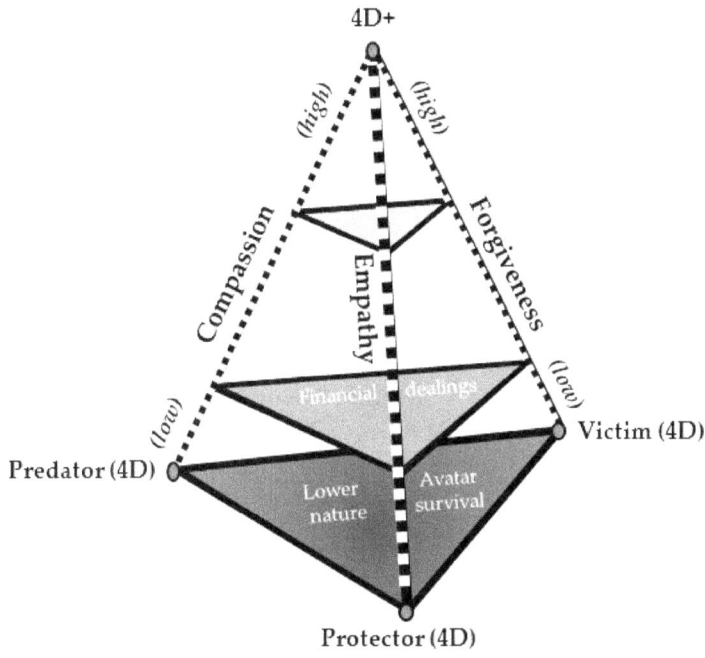

Figure 9.2: Compassion, empathy, and forgiveness: a dimensional view.

In this 2D triangulation relationship, the *predator* likely experiences low compassion for the victim, the victim may experience low *forgiveness* for the predator, and the protector may have low *empathy* for the predator. In a crime show, these roles may be represented by the criminal, the victim, and the police.

Although most people are familiar with this triangle, only those progressing toward hyper-D territory (seeking to add new dimensions to their perceptions) may perceive this familiar 2D triangle as just the base of a 3D tetrahedron. In adding a new dimension, those with a hyper-D mindset may utilize empathy, compassion, and forgiveness as ladders to ascend from lower to higher levels of those traits, with different experiences along the way.

When we decide to bring a higher frequency or dimension to each situation, we bring a new normal to our personal and collective world.

Slightly elevated levels of empathy, compassion, and forgiveness in this new dimension may be experienced in financial and other types of interactions where some form of regulatory body plays the role of protector between sellers and buyers.

At *mid-levels* of empathy, compassion, and forgiveness, where a balance is found between our fear-based lower nature and our Love-based higher nature, all the roles may be covered by either two people or only one person. For instance, a self-actualized buyer with sufficient self-esteem may play the role of their own protector. When a mid-level of empathy, compassion, and forgiveness are rolled up into a single 4D person, we often call them *Mom*.

At the *highest* levels, empathy, compassion, and forgiveness may converge at one point for some people. I call this hyper-D territory because, in elevating empathy, compassion, and forgiveness toward a common point of consciousness, one may notice not only nonlinear and bi-directional time but also increased multidimensionality.

My point is that given[111] that most of us experience only four of the countless dimensions, one thing we're *not* experiencing is a full, accurate view of reality. Hence, looking for extra dimensions could upgrade most every area of science and medicine. This won't negate the current laws of science. It will expand them in more elegant ways as we step into a new world that makes our old world seem like we were seeing it in black and white. For instance, if a dot were to begin to consider the possibility of extra dimensions, it might first notice being part of a line, then notice being part of a square, then notice being part of a cube, etc., realizing that it was always more multidimensional than it had been told.

Multidimensional information and communication are happening around you all the time, but your minds have been trained to not see it. In a more multidimensionally aware society, you could look at a friend for a minute or two and not need to ask how they've been. Your energy fields are more informational than your mind. —The Z's

When in meditation, the current version of you gives comfort to the prior version of you at the moment of a historical trauma, and the sting of the memory suddenly feels softened, less charged, and more healed, you've begun to practice self-care, or hyper-D alchemy. Alchemy of this type is possible when high levels of empathy, compassion, and forgiveness are combined with a more fluid perception of time.

In my experience, consistent application of increasing levels of *empathy, compassion,* and *forgiveness* regarding oneself and others is a game changer. With each higher level, upset, anger, and outrage become slower to arrive and quicker to leave. This allows for increased breathing room so that a self-sovereign mind might *respond* rather than react, allowing room to consciously choose whether to change, accept, or reframe a situation.

Masters don't react to or judge emotional trigger bait. They observe and respond from a place of Love. A visible response is optional because, between sending a blessing and the impact of the observer effect, they've already responded.

Higher levels of empathy, compassion, and forgiveness become increasingly conducive to peace, balance, physical and mental health, and reconciliations not available to or necessarily understandable by two-dimensional triangle people. What will it be?

Ch. 10: Leaning toward mastery 103

Evolution or intelligent intervention?

Science and the courts have historically avoided areas that might step on the toes of religion, leaving us with controlled narratives instead of knowledge in some very important areas. It's time for religion to help with this situation.

If religion started teaching a combination of evolution *and* intelligent intervention regarding how anatomically modern humans got here, science and the courts would be forced to either abandon both views because they come too close to religion or follow the latest evidence wherever it leads, which is what they should have been doing all along.

If this happens, spiritual people (who've pondered the question for millennia more than science) may not be surprised when the data supports a case of *and* as opposed to *or*.

Science says that humans evolved, like other hominids, with 24 chromosome pairs. That is, until about 200,000 years ago, when humans somehow began having 23 chromosome pairs. What it took to merge two of our chromosomes while snipping off the excess might be accomplished in a precision biolab, but likely *not* by random mutation.

In short, science points to 24 chromosome-pair humans benefiting from ~600,000 years of evolution until *some* type of intervention occurred ~200,000 years ago, when we somehow became 23 chromosome-pair humans. This strongly suggests intelligent intervention *in addition to* what was provided by evolution.

The esoteric and indigenous version of the story holds that Pleiadean women teachers arrived from the stars and had children with 24 chromosome-pair men ~200,000 years ago, with the resultant offspring *appearing* to have 23 chromosome pairs.

Part of a Pleiadean mother is seeded inside you…to…bring beautiful, magnificent, soft, sacred balance… Balance is the key for guiding this new consciousness into the future. —Onyah (Peggy Phoenix Dubro)

These were reportedly tall women with translucent skin and split vocal cords, capable of singing their own two-part harmony. I emphasized *appearing* above in that (besides nature preferring divisible by four numbers), a future invention allowing us to see quantum fields will reportedly reveal our (previously unnoticed) hyper-D 24th chromosome pair, compliments of our star heritage.

You are seeing a biological activation of your (so far) unseen 24th chromosome pair you have by intelligent intervention that will start to increase your compassion and caring…integrity will increasingly matter. —Kryon

This comingling reportedly occurred on a large, Eden-like garden island in a remote part of the Pacific Ocean. This Lemurian (*Mu*) subcontinent was reportedly formed when the Earth's crust pushed up to form a much larger and higher[112] land mass than we see today. The area was reportedly pushed up so much that mountain-top ceremonial structures were forced to burn charcoal to augment low oxygen levels.

When, after thousands of years, the underlying crustal bulge began to subside[113], there was reportedly a <u>fall</u>, at least[114] in the average altitude of the <u>garden</u> island to the point that fleeing people must have felt <u>cast out</u> as they sailed across the oceans in search of a non-sinking home.

As most of that subcontinent sank, all that was eventually left (other than perhaps the stretch marks still visible in the seabed) were the exposed mountain tops we now refer to as the Hawaiian Islands. This narrative holds a striking resemblance to what the indigenous Hopi refer to as the "end of the first world" in the form of a sinking[115] island.

> *Spirit…made an appearance…on an island…now beneath the water…said "I'm going to give you…Original teachings…share these so that you can have peace on Earth.* —Lee Brown, Salish Tribe 1986

In short, sky *women* arrived at a tropical subcontinent *garden paradise,* mated, and taught people that they were born magnificent children of the heavens. They also taught (at least until the elevation of the land experienced a great *fall*) that people, via intuition and logic, have *direct access* to their larger (spiritual) selves as well as universal Truth. At some point, our modern society discounted this intuition, to its great peril.

> *The intuitive mind is a sacred gift…the rational mind is a faithful servant. We have created a society that honors the servant and has forgotten the gift.* —Albert Einstein

Old, dark energy has long known that the best way to mislead is by rearranging details that are true. In fact, modern marketing and politics have turned this into an art form. So, how did religion rewrite the Lemurian story using the true elements of *garden paradise, women, fall, heaven,* and being *cast out*?

> *There was an idyllic <u>garden paradise</u> where <u>women</u> tempted, leading to a <u>fall</u> and being <u>cast out</u>. Women, because they created the problem, could be subjugated, and the most intuitive may be executed as witches. We're born dirty (without <u>direct access</u> to God), needing a man to intercede on our behalf.*

If I were in charge of rearranging the Lemurian story details in a way that would best throw humanity off the trail toward ascension, I would make those exact same changes. All in all, which of the two versions resonates strongest with your intuition and logic?

> *We're constantly offered true-untrue-true sandwiches. The wise look under the bread.*

Logic dictates that the planetary nursery of our Milky Way galaxy likely created a huge litter of Earth-like planets at around the same time, each with access to similar seeds of life.

Most of you, in your lifetime, will become very aware of your galactic connections. There is nothing off Earth to be more afraid of than some of the most difficult energies on Earth. —The Z's

Earth was the developmentally delayed runt of the litter (by perhaps a million years) for two reasons. One was that Earth only has access to a single viable sun, while most planets have two. The other reason was that disasters, like asteroid strikes, forced life on Earth to start over several times. Hence, if we've reached the point of hominids with cell phones, similar beings[116] on other planets in our galactic litter are likely a million years more advanced and monitoring our progress. Using the Drake equation, science predicts many advanced civilizations within our galaxy.

This planet is increasing in light…measurable by other planets…some of whom are very aware of you and are waiting for you to… understand…. What you do in the next 100 years will change the light quotient of the galaxy. —Kryon

Is it reasonable and logical that a million years from now (when we've caught up to where much of our galactic family is today), we could have interplanetary travel abilities and may also want to lend a helping hand to a less ascended planet? Yes, it is.

In that I've encountered both the unique energy of Hawaii and the positive, transformative influence of wise, intuitive women teachers, neither my logic nor intuition have a problem with the notion of a garden sub-continent of Lemuria. I can't say the same for the Garden of Eden story. Part of the road to mastery involves utilizing our intuition to decide matters such as this. Which will it be?

Building blocks

Imagine a dimension where only a single building block exists: tiny LEGOs made of pure gold. Your *body* is nothing other than that. The *good* you encounter is nothing other than that. The *bad* you encounter is nothing other than that.

The religious "authority" trying to convince you that you're less than gold and separate from true gold is nothing other than that. You briefly consider the narrative they're trying to sell before noticing the perfection of the building blocks making up your body and concluding that rather than invalidating you, they've invalidated their "authority."

This is a metaphor for our universe, where all matter is made of the lone building block of multi-D divine consciousness energy. I refer to this consciousness energy as "multidimensional" in that enfolded within it are Truth and the binding agent of Love.

> *...love...binds everything together.* —Colossians 3:14

Just as there is ultimately only one building block, there is only one ultimate law, the law of universal oneness.

> *There is only one law...the law of one. Other...so-called laws are distortions of this law, some of them...important for progress.* —Ra

What if oneness is the underlying mechanism behind the gravity that binds all matter together? If so, the source of gravity may be both spiritual and scientific. All mass is drawn toward oneness with other mass because oneness is a higher law.

Energy blowback from best and worst wishes

Where will humanity's long path toward ascension ultimately lead?

> *The "path": investigate, contemplate, substantiate, emulate.*

Our hyper-D ascension path will likely lead us to embrace reality in broader and higher dimensions until we ultimately reach the unifying point of All-D.

Along the way, the path will no doubt offer great rewards, especially to those with the initiative and courage to be early adopters of broader and higher dimensions. For now, the stairs from here to there might best be climbed by first embracing that which is broader-dimensional and then that which is higher-dimensional.

For instance, a person who operates from only their analytical left brain may become broader-dimensional by integrating their creative right brain, becoming much improved. That broader-dimensional upgrade makes them a candidate for a hyper-D upgrade by way of embracing inspirations from unseen (beyond 4D) sources. Creative types such as poets, writers, and artists may find this to be old news, whereas largely analytical types may see this as a new concept. Either way, this book seeks to address the "Why do I care?" aspect of increasing our wisdom and abilities by leaning into both broader and higher dimensions.

A hardnosed scientist may fallaciously cling to the dogma that if we observe something that can't be explained by the "currently" known four fundamental forces (*gravity, electromagnetic, weak nuclear, and strong nuclear*), it must have been imagined.

You are not thinking; you are merely being logical. —Niels Bohr

They've invented fictional placeholders such as "dark matter" and "dark energy" in an attempt to explain what's being observed through telescopes only in terms of (clearly insufficient) known forces. For those of us who pay attention to unusual events that clearly *did* happen and likely are *not* explainable in terms of the traditional four forces, those scientists are more likely to invalidate their position than our experiences.

With an open mind, there are obviously more than four fundamental forces. To that end, esoteric[117] sources have identified two additional forces that science may eventually discover: the *weak and strong interdimensional forces.*

For those willing to view unusual occurrences through the lens of six (as opposed to four) fundamental forces, metaphysics is just future physics, and "spiritual" often translates to *leading-edge lay scientist.*

Metaphysics is future physics, available today. The less courageous can learn about it in the future...via tuition. The more courageous can learn about it (and potentially use it) today...via intuition.

That same esoteric source reports that science will someday be able to see those two additional interdimensional forces in action by way of a special lens. This lens will reportedly make visible hyper-D aspects of the human biofield, our biology, the air around us, the night sky above us, and Mother Nature.

Nature is an alive being, which is why you feel better after taking a walk. You reconnect with your sensory body. —The Z's

Everything is energy. Specifically, everything is polarized energy. Beyond electricity and magnesium, many things we might think of as stand-alone may actually be part of a polarized, broader-dimensional continuum, if not a grid of polarized hyper-D energies.

As a Reiki practitioner, when I move my energy-scanning left hand near someone and it stops, it's likely because I've felt a change in polarization. By sending counter-balancing polarization energy until that spot matches the rest of their body, I've not *healed* the body but balanced it. A balanced body may heal itself.

Consciousness is part of a broader-dimensional low-to-high-vibration *continuum* that becomes a higher-dimensional *grid* when combined with some other factor. Consciousness energy, with some hyper-D properties, likely moves superluminally (faster than light) from the thinker to that which is being thought about, inferring that a polarization has been established and that consciousness, beyond being polarized, may also be polarizing.

Love is another example in that its broader-dimensional polar opposite may be fear. Motives driven by the *fear* side tend toward worst wishes and isolating win-lose outcomes, while motives driven by the *Love* side tend toward best wishes and cooperative, win-win outcomes. This leads us to a broader-dimensional Best-to-Worst Wishes *continuum*, which may be part of many possible higher-dimensional *grids*, including the one shown in Fig. 10.1.

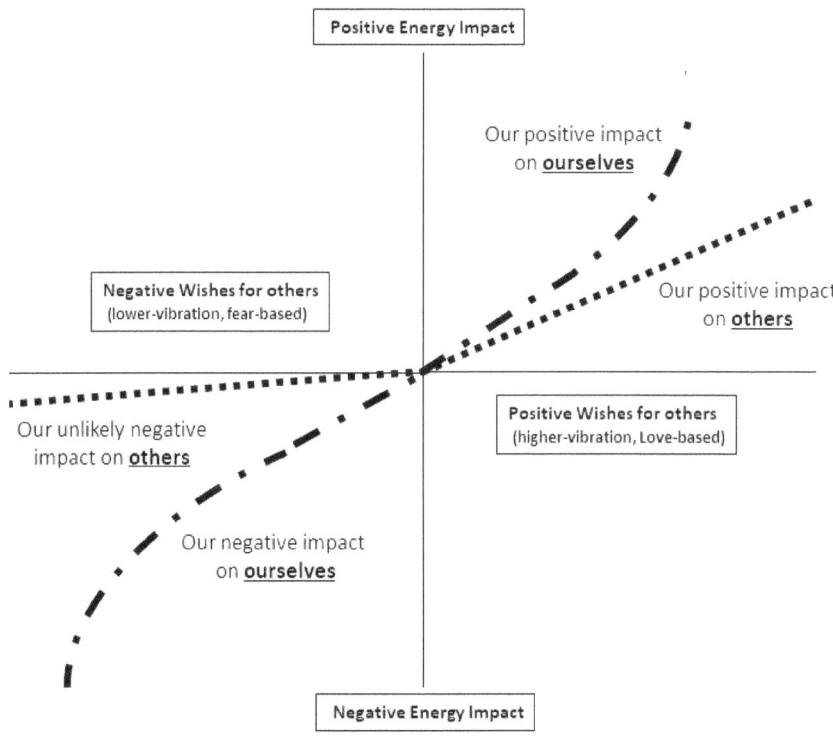

Figure 10.1: Best and Worst wishes for others…Energy Blowback

When we try to send positive or negative energy to someone, the graph suggests that the impact on us far outweighs the impact on the other person. The graph is a combination of three factors that either aid or hinder each other: *Free will, self-esteem,* and *universal energy bias.*

Upper-right quadrant: The lower line in the upper-right quadrant posits a linear rise in positive energy received by a targeted person based on positive energy sent, boosted by the universe's positive energy assisting bias but resisted by both the target person's (not completely onboard) free will and their (not sure I'm deserving) subconscious self-esteem.

This touches on an energy practitioner's (e.g., Reiki) concept that rather than *sending* ego-directed energy to the client that would be resisted by their subconscious free will, we should *channel* divine energy that decides for itself how it should be offered to the client for their highest good.

> *Infringement of free will won't occur if the energy or information we offer another is channeled through us, which is chosen and targeted by Spirit. If it's offered by us, it may violate their subconscious free will since it's chosen and targeted by our ego.* —Ra (paraphrased)

The upper line in that quadrant posits that we receive energetic blowback for *channeling* divine Love energy (as opposed to sending egoic love energy). What we receive far surpasses what the other person receives, because our free will is completely on board, *plus* the universe's positive energy matching bias, *plus* our subconscious self-esteem may accept a blessing for sending a blessing.

Lower-left quadrant: The upper (straight) line in the lower left quadrant posits that it's questionable that a targeted person will receive much, if any, of the negative energy we attempt to broadcast to them. While our negative energy may be partially allowed by their subconscious low self-esteem (*I deserve it*), it will likely not be assisted by the universe or allowed by their free will.

On the other hand, for having sent negative energy, the lower (curved) line shows us receiving an extra helping of negative energy blowback. Neither our free will nor sub-conscious self-esteem will likely block the negative blowback in the sense that we're consciously trying to cause someone harm.

In short, like when one finger points away and three fingers point back, it's the same for how we experience broadcasting either positive or negative energy to someone. Hence, a good health and longevity[118] plan (known to the masters) is to constantly channel a blessing to everything and everyone we see and never wish ill for any reason. As divine love channels through us, we get to keep *what sticks to the pipes*, and we are also blessed. What will it be?

Thought Patterns

How many thoughts does it take to make a thought *pattern*? From the perspective of those who can see thoughts projected around us as geometric energy patterns, perhaps only one is required. Each thought likely enhances or degrades our overall auric (Merkabah) geometric pattern, which unseen beings may notice, which is why negative, low-vibration thoughts and media influences are less than ideal.

Since energy flows where attention goes, managing our thoughts is managing power. Since thoughts alter both physics and biology, negative thoughts are an act of harming the self—a misdirection of power.

How we interact with energy patterns somewhat identifies us. One who enhances them and brings them back into coherence may be called an energy *healer*. One who interprets them within an object is said to perform *psychometry*. One who interprets energy patterns around people is said to give *readings*. One who interprets them around our biology may be called a *medical intuitive*. Those who temporarily bring their energy pattern into coherence with another being may be called *empathetic*, or "whisperers." One who temporarily brings their energy pattern into coherence with the physical world may be called a "spoon bender," "rain dancer," etc.

See a "pattern?" They're all interacting with energy patterns. One day, a special cryogenic (*quantumscope*) lens will reportedly make these energy patterns visible to a world that currently believes only matter *matters*. Until then, those who understand that everything is energy have advanced access to a more complete, healthy, and colorful world.

Hacking 4D

Is it possible to hack a 4D place, time, and all that resides within it? Beyond the stories about spiritual masters, we hear such stories from average people all the time.

- Stories about a traveler who reached their destination much faster than physics should allow
- Stories about a person who was in two places at once
- Stories about energy healing or spontaneous remission
- Stories about those who, via the placebo effect, alter their biology with only the power of their mind
- Stories about those who, with only their minds, collect intelligence at a distance

How have these people managed to *hack* or pull rank on the default 4D laws of physics? They did it by employing the superior *law of consciousness* from a hyper-D vantage point. Welcome to the path to mastery!

> *Art is what we create based on the universe's suggestions. Manifesting is what the universe creates based on our suggestions. Mastery leans into both, plus Love, wisdom, Truth, oneness, self-empowerment, sovereignty, etc.*

Judge, discern, or bless?

The longer we contemplate something, the deeper our discernment goes—until we judge it. From the point of "I've made a judgment," discernment rarely goes any deeper. Hence, it's wise to remain in *discernment* and out of judgment for as long as possible.

> *Discern if you want to see what is.*
> *Judge if you want to divulge your past.*

That said, our subconscious likely fears that if we withhold judgment for too long, our ever-deepening discernment may shift control away from our (*separate* for survival) head to our (*get along* for survival) compassionate heart. These fears may subconsciously prompt us to judge, to our detriment, before the depth of our discernment or feeling goes very deep.

> *The quicker we judge, the less we see, and the*
> *more separated and dangerous our world becomes.*

The opposite is also true. The deeper the discernment due to suspended judgment, the more we can accurately see and feel, and the more collaborative and safe our world becomes.

Why do we typically live less than 100 years in bodies designed to last for centuries? It may come down to toxins building up in our bodies over time. That is, not just chemical toxins, but energetic toxins from thoughts and judgments. While we may be able to somewhat minimize chemical toxin buildup by donating blood[119], thought toxin buildup may be more impactful. This is because the body is capable of accumulating energetic residue from a lifetime of thoughts, words, and deeds.

When someone cuts us off in traffic, how can the universe tell whether our thoughts went to judgment, discernment, or blessing? If an energetic poison lodges in or around our body, potentially lowering the quality or quantity of our life, it's a sign of judgment and grievance. If there was little change in our body, it was likely experiencing the neutrality of discernment. If the quality or quantity potential of our lives is improved by the experience, our response was likely to send a blessing.

> *We're seeing the slow death of judgmental energy. In the meantime, judgment is holding back your evolution. You can speed up your evolution if you can get past this.* —The Z's

Hence, when we see a "bad" person or group in the news (or even in a fictional story), we have a decision to make. Ask yourself, "How will my tissues permanently record what I'm currently thinking?" Could a cancer diagnosis years from now result from judging a fictional character in "harmless entertainment" today?

Our biology and longevity reflect the accumulated impact of our thoughts, which is why sovereignty of mind is worth the trouble. What will it be?

Your holographic approximation

As a futurist, I can predict that (in addition to your social media posts), you've already been near enough cameras and microphones so that sociologists and descendants, centuries from now, using your digital footprint, will likely be able to interview and interact with a walking, talking hologram approximation[120] of you. As such, they will likely be evaluating whether you were one who led the way toward their more mature way of being *or not*. In other words, were you part of the solution toward ascension, or were you part of the problem?

Being at peace with and transparent about our imperfections is authenticity. At the same time, seeking to shrink our imperfections while growing our areas of perfection is the process of ascension.

Which ways might we lean today so our digital approximation will eventually be seen as ahead of our time and part of the solution?

Lean toward being increasingly balanced, tolerant of others' beliefs, slow to anger, patient, compassionate, kind, and a person with strong self-esteem. Lean toward trusting intuition and toward that which protects and increases our soul *flame*.

> *Some will see your flame and want to blow it out...others will approach with a candle....* —Lenita Vangellis

Lean toward demonstrating that cooperation in pursuit of oneness beats competition in pursuit of separation. Since the future will know that these were all well within our reach today, what will it be?

The future of healing

Future medicine may eventually grasp that most healing is self-healing and shift to offering the mind and body *suggestions* rather than harsh chemicals with side effects.

Homeopathy does this today in a generic way, via water's ability to retain an energy signature, or signal. Energy practitioners do this by offering a client's body an energetic template for wellness. Hence, neither homeopathy nor energy practitioners *heal* in the sense of brute-forcing an outcome. Rather, they *suggest* a self-healing roadmap for the client's subtle body.

As such, how much the body heals in response to homeopathy or energy work may be more about our subconscious, or soul's, willingness to be healed than practitioner or modality efficacy. Hence, rather than charging for results, practitioners might charge for their time. While mundane maladies tend to heal automatically, unusual maladies may prompt the cells of the body to wait for instructions from *the boss*. Because most are out of touch with their bodies, many perish as the body awaits a response to a request for instructions we've never noticed.

What if we could offer customized guidance to the body? While programming the same healing instructions into each of our trillions of individual DNA strands may seem daunting, what if those instructions were already built in? Reportedly, encoded within our *junk* DNA is the record of every past life, including those in which the body knew how to beat a particular disease. If so, what if it's just a matter of us, as *the boss,* sending a body-wide directive: "Execute the disease-beating DNA instructions prerecorded from a prior life?"

DNA instructions can facilitate healing, but what if stubborn issues require more supplemental energy than an energy healer can provide? Imagine tumblers in a lock that must line up in order to access supplemental universal energy; tumblers that may have names like *ego-mind, subconscious, super-conscious,* and *soul.* When they all align, if only for a moment, science may call the results of the ensuing energy surge *spontaneous remission*.

Since some tumblers (e.g., the ego mind) tend to be in constant, erratic motion, lining them up is easier said than done. Hence, developing sufficient sovereignty of mind to send body-wide directives while lining up tumblers could be the very game changer that takes us from yesterday's level of healing success to that of tomorrow. What will it be?

Describing the hyperdimensional

Because no description is perfect, to describe something is to distort it. Any description is first distorted by the perceptions, experiences, biases, language, and cognitive filters of the speaker and further distorted by a completely different set of perceptions, experiences, biases, language, and cognitive filters with each listener. It's like layering two or three polarized lenses at different angles in front of our eyes, so what's in front of us is distorted, if visible at all.

In addition to that handicap, imagine trying to describe that, which is nonlinear hyper-D, with 4D, linear words, attempting a structured description of something that has no structure. Accurate information transfer becomes so challenging that we're left with only metaphors, parables, or simple, all-inclusive responses. For instance:

God, how would you describe yourself? "I am."
God, where are you? "Yes."
God, what are you? "Yes."

Some seek to understand the hyper-D in an intellectual way, such as the quantum biologist, who studies the hyper-D aspects of human biology. Others seek to understand the hyperdimensional in a first-hand, visceral way, such as through spiritual experience.

When an ancient spiritual experiencer distorts a hyper-D experience by writing it down (perhaps years after the fact), it's often further distorted by language translation, editing, reading, and seminary teaching before being further distorted by preaching. Listeners will further distort what was preached through their cognitive filters and then claim (ironically) that their beliefs are *flawless Truth*, even when they conflict with common sense.

Hence, one on the spiritual hero's journey of enlightenment realizes that theirs is largely an intuitively followed path of unlearning, from narrative to Truth.

You have so much to unlearn. —Kryon

This journey often leads away from the narrative-embracing crowd to a solo path toward a Truth-embracing crowd—from an assumed relationship with Truth to one closer to actuality, in a better place to attempt a description of that which is hyper-D.

How is dark energy created or increased?

There's a single building block for everything: universal consciousness, which constantly beams light energy to us in forms such as compassion, love, benevolence, joy, and laughter. Sometimes we align with that light energy to receive it, and sometimes we block it, creating shadow.

A good pre-life, life, and afterlife plan: seek the light, hold the light, repeat.

If dark energy is the shadow of light energy, what could possess enough of the divine that it could block divine light to create a dark energy shadow? Our divine free will is that capable.

The biggest dimmer switch between us and our infinite potential is our free will. Therein lies our work and the path.

Anything created from universal consciousness is at some level conscious, so the dark energy shadow created when our divine free will blocks compassion, benevolence, etc. to opt for condemnation, grievance, etc. is at some level *conscious*, with a survival instinct.

> *Everything is alive and has its own consciousness.*
> —Lakota elder Tiokasin Ghosthorse

The metaphor in the diagram (Fig. 10.2) illustrates the shadow's survival instinct. Our rising soul flame may trigger the shadow to react and try to dampen our flame. In fact, we may be encouraged to believe that if we dampen our flame enough, the shadow might leave us alone. By way of translation, shadow sees that our light threatens it, so it prompts some to deluge us with fear and imbalance-inducing narratives in order to dim our light. That is, if we cooperate.

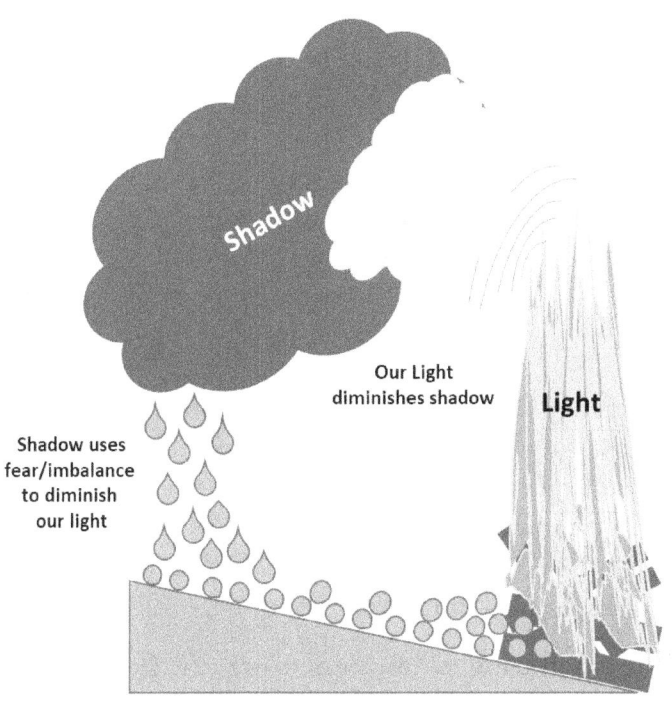

Figure 10.2: Every thought aids one side or the other.

You cannot be stopped unless you stop yourself...You have the power...you simply have to take it back...The...no power dynamic is just a con/illusion that humanity believes...If you refuse to give up...you will get somewhere. —David Icke

Every thought, action, and information or entertainment choice provides a boost to one side of the light/dark balance or the other. Does that newscast, song, TV show, movie, etc. strengthen our personal shadow, diminishing our personal light? Or does it strengthen our personal light while diminishing our personal shadow?

What's the difference between darkness and evil? Darkness is a blind/unintelligent force that, like gravity, seeks to survive by counterbalancing light. When humans choose to imbue

darkness with consciousness, it becomes conscious evil. Humans are that capable. —Kryon

Whether we realize it or not, we are accountable for the global impact of every thought, so we might as well own it as part of our self-sovereignty and path toward mastery. What will it be?

Keep growing until things make sense

When we knew only simple math, a day came when higher math made no sense—until we took the trouble to *grow* into algebra, when it all made sense, and peace, joy, and balance returned. Then, a day came when yet higher math made no sense—until we took the trouble to *grow* into geometry and trigonometry, when it all made sense—and peace, joy, and balance returned.

The concept is the same for our lives in general. If the world doesn't make sense using only the brain, keep growing into your *brain-heart-pineal complex* until it all makes sense and peace, joy, and balance return. What's the scientific equivalent of "As above, so below?" Fractals.

Figure 10.3: Fractal-like patterns in Romanesco cauliflower

From infinitely large to infinitely small, fractals are geometric patterns that endlessly repeat in both directions, no matter how much we zoom in or out. What if hyper-D fractals are within and around us? While the universe varies, it's generally biased toward the symbiotic, self-balancing, benevolent, and harmonious. Otherwise, statistics say our chances of currently being alive on Earth are virtually nil.

> *It is consciousness that creates the material universe, not the other way around... the laws, forces, and constants of the universe appear to be fine-tuned for life, implying intelligence existed prior to matter.* —Dr. Robert Lanza

Since the universe is biased in those ways, fractals tell us that we, who come from that universe, are also likely to be biased toward balance, benevolence, and harmony. That said, these traits may be apparent only at the correct zoom level. The universe's bias for progressing things to a higher level of order may seem quite chaotic at some zoom levels. Since the universe has proven its ability to progress building blocks from dirt to dolphins, it's reasonable to conclude that it also knows how to progress us from a human planet to a humane planet. Hence, when our collective world seems chaotic, we can zoom *out* (like going lucid within a dream) until harmony, balance, and benevolence become apparent.

> *You will be no good to the evolution of humanity if you are not taking time to find peace...connection within yourself.* —The Z's

Likewise, if we feel personally unbalanced, we can zoom *in* until harmony, balance, and benevolence become apparent. What will it be?

Choosing our "ate"

When someone pushes our buttons, our response is often some type of "ate." If we're not feeling very confident, perhaps we try to negoti*ate* or plac*ate*. If we're feeling confident, we may choose to deb*ate*, retali*ate*, implic*ate*, invalid*ate*, mand*ate*, manipul*ate*, intimid*ate*, etc. What impact will this approach likely have on our relationships? Deterior<u>ate</u>. What if we were to catch ourselves before our ego commits us to a low-vibration slippery slope and instead try to rel<u>ate</u>, appreci<u>ate</u>, accommod<u>ate,</u> or collabor<u>ate</u>, bringing a raised level of vibration, compassion, and divine light?

What impact is <u>this</u> approach likely to have on our relationships? Elev<u>ate</u> and illumin<u>ate</u>. When we learn to go beyond choosing between plac<u>ate</u> or escal<u>ate,</u> we can navig<u>ate</u> toward the path to mastery! What will it be?

Empathy or compassion?

We often use the words "compassion" and "empathy" interchangeably. Are they really interchangeable? The difference may be noticed when observing someone who has a choice to be *bitter* or *better*. If you have *empathy* for them when they choose to be *bitter*, you may feel their heavy, low-vibration grievance energy as if it were your own. If you feel *compassion* for the person making the same choice, it may be from a more loving, impartial-observer perspective. In this case, empathy and compassion are massively different.

On the other hand, if the person chooses to feel *better* by way of forgiveness and release (via compassion for self and others), it may feel very much the same, whether having empathy for their compassion or compassion for their compassion. Hence, the other person, rather than us, may be in control as to whether our seemingly arbitrary choice to look with empathy or compassion has similar or very different results. Since a self-sovereign would not forfeit that decision to someone else, those on the road to mastery (as we enter the age of compassion) may want to embrace the difference between empathy and compassion and choose *compassion*. What will it be?

Stages of spiritual awakening

Sometimes, the best response to a question is to replace it with a better question. Spiritual awakening often begins when something shakes us from our unconscious sleep-walking routine so that we begin to ask bigger and better cosmic and spiritual questions. The bigger our questions, the bigger our growth.

> *You are not waking up your minds; you are*
> *waking up your heart and soul.* —The Z's

In response to our implicit permission to know, our unseen guides lead us to pertinent teaching materials and people. This may lead to an awareness that much of our childhood conditioning and controlled narrative programming no longer serve us. This often leads to reevaluation and reflection and the devaluation of toxic or draining people, information, and situations. As the *chains* of false narratives are cleared away, our true (holy) selves begin to emerge.

Want to become more holy yourself? Become more wholly yourself.

The emergence of our true, holy selves often involves an inclination to help others. This often involves sharing what we've learned. This is the upward spiral of ascension.

> *One day… everything feels right. Your heart is calm. Your*
> *soul is lit. Your thoughts are positive. Your vision is clear.*
> *You're at peace…with where you've been…what you've been*
> *through and…where you're headed.* —TheMindJournal

Caring may take the form of compassion, laughter, *joy,* or the sending of positive energy. Esoteric sources have long claimed, and science is now confirming, that our thoughts possess energy and have interdimensional reach. Because all points in space and time are connected, our thoughts and intent can change things, not just at the 4D level but also at the quantum and hyper-D levels.

Our thoughts can also select between the *great, so-so,* and *not-so-great* futures that are constantly offered to us, like a mind-reading car radio jumping from station to station in fast-scan mode. Like with a radio station, the future we receive is that which is closest to the vibration level of the thoughts we're currently having. In short, our thoughts are constantly altering our future by selecting from a buffet of what might happen next. When in doubt, choose helpfulness and joy.

> *Joy chases away darkness. If you concentrate on the joyful, the lights will never go out, even when you sleep, [This is] the answer to finding God.* —Kryon

Scientific studies[121] with only a *mental intention to help* have been documented to lower others' pain levels, alter the output of random-number generators (that rely on quantum effects), improve the outcome of experiments, and alter the pH and atomic hydrogen-oxygen bonds of water. Those same studies noted that hyper-D non-physical beings, especially when requested, may show up to assist in carrying out those helpful intentions.

To appreciate this, and that the placebo effect demonstrates the power of belief, is to appreciate our magnificence, which is the trailhead toward mastery. Full disclosure: the intent to send loving, helpful energy may result in side effects. According to esoteric sources, our double-helix DNA contains an antenna or tuning fork of sorts that only vibrates when we are both receiving and transmitting the frequency of divine Love, as when sending loving, helpful energy. The resonant vibration of our DNA in that way can reportedly trigger a biological cascade, resulting in a personal side effect of improved health and longevity.

How might we put this information to use? What does that negative news item need most? Yet another disturbed onlooker, or a transmitter of hyper-D compassion, cooperativeness, peace, and balance? What will it be?

Ch. 11: Leaning toward mastery 104

Our boundaries... a shield and a cage

The more we train the world around us about the edges of our personal boundaries, the less action the shield part of our boundaries tends to see. At some point, we may not even be able to recall the last time the shield (the *up side* of our boundaries) became necessary while the cage (the *down side* of those same boundaries) continues to see lots of action.

The cage side of our boundaries likely causes valid opportunities, energies, concepts, and ideas, requiring an open mind, to bounce right off. If you've ever wondered why healing energy sometimes seems as if it's bounced off, this is one way it can happen. What if we checked our boundaries for necessary updates as often as our phones and computers?

> *Those who do not move do not notice their chains.* —Rosa Luxemborg

When a judge says, "I disallow that," it says nothing about whether it's true. How the universe honors our free will is similar. When it comes to the spiritual, subtle, or unseen, we might not realize that "I don't believe that" is heard by the universe as "Whether true or not, I disallow it." To honor our free will, the universe may not seek to overpower our disbelief with evidence but to ensure that no one will. That's how powerful our thoughts and intent are, and how easily we can build our own ever-shrinking cage out of rigid, petrified thoughts.

> *I started to be free when I discovered that the cage was made of thoughts.* —Unknown

"I don't believe that [fill in the blank] could help me heal," may be heard as "I disallow [fill in the blank] from helping me heal." Likewise, "I don't believe a medium could gather accurate information from my deceased loved one" may be heard by that loved one as "I disallow a medium from gathering accurate information from my deceased loved one."

Imagine how many possibilities we have allowed our fear-constructed cage to disallow. Yes, our free will and intent are really *that* potent and honored by the universe. Our world can get so much larger and more magical when we periodically examine our boundaries. For instance, we could change our "I don't believe or allow it" cage to "I'm unconvinced but open to new evidence," or we could start and end each day with, "Spirit, show me what I need to know." What will it be?

To heal others, heal yourself

Is it selfish to heal oneself before sending healing energy to another?

Selfishness is like a stick with two ends. In the *old* energy, selfish may mean nurturing oneself in a way that's often a disservice to others. In the *new* energy, selfishness, like woodworkers "selfishly" taking the time to sharpen their tools, may translate to nurturing oneself in a way that better allows one to be of service.

So, is self-love selfish? Besides the fact that one can't pour out love to others from an empty cup, love isn't a finite resource, so taking some for ourselves doesn't mean less for others. Actually, it's just the opposite. Focusing on self-love doesn't just fill up our own cup; it sets our mental tuner to a frequency that can unlock a larger supply than we could possibly give away. Yes, before sending healing energy to others, we should fill our own cup.

That said, what if sending healing energy to our inside world could lessen the amount of healing needed in our outside world? As the saying goes, "If you spot it, you've got it!" meaning that the only reason we've noticed someone in need of healing is that their issue may resonate with something needing healing within us.

...who looks inside, awakes. —Carl Jung

If so, prior to sending energy to that *other* person, what if we first applied Hawaiian ho'oponopono to our corresponding wounded part, as in "I'm sorry, please forgive me, thank you, I love you?"

To the extent that we project our reality, what if healing our own internal malady lessened or even erased the other person's malady? If the other person's malady was even partially for the purpose of triggering our introspection and healing, it may have fulfilled its purpose. If so, a universe that seeks to conserve energy may have no more need for the other person's malady. Projecting to a global stage, which global maladies, viewable on the outside, may at least in part be ours to heal on the inside? ...the ones we've noticed.

Quantum science may provide a theoretical basis for how nothing more than mental intent could improve a body issue. The wave-particle duality suggests that a sore toe is, at the same time, a group of quantum particles and a group of energy waves. Hence, sufficiently tuned, directed, and powerful thought-intent energy waves may alter the energy waves in a sore toe, resulting in the toe having altered particles, leading to improvement. That said, the energy of the sender can, and often is, blocked by conscious or subconscious mental waves coming from the receiver. These waves may translate to "I don't trust or deserve the sender's energy, or I'm getting too much of a payoff from this malady." Yes, both the sender and receiver (whether oneself or another) may really be that capable.

Ideas in the field

Although we may think of our ideas as original, unfettered, and without limits, our mind is inextricably and holographically intertwined with both the Earth's collective quantum *field* and the one infinite mind. As such, our "it just came to me" ideas, rather than arising independently from our gray matter, may be metered out to us from the conscious *field* according to what we're likely to do with them.

The synergistic impact of trillions of human-cell energy fields likely creates our personal toroidal biofield, capable of holding a tremendous amount of information. We call those who read and interpret this information "psychic readers," etc. For those who want to read and interpret their own information field, we call these people meditators, dowsers, or practitioners of kinesiology. For those interested in reading and interpreting Earth's collective field, we call these people dowsers, remote viewers, prophets, futurists, and innovators.

All these labels represent people who cultivate and utilize intuition and the *clair* (clear) subtle senses in order to notice and interpret the symbolic or metaphorical subtle energy and information available in the quantum field. Far from "woo-woo," these are birthright skills, available to all but only utilized by some.

Part of this skill can allow some to perceive *nonlinear* information in the field. A matching skill may allow some to interpret nonlinear information so that it's useful in a linear, 4D world. This is an example of metaphysics representing future physics, decades before someone is granted scientific recognition for describing the same concept with fancier words.

> We see science climbing the proverbial
> mountain of knowledge, only to find Buddha
> sitting on top. —Dr. Bruce Lipton

Some people believe that the best new ideas are metered out by the quantum field. As a creative associated with many computer technology patents, I have long felt that ideas float within the field like sentient beings in search of the right recipient. The ideal person would be someone willing to birth an idea into reality without weaponizing it.

Talent hits a target no one else can hit;
genius hits a target no one else can see.
—Arthur Schopenhauer

As a futurist, I agree with esoteric sources that foresee "energy generation at the point of consumption" coming to the aid of an aging power grid. In the same way that consumables (e.g., coal) are now being disrupted by renewables (e.g., solar, wind, etc.), renewables may one day be impacted by "perpetuals" (e.g., generators making use of the perpetual force of permanent magnets). This could take the form of a generator per building. If perpetual-force engines/generators become real, their miniaturization could also disrupt the battery industry.

Even a futuristic perpetuals[122] industry may eventually be impacted, if not disrupted, by "inexhaustibles," as we discover how to draw unlimited zero-point energy from the quantum foam. Reportedly, ideas for inexhaustible energy will be held out of reach until those who would weaponize them are no longer a factor. The *right* recipients are known to the universe by the frequency of their thoughts, intent, and integrity.

Once the time is deemed right, game-changing ideas have been known to shift from being *embargoed within the field* to being ubiquitous and obvious almost overnight. As an example, although we've seen birds demonstrate flight and string instruments demonstrate vibrational sympathetic resonance for thousands of years, the game-changing ideas for powered flight and radio suddenly *came* to innovators on both sides of the Atlantic at virtually the same time. Rather than being an accident or coincidence, the availability of these key ideas was reportedly in response to the vibration level (thoughts, intent, and integrity) of general human consciousness, demonstrating that we were ready for it.

Do you want to be the recipient of the next great creative idea? Clean up your thoughts, intent, integrity, and vibration level as if they're being monitored (because they are) and, if you're fortunate enough to be chosen as a recipient, be prepared to follow through.

Thoughts bend the odds

As we get further into the shift, every positive or negative thought goes ahead of us like a ship's bow wave to increasingly bend the physics and odds of chance that shape our personal and collective reality.

> *Why is it worth the trouble to strengthen our light?*
> *The farther our light projects into our future, the*
> *more effectively it can select from future possibilities.*

Besides the time delay between thought and result, it's only the *seemingly* random results of our conflicting, chaotic, runaway thoughts that have thus far kept the general public from noticing the connection. What may hasten that day of noticing are augmented reality glasses that let everyone see the geometric thought *patterns* in our energy field, as some animals, psychics, and infants apparently see today.

> *Your energy field has everything to do*
> *with what you've lived through.* —The Z's

Those glasses may also highlight negative energy litterbugs who practice poor energy hygiene. Not unlike someone leaving a trail of trash as they walk down a city sidewalk, negative thinkers may leave behind steaming piles of negative energy for others to step into. Those who can see or feel energy often notice such "thought forms" in rooms, sidewalks, or public spaces. These negative energy piles may persist until neutralized by intent, such as with smudging, or by chance, such as due to the passing by of an animal or person in their high-vibration "happy place."

With or without special glasses, our level of *thought hygiene,* or sovereignty of mind, may soon become noticed and deemed important by those around us. When that happens, it may take years for the average person to catch up to the skill level that some readily demonstrate today.

Those who see this coming and begin cultivating sovereignty of mind today may be among those most noticed and admired when this inevitably becomes a big deal. What will it be?

Seeking imbalance and balance

A master may seek to have some things very much in balance and some things very much out of balance. The more one realizes the extent to which society encourages the opposite of how a master would do it, the more one suspects it's not by accident.

Different kinds of balance and imbalance can be mileposts for spiritual growth. Is your love for others, or your opinion of others, greater than for yourself? It may need to be brought into balance.

Are you stuck at a point of mediocre, blue-pill balance between fear and peace in the grip of your "programming"? Perhaps, as students of mastery, you should imbalance your current point of balance?

We've likely been subconsciously programmed to believe that the *unknown* equals *danger*. So, instead of becoming increasingly comfortable with the unknown, we often prefer to imbalance a situation in favor of knowing what to expect. Perhaps, as students of mastery, we should bring balance to that imbalance?

Most, including a court of law, are highly imbalanced in favor of *apparent* evidence over intuition regarding what's True. Students of mastery may be imbalanced in the opposite direction, in favor of intuition[123].

When we go into our *closets* and quiet our minds, some think we're imbalanced toward being alone. Instead, those who experience hyper-D connectivity or oneness during these times might say that this is when they're most balanced and *least* alone. What will it be?

Thoughts as currency

At some point in our ascent up the enlightenment staircase, we internalize ("cognize") that the subtle thought energy of our consciousness is readily transacted as interdimensional currency. In other words, as far as the quantum field of potential futures is concerned, *"if you thought it, you bought it."* If you're not sure what your thoughts have placed in your quantum field shopping cart lately, take a look around. The deeper we get into the shift, the more pronounced this cause-and-effect relationship will reportedly become.

To see the quality of one's life is to know the quality of their thoughts.

This ties in with free will. When we've reached high enough on the enlightenment staircase, spiritual logic makes it apparent that either divinely gifted free will is true or divinely imposed judgment and commandments are true. We can't have it both ways. While *lower-*enlightenment stairs fixate on the second, judgmental possibility while ignoring the contradiction with the first, the maturity of *higher-*enlightenment stairs won't allow this. It eventually dawns on us that low-vibration people, groups, and institutions are not necessarily judged *for* their thoughts and choices, but at the level of quantum field potentials, *by* their thoughts and choices.

We live in a world where both metaphorical flowers and weeds exist—where our current and future experiences increasingly depend on where we choose to place our attention. More importantly, having the sovereignty of mind to hold our attention on the *flowers*, versus letting our attention drift into the *weeds*, plants (at a quantum field, potential level) the seeds for more of the same. It's remarkable how few seem to be monitoring and redirecting their thoughts in recognition of this.

> *Your mind is a garden. Your thoughts are the seeds. You can grow flowers or you can grow weeds.* —Clever Classroom

Floating on a turbulent sea of quantum potentials, we can either let the karma of our carelessly thought-planted seeds be the waves that push us around, or we can take ownership of our boat's rudder by way of consciously directed thoughts and focused intent.

If we can think about it (*especially if we can feel and verbalize it in the present tense*), it already exists fully formed in the quantum field of possible futures, and like it or not, good or bad, our consciousness will be its homing beacon until some form of delivery is made. The combination of all these factors is why, ironically, sovereignty of mind, as rare as it seems, is so important. What will it be?

Steps of learning

Just about any institution you can think of (science, medicine, religion, education, etc.) likely started with pure intent but has now, to some extent, been coopted by special interests. This results in *today's version* of most institutions representing some truth and some agenda-serving narrative. As part of the shift, intuitive assistance in sorting Truth from narrative is increasingly at our disposal.

> *All humans are intuitive; some just haven't turned that faculty on.* —The Z's

Realizing this, our self-sovereign ascension process starts with the courage to test and rethink our previously unquestioned learning. This ongoing learning, unlearning, and relearning process can be viewed as a repeating process:

1. I adopt what I or someone else thinks is true and assume I've found Truth.

2. I note that parts of what I "know" don't hold up. I'm confused and conflicted—reluctant to be disloyal to teachers and their teachings. I begin a path of investigation and thinking, updating parts of what I thought I knew with that which more resonates as Truth.

Early in our journey (*the indoctrination and intellectual training wheels phase*), our learning comes mostly from others as we prioritize training over Truth, never making it beyond step one. Step one is home base for some religions. Later in our journey (*the investigation and thinking phase*), lightworkers tend to develop sufficient courage to venture into step-two territory. After that, learning comes less from others and more from our own conclusions, assisted by intuition, critical thinking, and hyper-D inspiration. Step 2 often inspires a "more spiritual than religious" stance.

Eventually, when higher-dimensional inspirations can no longer be verified by lower-dimensional resources, intuition and hyper-D assistance (divine inspiration) account for most new spiritual learning. Ironically, most of the negative judgments about the conclusions arising in step two territory are from those who may have been tempted to go beyond step one but never found the courage.

> *Many [in] the early stages of the awakening process are no longer certain what their…purpose is. What drives the world no longer drives them. Seeing the madness of our civilization so clearly, they… inhabit a no-man's-land between two worlds. They are no longer run by the ego, yet a rising awareness has not yet become fully integrated into their lives.* —Eckhart Tolle

For me, "truth" is something that's held up at the level of step two for quite a while. Prior to that, I treat what I think I know as only my current *working theory*. What will it be?

Which currency warrants investment?

How can we tell what's "red pill" real, versus what's "blue pill" illusion? If it's of a high enough vibration that it can cross the veil between 4D and hyper-D, it's likely real, inexhaustible, and persistent. Hence, positive heart-type energies such as love, compassion, kindness, compassionate laughter, and joy are real. As such, we can source them from across the veil, increase them, and take the results with us when we return home from classroom Earth.

> *Heart energy is the currency of the future. Honor your heart and let in the light as a daily practice. The result will be an extraordinary upshift for you. —The Z's*

What about high-vibration music and singing? Since most of the universe lacks the vibrating air required to support music and singing, music and singing reportedly exist across the veil in the form of vibrating light.

On the other hand, low-vibration fear, drama, anger, and judgment only *seem* real but can't return home across the veil with us and therefore may be more of a time-wasting, yet educational, snare. We know we're collectively snared in a blue-pill illusion when so many are willing to lose all sense of work/life balance in order to increase their (not real) bank account while *not* being willing to suspend their daily video programming to increase their (real) vibratory rate.

Since money can't return home with us beyond the veil and our personal vibratory rate is recognized interdimensionally as real, universal currency, which of these might an un-snared person prioritize?

Nikola Tesla once said, "*...to find the secrets of the universe, think in terms of energy, frequency, and vibration.*" Probably not by coincidence, all three of those are components of consciousness, the fundamental building block of the universe.

When we've raised our consciousness' vibratory rate sufficiently, the energy field around us may be seen as an aura of light. This (real) light vibration is universally recognized both as currency and as a calling card, capable of going before us like a bow wave to prompt beneficial synchronicities while promoting enhanced health and longevity.

> *In the energy world, it's all about authenticity... The energy world sees you for who you genuinely are.* —Abbey Normal

Our light vibration currency is built in, requiring only the courage to protect it, enhance it, and let it out. For new-energy (shift) people, someone showing their divine attributes may be a source of inspiration and illumination. For old-energy people, it may be more of a source of irritation.

How do we know what divine attributes are inexhaustible, like water bubbling up freely from the ground? A good place to look is at whatever dark-minded men have spent millennia trying to neutralize by way of fear, intimidation, and executions, only to see it continually reappear. Soul attributes such as *compassion, love, empathy, joy, intuition, and faith* have persisted against long odds and are still available to us today.

There is little the dark-minded fear more than coming up against those displaying the power of soul attributes. That is, except when several soul-attribute people follow an intuitive, wise, soul-attribute leader. Watch for this, and notice how society becomes better for it.

Ascending dimensions via intent

We too often allow fear to choose "or" when "and" would serve us better.

"Or" often leads to separation, the disintegration of relationships, and lower levels of order. "And" often leads to integration, synergistic coherence, and ascending levels of order.

Or-thinking signals to the universe that we may be stuck at our current level, whereas *and*-thinking may signal that we're ready to reach higher.

Or thinking is why institutions and corporations fail—by refusing to embrace new ideas. *And* thinking is how they integrate new ideas and survive. Hence, evolving people and institutions may want to lean away from the devolving influence of "or" while leaning into the evolving influence of "and."

Many live in their analytical and fearful left brains, believing themselves to be fully enabled, informed, and authentic. Sorry, but to be completely authentic and in integrity is to fully integrate all the dimensions of who we really are, *no matter how magnificent and fear-free*.

Like stairs, we can climb levels of authenticity, integrity, and self-realization by perpetually leaning into "and." Unless, that is, we've become stuck at one of the levels. Like the step of being a *yearling* was never intended to be permanent, it's the same for the step of being a *fear-ling*, where fear pushes us toward the separation of "or." Rather than fear being just one wisdom-building step on the way to a higher perspective, many get stuck as *"fear-lings"* in a state of arrested development.

We could ask, "Should I experience *this* dimension *or* one of the higher dimensions of my true self?" A better question to ask is: how do we reach coherence with, or integrate, this *and* that next dimension? In the same way that free will is honored in higher dimensions, the universe requires our permission to activate a hyper-D assistive hand toward each more perfect version of ourselves. This touches on why we're even here: to see how much self-realization may occur when free will allows us to lean toward the light of expanded dimensions or lean the opposite way toward contraction. As shown in Fig. 11.1, two pyramids joined at the base form an octahedron.

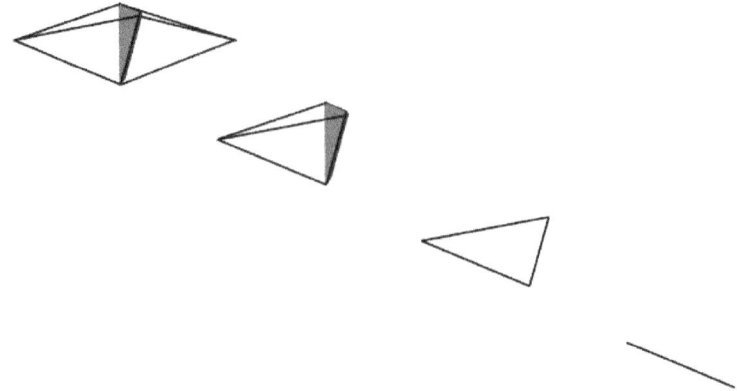

Figure 11.1: A line embracing higher dimensions

Consider an imaginary world in which our most highly realized self was to be a hyper-D octahedron capable of flight. As such, you understand that you could be dismembered into two 3D pyramids capable of only running, and that each of those could be further dismembered into three 2D triangles capable of only walking, and that each triangle could further be dismembered into three 1D lines capable of only crawling.

Now, imagine that, before incarnating into this fictitious world, you agreed to the ultimate test of (seemingly) coming in as a single, crawling line with amnesia about your true dimensional nature. When dark was stronger than light, what historically happened when masters presented themselves as fully assembled octahedrons? Fearful, crawling lines were convinced to support their elimination as evil or dangerous.

This is a metaphor for how we incarnate into Earth with amnesia regarding our amazingness but with the free will to lean toward the expanded dimensions of the light or the contracted dimensions of the dark. Since the shift is increasingly making the light stronger, the risk of choosing light and mastery is now much less. Given that, will we continue to follow fearful narratives, content as crawling lines, or employ courage and free will to reclaim our true selves, dimension by dimension?

What if we did and woke up one morning to realize that we were always unknowingly part of a two-dimensional triangle capable of walking? You would then begin to experience those still in a 1D lower dimension from the perspective of a 2D higher dimension. You'd see things with a new level of context and wisdom that straight-line people would have no way to understand.

Consciousness can vibrationally see downward better than upward, so if you try to explain your new 2D walking triangle perspective to 1D straight-line inch-worm people, they have no frame of reference and may think you odd, in need of help, or someone to be ostracized. Welcome to the courageous path of the hyper-D black sheep.

> *The opposite of courage is not cowardice; it is conformity.*
> *Even a dead fish can go with the flow.* —Jim Hightower

Imagine further using our free will to become even more of who we really are and waking up on a future day to realize that you were always part of a three-dimensional tetrahedron (pyramid) and capable of running. You then see things in a higher-dimensional context that walking triangle people can't understand and straight-line, crawling, inch-worm people may view as certifiable.

Still, you courageously push forward until you wake up, realizing that you were always an octahedron that could fly. And on and on it goes. Since there are likely hundreds of dimensions, our birthright path of self-realization doesn't need to stop there. While straight-line people may see triangle, tetrahedron, and octahedron people as society's problematic oddballs, what they're really seeing is a peek at Earth's ascended future.

The 100th monkey gets all the attention. The 99 did most of the work. The first few were thought to be a bit odd. Those over 100 get the benefits for free, perhaps after making fun of the first 100. As the world slowly enlightens, which monkey do you have the courage to be?

At each stage, it was never about *becoming* something more, so much as removing the veil to realize we were *always* more. This is the path to mastery.

So, what specific steps and assistive hands might be involved in left-brain dominant types growing into birthright higher dimensions? Left-brain people with the courage to lean into their hyper-D selves may find their first assistive hand in the form of their right brain. This represents *you* inviting *yourself* into the higher dimensionality of right-brain, left-brain coherence, and basic intuition.

Those willing to lean into yet higher dimensions of their own authenticity and consciousness expansion may next encounter an outstretched hand from their heart as an invitation to experience the higher dimensionality of *whole-brain + heart coherence*, which comes with expanded intuition. Since the heart may be thought of as our spiritual brain, this is an important step.

Because there will always be differences among us, a free, ascended Earth may never experience hive mind, but what if we strived for hive heart?

> *Your heart has universal intelligence, which is why you've been divorced from it by heart-absent hierarchies that don't want humans to remember their sovereignty and heart power, leading to soul power, leading to Source. An ancient energetic war has been playing out for a long time. You are now in a final battle. Your job is to lay the foundation, usher in, nurture, and support the era of heart consciousness. Heart energy is flooding into the Earth. Experience it rising, in tandem with the exposure of all that lacks it. It will become increasingly difficult for heartless actions to stand unchallenged.* —The Z's

Those willing to lean into yet higher dimensions of authenticity may next encounter the outstretched hand of the brain's "6th chakra, singular eye, window to the soul" or pineal gland (with its piezoelectric rambohedral crystals) as an invitation to integrate hyper-D send/receive visual ability.

If...thine eye be single, thy whole body
shall be full of light. —King James Bible

That is, *brain + heart + pineal coherence,* along with game-changing hyper-D intuition. Interdimensional send/receive ability, plus intent, leads to the outstretched hands of our unseen hyper-D guides as an aspect of our own soul. These (*You-leading-you*) guides may lead us to the outstretched hand of a conscious Gaia with an invitation to restore our birthright Mother Earth connection.

Irony: Nature is conscious, while generally believed to be unconscious, while the masses are unconscious, while generally believed to be conscious.

Our guides may then lead us to the outstretched hand of our innate, or *smart,* body, which may know far more than our brain. It's part of the conscious, coherent, hyper-D field created by the overlapping of the field around trillions of cells. This is but one more example of *You* offering assistance to you. Our guides may then lead us to the outstretched hand of higher-self dimensionality as an aspect of our soul, which can increase and balance the energy and vibration level in our Merkabah biofield and body. This may encourage better health and longevity.

If we were operating from the [higher dimensional] oneness and interconnection of our ascended future, most of what's happening would not be happening. Because consciousness keeps rising, controlling groups must double down, creating tumultuous times. Don't get drawn in. This is the generation where the break occurs. From 2030 on, the baseline for old souls will be a higher dimension, exemplified by living more in synchronicity/flow, thinking about something and seeing a sign, being more creative, and experiencing increased heartfelt oneness. —The Z's

Even after one has reached high levels of individual dimensionality, higher levels are still available by way of forming coherent groups.

On a quantum "all are one" level, this is an even higher expression of *You* assisting you. A critical mass of those who are fully authentic can change our world.

Is there a place where the upward-dimensional or interdimensional path to our authentic selves ends? The path doesn't end until our balanced, peaceful selves have found their way back to divine oneness. Along the way, first seek balanced coherence within and then without via coherent groups. Then seek coherence with *all that is.* Now that you have a roadmap, what will it be?

Faith

Faith comes in both empowering and disempowering varieties. An example of disempowering faith is having unquestioned trust in a committee's written, assembled, edited, and interpreted book full of metaphors and controlled narratives as literal, absolute Truth or as a justification for being unkind.

> *Too often, "faith" translates to "I forfeit my first-hand Truth-seeking power to hand-me-down, agenda-serving narratives." The courageous prioritize first-hand research and experience.*

My writing often concentrates on where science and spirituality describe similar things using different semantics. For those on the science side who think they have little use for the empowering version of the spiritual term *faith,* allow me to translate into science speak:

> *Faith is the ability to exercise sovereignty of mind to observe, as tangible, that which is still one of many potentials in the quantum field until the Observer Effect biases potentials to collapse the wave function into the pre-visualized (or better) reality.*

In short, empowering faith rather than the futile, wishful thinking of the disempowered is an advanced skill for biasing quantum potentials. Hence, regarding faith, one should not confuse "I'm not up to the task" with "I have no use for it." What will it be?

Vibrational neutral buoyancy

Since our rate of vibration impacts how much our thoughts alter the physics and quantum potentials around us, we often make the mistake of focusing only on how to raise our vibration rate rather than on what's holding it down.

Scuba divers understand that *neutral buoyancy* is the point where upward and downward forces cancel. If their weight belt is set for neutral buoyancy at a depth of 50 feet, that's where their descent will stop. At that point, they can apply effort to temporarily go higher, but the moment they relax, they'll settle right back to 50 feet. If they want a higher (with no effort) neutral buoyancy point, one way is to release some ballast weight.

What if the neutral buoyancy point of our vibration rate is similar? What if finding and dropping vibrational ballast weights is as (or more) effective and lasting than efforts to raise our vibration rate? What if we're born with a much higher vibratory rate (conducive to play, joy, laughter, giggling, dancing, and compassion) than we have today? What if our vibratory rate has greatly dropped since childhood due to our figurative vibrational weight belt being systematically covered in weights? Weights the well-intended have helped us attach since childhood?

If so, the wise may give priority to recovering our inner child and identifying and dropping as many vibrational ballast weights as possible. Weights holding us down come in many forms. For starters, any grievance (since birth) has attached a weight and lowered our vibrational neutral buoyancy point. The rope that holds each grievance weight in place is a judgment. A thousand years from now, when Earth is more ascended and at peace, it will be because we've figured out that discernment is a skill while judgment is more of a toxic habit.

> *When we stop analyzing, judgment ceases...we become observers...the state of our soul.* —Rev. Lee Wolak

What's the knot that holds each rope in place? It's the assumption that the universe made a mistake in letting whatever you judged occur. This gives us two ways to release each grievance weight: untie the knot by trusting the universe, cut the rope by way of forgiveness, or both. Does this include that kid on the playground decades ago? Yes, it does. Does it include that long-forgotten person who cut me off in traffic years ago? Yes, it does. Since weights don't have an expiration date, we likely have hundreds holding our vibrational neutral buoyancy point down.

> *If you want to fly, give up everything that weighs you down.* —Buddha

Once, during a silent meditation retreat, I was tasked with forgiving *everyone and everything* since it's reportedly the key to the lock between the 3rd and 4th chakras, which keeps our hearts from fully opening. I forgave for two days straight before I felt the physical sensation of my heart opening. The first day concentrated on the role of others (insufficient by itself), and the second day concentrated on my part in each situation.

Since long-forgotten grievances are hard to recall in order to be released, I recommend releasing grievances as you go, boosted by an occasional affirmation of "I forgive everyone everything... and I trust that the universe knows what it's doing."

Besides grievances, there are other ways to add vibrational ballast weights, such as internalizing, as Truth, lower-vibration narratives or beliefs (petrified narratives).

As mentioned in my first book, most of us base our conclusions and actions on a foundation stack of underlying premises, perhaps 16 layers deep, with each (upon deeper examination) turning out to be somewhere between flawed and completely fictitious. Since each premise holds up all the premises, conclusions, and actions above it, only one needs to be flawed before most everything we think and do looks misguided to those in our future. Unless, that is, we end each current statement of "certainty" with "Or so it might currently seem."

> *You are not responsible for the programming you picked up in childhood. However, as an adult, you are 100% responsible for fixing it.* —Rev. Jamie Sanders

Once you start looking for ballast weights, you'll likely find a vast supply. Dropping ballast weights is worth the effort because each one we locate and drop may allow us to reap the rewards of an effortlessly higher level of vibrational neutral buoyancy. What will it be?

Soul reintegration

What's the purpose of our countless Earth incarnations if not to make progress on the path toward reintegrating with our soul? To explore reintegrating with our soul is to eventually stumble upon the hyperdimensional. To explore the hyperdimensional is to eventually stumble upon our innate (smart) body, guides, and angels as aspects of our higher self, or soul.

> *Each and every soul will become consciously aware of the ability to communicate with the divine.* —Edgar Cayce

Whispers from this higher-self *group* (*higher self*, for brevity) may account for much of our intuition. Other potential members of that group may be former and future versions of ourselves. If the *veil* is a barrier between us and the hyper-D, our higher self may represent multiple points of access through that veil.

How our higher self cooperates with the higher self of others likely accounts for many of life's synchronicities. To fear or deny either our higher self or the synchronicities it generates is to fear or deny aspects of ourselves, slowing the integration process with our soul.

Our free will keeps our higher self from forcefully educating us about the advantages and gifts it has to offer. Indeed, our higher self will wait as long as necessary for us to willingly pursue our sacredness. When this finally occurs, it's often in stages.

> *Everyone is gifted. Not everyone has*
> *opened their package.* —Myrian Galler

It often begins with "Soul, how do I know you're there?" which gives permission for our soul to lead us to the "If you're there, prove it" stage. The next stage is likely "OK, soul, you exist, so what's next?" which gives permission for us to notice how our soul may inform and steer us through synchronicities. The next (leaning toward mastery) stage may sound like, "My thoughts, expectations, and intent work with my higher self to bias reality for the highest good."

Have you ever felt a loved one's presence more strongly *after* they've passed? That's called "soul splitting," where some of their soul (for the duration of your life) may join your higher self group for the purpose of healing, unification, education, and empowerment.

> *Spirit seeks to unify and heal.* —A Course in Miracles

As we get closer to the path of mastery, we may have one foot in our personality ego and one foot in our higher self. Hence, how we shift our weight between them, from thought to thought, can change both our perceptions and experiences. Shifting our weight toward our higher self causes us to more actively engage the world with the higher vibration, Love-based win-win energies of wisdom and compassion. This results in increased, authentic power as we lean toward higher self-integration and mastery.

On the other hand, shifting our weight toward our ego encourages us to more actively engage the world with the lower-vibration, fear-based win-lose energy of competition and gains at the expense of others. This results in decreased authentic power as we lean away from higher self integration and mastery.

Along the path to integration with our higher self, we stumble upon increased personal sovereignty and power reintegration. The path of personal power recovery may cause us to stumble upon a multi-step path toward a healthier body as we progress from:

(1) It's exclusively the doctor's realm when something hurts, to…
(2) My thoughts impact my body's chemistry. I can research my body's needs with kinesiology, pendulums, etc., to…
(3) My smart body is intimately integrated, communicating and responding to my intent to change its chemistry, etc., improving the quality and quantity of my health.

Past-life persistence

For those who prioritize common sense and the pursuit of Truth over society's narratives, the notion of past lives connects a lot of *dots* while causing many anomalous things to fall into place.

We can only connect the dots if we're willing to collect them. When an occurrence could have been either magical or mundane, automatically dismissing it as mundane rather than staying open to the magical possibility may eliminate a loose end at the expense of losing an important "dot." Breakthroughs occur when a tapestry pattern emerges from loose ends.

There's nothing new about the notion of reincarnation, which has been an intuitive part of belief and thought systems (including Plato's) as far back as we've kept records. For its first ~553 years, the Eastern Orthodox and Catholic churches kept it an open question until the *Second Council of Constantinople*. Even then, the debate was not about whether it was real but whether it (as Truth often does) conflicted with some of the church's narratives.

Assuming we've experienced physicality hundreds of times, a divinely designed system of kind practicality makes sense. Transitioning at the "wind of birth[124]" from an all-knowing hyper-D consciousness to a 4D baby with amnesia isn't easy. Thus, a kind universe would provide a system of support for that traumatic transition. Enter *the persistence of inter-life knowledge, skills, and preferences*.

The easiest possible transition would involve being born into the same region, culture, language, gender, and even blood line as before. That is, plan for a life that includes mastering the same knowledge and skills that you've mastered many times before. We call these people fast learners, naturals, or prodigies. Are these people more intelligent or just better at drawing from *multi-life skill persistence*? At the other extreme, is that one student really slow, or are they just the only one in the class truly encountering the material for the first time?

For instance, you may choose to be a guy with a talent for woodworking for 15 lifetimes in a row. While making use of persistent knowledge from past lives allows for the easiest path, it doesn't promote a lifetime with the most growth. As stated in my first book, we can intellectually know the game of tennis inside and out before we're born, but we don't *really* know the game until we've moved beyond being a tennis player to the more challenging lifetimes of being the metaphorical ball, the racket, the net, the court, and the wind. Only then will we truly, viscerally, and experientially understand tennis.

Learning sometimes requires us to play the part of the figurative *windshield*, while other times we play the part of the *bug*. That is, sometimes the *predator* and sometimes the *victim*—sometimes as the husband who dies in battle and sometimes as the pregnant wife who is left behind. Learning sometimes requires us to be the one who departs too soon, or perhaps the one left to pick up the pieces.

Thus, as easy as it is to be a guy who likes girls and dogs for 15 lifetimes in a row, spiritual growth will eventually require a significant change of perspective. Since inter-lifetime preference persistence can be strong, don't be surprised if the next life is as a person with girl plumbing and guy mannerisms who likes girls and dogs. This represents a soul undergoing a natural transition that reportedly takes around two lifetimes to complete.

The next lifetime may be as a person with girl plumbing and girl mannerisms who likes girls and dogs.

With the transition nearly complete, the following dozen or so lifetimes may be as a person with girl plumbing and girl mannerisms who likes guys and dogs.

That is, until it's time to change plumbing again, when the next life may be as a person with guy plumbing and some girl mannerisms who likes guys and dogs.

Next, they may be a person with guy plumbing and guy mannerisms who likes guys and dogs.

Next, they may be a person with guy plumbing and guy mannerisms who likes girls and dogs. Thus, the cycle of ~30+ lives repeats.

Hence, the wise are accepting of the percentage that will always be undergoing *multi-life gender transition with preference persistence* because they realize that anyone who's had hundreds of lifetimes has themselves been in that position many times before and that (fear-based narratives aside), it's a natural and normal part of the divine ascension plan. However, if someone doesn't like dogs, that's different!

Compassion soup

Like aircraft carriers, civilizations turn slowly when something new influences the rudder. That said, what influence might be capable of moving the rudder of our civilization in a positive way? In the movie "My Big Fat Greek Wedding," the quirky father believed that a spray bottle of blue window cleaner could improve just about anything. If there was a real-life (make everything better) equivalent of that blue window spray, so capable and versatile that it could heal memories, relationships, and even civilizations, what might it be? Perhaps the most amazing, underrated, hidden in plain sight, and multidimensional tool at our disposal is *compassion*.

> *Compassion, as a living energy and consciousness, provides the healing balm to the wounds of humanity.* —Sirian Blue White Collective

It's said that compassion, sometimes associated with vagus nerve activation[125], represents a heart-opening connection to the creative Source that can be applied in remarkable ways. How many other things can you name that, like the blue liquid in that movie, are magical enough to be at the same time a *balancing agent*, a *bonding agent*, a *solvent*, and a *catalyst*?

Compassion, as an aspect of feminine energy, is capable of bringing male-energy-heavy situations back into proper balance. Thus, it's a *balancing* agent. Balance tends to be greatly undervalued in that most, if not all, destructive things occur from a place of emotional imbalance. On the other hand, many, if not most, healing and constructive things occur from a place of emotional balance. Balance is fundamental as a launching pad toward good things such as intuition and the type of inner and outer peace that can quiet fear and promote healing.

Balance can also be a launching pad for the courage to reach higher. Balance is so important that it should be prioritized within our daily routine, well above staying entertained and informed. Even when information and entertainment *seem* free, they come at far too high a price if they take us out of balance.

If you take care of your inner world as much as your outer world, you will become quite strong, robust, and balanced. —The Z's

Compassion is also a *bonding* agent in that we tend to become more trusting of and loyally bonded to those who treat us with compassion. It's no secret that compassion-based solutions are the ones most likely to *stick* while creating a minimum of new problems, such as grievances or a desire for retribution.

Compassion is also a *solvent* in that it can soften our hardened, well-entrenched positions to the point that we can once again hear each other. It's capable of dissolving grievances that would anchor us to the past and limit the possibilities for our future.

Compassion is a *catalyst* in that it can transform and elevate whatever it touches without itself being altered. For instance, if compassion elevates our conversation from confrontational to cooperative, we are changed, as compassion remains unchanged. In short, compassion, applied from a place of emotional balance, is such an amazing tool that failing to employ it in many (if not most) situations leaves perhaps our most capable tool unused. Compassion is literally capable of making the difference between us destroying ourselves and ascending as a peaceful planet.

It's been said that we won't even be at the starting line toward where we want to ascend as a civilization until we've *shifted* away from fear and, via compassion, left behind war as an option. If that's true, how do we get from here to there? Apparently, we will be assisted by Earth itself.

The more you experience elevated, compassionate consciousness, the more you notice its absence, such as with those still supporting ancient separation, manipulation, control, and war energies. Non-heart, invasive energies, long ago injected into humanity for disempowerment

and containment. Earth will increasingly bathe you in crystalline energy until you shed those [invasive] energies. Within 2-3 decades, the masses will begin to see through not only those invasive energies, but those who promote them. –The Z's

Although compassion has many uses, we tend to think of it as one thing. Actually, it's a soup made of several ingredients. The fact that compassion's ingredients are similar to what compassion inspires attests to its multi-D nature. In fact, many of the ingredients making up compassion soup (perhaps not by accident) exactly match the steps that can help us climb toward a safer planet.

It's unlikely that we could get all the way to civilization-saving global cooperation in a single jump. Instead, we can climb the steps toward global cooperation by repeatedly applying compassion as a catalyst. But how?

Balance is one ingredient of the compassion soup that can propel us from emotional *imbalance* to the launching pad of emotional *balance*. Whether healing, growth, or just staying calm in turbulent times, it all starts with emotional balance. A critical mass of individuals finding and staying in emotional balance can change the collective.

> *When a complex system is far from equilibrium, small islands of coherence in a sea of chaos have the capacity to shift the entire system to a higher level of order. –Llia Prigogine, Nobel Laureate*

From a place of emotional balance, we can further apply the compassion catalyst (which has *tolerance and empathy* as ingredients) to propel us to a place where tolerance and empathy are our home base. As a critical mass of us make the jump from emotional balance to tolerance and empathy, so goes the world.

> *Our soul is said to be the multi-D 2/3 of us that stays beyond the veil, so our bodies don't vaporize. For every "not nice" 1/3*

of a person you encounter, their unseen 2/3 asks your unseen
2/3 for tolerance, empathy, and compassion.

From a place of tolerance and empathy, we can apply the compassion catalyst again (which has *forgiveness* as an ingredient), allowing us to soften toward forgiveness for others and ourselves. This can break the endless "eye for an eye" cycle of suffering until *forgiveness* becomes our home base. As a critical mass of us moves from tolerance and empathy to forgiveness, so will the global collective.

Compassionate forgiveness sorts us into two groups: those who need a reminder from the universe that they also screw up, and those who don't.

From a place of forgiveness, applying the compassion catalyst again (which has *cooperation* as an ingredient) allows us to soften toward cooperation, until cooperation becomes our home base. As a critical mass of individuals moves from a home base of forgiveness to cooperation, so will the world.

Once we get to a place of global cooperation, compassionate action can keep us there. As a critical mass expresses consistent compassionate action from a home base of cooperation, so will the world.

So, if we had no ideas about how to get from *here to there*, now we have a potential roadmap. Whether it's this roadmap or some other, each of us needs to get moving. In this game called *Classroom Earth*, where the fate of our civilization is at stake, there are no spectators. The future will see each of us as either part of the problem or part of the solution. What will it be?

Why compassion promotes evolvement

If compassion, benevolence, and Love represent *streams* of positive, constructive energy, the headwaters for those streams would be divine Source. Hence, those attributes, especially when found in combination, can provide us with a directional beacon.

As individuals and as a society, we have the option to continually course correct in the direction of those traits until we reach *home* as an enlightened ascended society. Along the way, we can track our real-time progress, either closer to or farther from *home*, as thought-by-thought (Fig. 11.2), we either move up the spiral toward "evolved" or down the spiral toward "devolved."

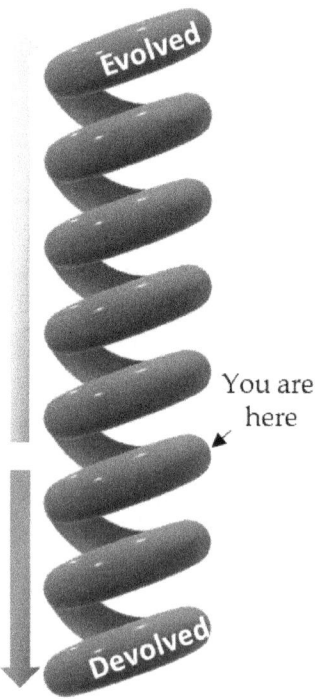

Figure 11.2: Evolving or devolving spiral.

Above our current point on the spiral, wherever that happens to be, is the ascending harmony/thriving spiral toward our divine Source home. Symptoms of movement in the *ascending* direction may include increased peace, balance, perspective, altruism, and positive synchronicities conducive to happy outcomes.

Below our current point on the spiral is the descending, *competing, and surviving* spiral away from our divine Source home. Symptoms of movement in the *descending* direction may include decreased peace, decreased balance, decreased perspective, decreased altruism, and decreased positive synchronicities conducive to happy outcomes.

Yes, the power of our thoughts and free will, whether intended or not, is really that impactful. Moment by moment, our random thoughts and emotions move us up or down relative to our prior point. Unless, that is, we actively intervene by way of sovereignty of mind. Otherwise, by default, constant societal fear and outrage triggers encourage movement down the spiral.

> *Whether your mental tuner is set to view the world as fear and division or as love and unity, watch your experience increasingly reflect it. Since someone's going to control your tuner, why not you?*

An ascending alternative is to emphasize compassion, gratitude, and joy, such as with an upwardly buoyant mantra like "Thank you, God!" consistently placed in the gap between our thoughts. Such a constructive use of our sovereignty of mind can not only counteract downward influences but also propel us upward toward evolvement and joy.

> *How to be joyful... turn to the infinite One and, instant by instant, ... in all things giving thanks; in all conditions rejoicing...rest in the peace which the world does not know. Joy is a living energy as powerful and effective a teacher as sorrow. However, it demands of the seeker a self-imposed discipline....* —Q'uo

Compassion increases gamma brain wave activity in our problem-*solving* left prefrontal cortex while decreasing activity in the "fight or flight" and "we're all separate...as long as I get mine"—problem *creating and perpetuating* amygdala brains. Compassion-promoted gamma waves may be associated with "in the moment/zone/flow" peak performance, collaboration, and heightened sensory and extra-sensory intuitive awareness. Hence, compassion and gratitude promote positive outcomes: happiness, balance, lower stress, better health, and a longer life.

> *If you feel you don't fit in with this world, you may be here to help birth a new one.* —Unknown

Or, we can allow the media to constantly trigger our amygdala, turning down our higher brain function and making us less intelligent and more combative—becoming more *infirmed*[126] by the media under the guise of becoming informed. Besides the devolved personal and collective world this encourages, it promotes stress, unhappiness, imbalance, poorer health, and a shorter life. Every thought and interaction provides a decision point at which we can either consciously or unconsciously change our distance (up or down the spiral) relative to *home*.

> *Whether focusing on love or fear, whatever we concentrate on, we may concentrate within.*

This is accomplished by responding in either an up-spiral or down-spiral way—either toward compassion, altruism, benevolence, and Love, or away from them.

Now that we have a way to navigate directly to the benefits of an ascended individual and society, we're out of excuses. Free will allows us to collectively navigate there within generations or stretch out our collective suffering for eons. What will it be?

> *Suffering is necessary until you realize it is unnecessary.* —Eckhart Tolle

Ch. 12: Leaning toward mastery 105

Markers along the path to mastery

When our mind fully integrates and aligns with our soul, we've attained spiritual mastery—perhaps the end goal for classroom Earth.

> *The path to mastery: stillness amidst chaos, silence amidst roar, balance amidst imbalance, a lighthouse on the shore.*

When a person who has attained spiritual mastery takes their last breath, how do you suppose they respond to meeting the spiritual masters they aspired to emulate? Would they prostrate themselves or just rejoin their peer group?

The point is that at some point on the path to mastery, our relationship to the spiritual masters who've gone before us must inevitably progress, from idol to role model to peer group. These shifts in perspective may serve as mile markers along our path[127] to mastery.

Do not give your power away to Spirit. Cocreate with Spirit. —The Z's

Those markers may allow us to evaluate not only where we currently are on our path but also whether each narrative, religion, or "truth" we encounter on a given day is doing us any favors. Did our encounter with it progress us on our path toward mastery, regress us, or temporarily derail us from the path? Since most of the information and media we encounter in a given day appear engineered to either regress or derail us, masters in training may want to be vigilantly protective of their balance and head space. What will it be?

Sovereignty of mind—it's a thing!

A wise employer values positive thinking over skills. Skills can be taught. A positive attitude, which has even greater value, is more difficult to teach. Let's try a thought experiment for the purpose of making a point.

TV commercials represent a significant investment in capturing and holding our "thought seconds." What if a teaching and rewarding tool was available such that our employment compensated us not by the hour but by the *thought second*? Specifically, according to the *quality* of our thoughts in each second?

Imagine a not-too-distant employment future where, while *on the clock*, we wear augmented reality (AR) glasses with built-in brain sensors capable of monitoring the *quality* of every thought. That is, showing us moment to moment in our field of view how our thoughts are moving us up and down a sliding scale among a wide range of *compensation-per-second* rates?

The heads-up display in our AR glasses allows us to monitor in real-time how our "This could work!" thoughts momentarily place us on a pay scale on track for a new car by the end of the year. A moment later, when we are randomly thinking, "This could *never* work!" we see we've instantaneously changed to a pay scale on track for living IN a car by the end of the year. Suddenly, our sovereignty of mind becomes a priority.

> *We are increasingly experiencing both a shift and a split. As part of the <u>shift</u>, our thoughts are becoming increasingly powerful, capable of either degrading or upgrading not just our perception of a situation but the situation itself. The <u>split</u> separates those who, understanding this, choose to think more responsibly.*

For those who want the benefit of extended *thought-quality* feedback, the glasses could stay on all day. If so, when someone suggests watching a scary movie and then *talking trash* about others, the shifting pay scales in front of our eyes could indicate how costly that habit would be when our thoughts are being monitored. This would be important information in that there is no time in which the universe is not monitoring our thoughts.

Imagine flipping a switch on those AR glasses to also display quantum field potentials. Suddenly, you can see a hundred different levels of the universe's potential willingness to cooperate and collaborate with you based on the momentary vibration level of your thoughts.

At one extreme, when thinking positive, compassionate, loving thoughts, your glasses indicate the universe is tripping over itself to deliver beneficial synchronicities and outcomes. At the other extreme, low-vibration thoughts result in the glasses showing that "If it weren't for bad luck, you'd have no luck at all." It quickly becomes apparent that, whether on the clock or not, how your day goes is much more in your control than you once thought.

My point is that, thought experiment or not, encouraging individual sovereignty of mind can accelerate positive change for a person, but encouraging *collective* sovereignty of mind could accelerate positive change for our planet! What will it be?

Light worker, or shadow worker?

As part of the shift toward a higher vibration of consciousness, what might be increasingly controllable and possible? Reportedly, what's increasingly *controllable* via intent is our biology and longevity. Reportedly, what's increasingly *possible and productive* is reliable, unfleeting intuition that persists longer and is therefore more useful.

At the same time, some places where control used to be productive may now be increasingly unproductive. This may warrant a shift from "Universe, I know what's best, so do it my way" to:

Unseen guides, you see the constantly shifting quantum potentials, so thanks in advance for helping me in whatever way and timing are best. I'll intuitively cooperate with the experiences and connections you arrange for me as you show me what I need to know.

In short, as our consciousness rises into higher *octaves*, light workers will be increasingly comfortable trusting the nonlinear, hyper-D unseen. Hence, some things are increasingly *not* possible in our holographically connected, recorded, and quantumly entangled universe. When all things are one, separation and being alone are *not* possible. False hope is *not* possible because unseen forces are monitoring and standing ready to help. Likewise, a private conversation or act that isn't recorded and universally accessible across time is *not* possible.

Thoughts create while biasing the odds of chance at a quantum level, which is why it's worth the trouble to daily improve the *shadow-to-light* ratio of our thoughts and actions. That ratio, in addition to controlling what new ideas we're ready[128] to receive from the field, determines how much we'll be a *shadow worker* versus a light worker on a given day.

In a world of duality, where there may be multiple shadows for every point of light, it's all too easy to be deceived and ensnared by shadows and unwittingly take on the lower-vibration role of shadow worker. That is, unless we're among the growing minority employing intuition, logic, and courage to begin sorting narrative from Truth. If you're one of those folks, shadows can be used to find the light.

For instance, the "Consciousness soon ends" hijacked message, or *shadow*, can be used to point us to the Truth (light) of "Consciousness never ends." Likewise, the "We're born dirty, so fear God's judgment" hijacked message, or *shadow*, can be used to point us to the light of "We're born magnificent, with constant access to God's nonjudgmental Love." Also, focusing on the "I should take care about how others see me" hijacked message, or shadow, can point us to the light of "I should take care about how I see myself and others." Focusing too much on shadows may devolve us and lead to a certain mindset:

I'm a fearful mammal that must control things to survive and thrive, so I'll prioritize coming out on top over Truth and integrity.

As an alternative, letting the shadow point us to the light may evolve us and lead to a different mindset:

As my birthright, I'm a courageous, empowered soul, following intuition toward benevolent, win-win synchronicities.

Never underestimate the long-term destructive potential of a hijacked Truth when people haven't prioritized intuition enough to notice. Over time, *shadows* resulting from hijacked narratives have wired a tremendous amount of false fear into the human psyche. This has prompted many false premises supporting separation, judgment, and types of warfare that account for much human suffering.

One at a time, tackling symptoms of societal insecurity (bigotry, racism, bullying, inequality, etc.) is the hard way. Instead, let's use intuition and logic to return our false underlying premises to their original Truths, and watch how many societal symptoms of insecurity disappear on their own.

For those inclined to be light workers, few tools may be of higher priority than increasingly accurate, non-fleeting intuition. The more we heed and honor our intuition, the louder, more accurate, and less fleeting it gets. The opposite is also true. There are many perks for those who follow their intuition. Beyond a higher vibratory rate reportedly making it harder for low-vibration disease to reside, it may also improve our longevity in a way that's quite unexpected. Einstein's time dilation equations state that the more our bodies move per second, the more time dilates (stretches) for us. How might this relate to the 80-odd years a body often lasts by default?

Our body is completely encompassed within our biofield *bubble*, known as our aura, or Merkabah. The vibratory rate of our consciousness may impact the vibratory rate (non-traveling <u>movement</u>) of our biofield, which may slow down or speed up the aging time of our fully enclosed body.

If the biofield vibratory rate (non-traveling <u>movement</u>) of our bubble is *average*, the rate of aging time our body experiences would likely be average, taking our body 80 years to age 80 years.

If the vibratory rate of a light worker's energy bubble is *20% higher* than average, it might take 96 actual years for our fully encased body to experience 80 years of aging time.

On the other hand, if one's energy bubble vibratory rate is *20% lower* than average due to choosing fear and judgment in our thoughts, *news*, reading, and entertainment, it might only take 64 years for our fully encased body to experience 80 years of aging time.

While, as part of the shift and time dilation, those who are predominantly light workers might reportedly experience a 10–20% average longevity[129] improvement, esoteric sources project that improvement to reach perhaps[130] 100% within a few generations. For those following Lee Carroll's channelings, Kryon has stated that Lee experiences virtually zero aging while channeling. If the vibratory rate of the merged Kryon consciousness is quite high while channeling, time dilation alone might account for this. What about the rest of us who don't channel Kryon? We also have the ability to merge with a much higher vibration—that of our higher self, or soul.

What might we gain from an increased vibratory rate? Currently, our energy bubble follows our body. As our vibratory rate increases, however, there may come a point where we have the option of moving our body by moving our energy bubble through conscious intent. At that point, the buoyancy of our energy bubble may allow our body to levitate and travel without a craft.

Include the ability to consciously control other 4D aspects such as mass, density, size, speed, and dimensionality, and our Merkabah (Mer = light, Ka = vital force of our spirit, Ba = body, or sometimes loosely translated as "vehicle to ride") may someday transport us as the floating orbs occasionally seen today.

> *To take the form of..."light"...required for orbs...a transmutation of soul energy needs to take place.* —The Z's

Somewhere on that path is a shift from receiving to also giving back. For instance, how many times and in how many ways have we been blessed by being in the presence of a certain group, place, or body of water? At some point, groups, places, and bodies of water will be vibrationally blessed by *our* presence. This is not a new idea in that flowers reportedly grow where some have walked.

> *You cannot help but be of service...by the frequency... you hold. If your heart is open...the planetary heart is that much further open.* —Q'uo

The path to higher vibration rates begins with using intuition, logic, and courage to flip the script from shadow narratives to Truth and compassion. What will it be?

Can groups be hyper-D?

Just as individuals are undergoing a shift from old to new energy, so are groups. While most appreciate the strength of a group, few grasp the differences between growth-*limited*, win-lose groups, with their impact restricted to 4D reality, and growth-*unlimited*, win-win groups, capable of both 4D and hyper-D impact—going beyond additive to exponential.

We've all seen a win-lose company expand until its growth stalls. This occurs when something that resists growth or efficiency grows faster than the company. For a win-*lose* group, that something may include the universe's unseen resistance to a win-lose (force) group succeeding at the expense of others. Though normalized, a group that succeeds at the expense of others may eventually be viewed by our future as representing malevolent, unenlightened pathology. Like organs in a body or wheel spokes attacking each other, it will eventually defy common sense.

On the other hand, a (hyper-D power) win-*win* group that succeeds without being at the expense of others will eventually be viewed by our future as compassionately evolved and enlightened. Rather than the universe offering unseen *resistance*, it may offer unseen *assistance*, allowing the group's size and impact to keep growing.

Magic happens when win-win groups with compassionate intent reach a critical mass of coherence, such as when a meditating group reduces crime or group intent triggers someone's spontaneous remission. If the right kind of group can make a difference in these areas, perhaps this concept can scale to help our planet.

While win-*lose* requires at least two to experience a group effect, masters have demonstrated that a single win-*win* person can reach group-effect strength. This may be accomplished by forming a hyper-D *group* between one's physical self, one's past self, one's *future* self, one's innate self, and one's higher self, and then aligning that coherent group with the divine All. If a single master in training can create their own group effect in this way, imagine the compounded group effect that could be created with a group of such individuals.

> *You're existing in the past, present, and future simultaneously. It's all happening at once. Enjoy the now. Live in a way that lights you up….* —The Z's

This is why win-lose groups will someday be less relevant, if not obsolete. To hasten that day, we can support those who'll measure every thought or action against whether it works *for* or *against* compassionate coherence. That's the key to healing and transformation, not just at a personal level but globally.

This touches upon the very reason that many of us keep returning to classroom Earth: to tip our corner of the galaxy toward compassion by tipping Earth toward compassion, by tipping groups toward compassion, by tipping our self-group toward compassion—by consistently tipping our thoughts toward compassion. Care to join me?

Beam them up!

In "dream school" the other night, I was an astral-realm first responder. If a person or situation could benefit from a boost in vibration rate, I'd focus my heart center on divine Love until an energy bubble formed. I'd expand that energy bubble by picturing a beam of cosmic light entering my heart from the back and thinking, "Divine Love, light, joy, compassion, forgiveness, healing, balance, and peace," as a high-vibration bubble grew to enormous size. By simply thinking "Bless" while holding a target in mind, I'd then direct that enormous bubble of blessing energy to discharge where it was needed, with immediate results. If someone was having a bad day, you might say I *beamed them up* vibrationally, if not also dimensionally.

> *Whether dreaming or awake, when walking into any situation, if I first bless it up, I'm less likely to mess it up!*

Since the shift is supposed to add new ideas and abilities to a light worker's toolbox, I've added this to mine for use while lucid, whether awake or asleep. While the results in this dimension may not seem as instant, obvious, and dramatic as in an astral realm dream, rest assured that the universe not only notes such benevolent efforts but responds in kind with matching energy and benevolent energy blowback.

Besides having the same high-vibration energy returned to us, the increased quantum coherence experienced by both us and our target, per Dr. Kozyrev, slows the rate of (our/their aging) time by inducing localized biofield spinning or torsion. Want a near-constant slowdown in aging? Develop a habit of near-constant *beam-ups*! A coherent group may intensify this effect. The larger the group, the greater the potential benefits.

As the shift progresses, what are potential targets for our increasingly effective beam-ups? Perhaps we could beam up people, groups, situations, corporations, political parties, ideologies, religions, nations, or the entire planet? What will it be?

Choose your "ology"

Since "ology" means "the study of, or subscribing to," I'm coining the term "fieldology" to describe the study of what's possible through coherence between individual bio*fields* and with the quantum *field*.

The practice of *fieldology* is how government-sponsored remote viewers collect accurate information across space and time. It's also how some get their inventions. Nicola Tesla reportedly imaged complete schematic diagrams for inventions that resided in the quantum *field* and then proceeded to build them.

Accessing the quantum field is how my name came to be on patents. It's where futurists, akashic record readers, and medical intuitives get such accurate information. It may also be the source of that "It just came to me" song. In general, it may be where intuition, insights, and synchronicities come from.

> *Out beyond ideas of wrongdoing and rightdoing,*
> *there is a field. I'll meet you there.* —Rumi

Those who practice *fieldology* may also be considered *edgeologists*, in that they're on the cutting edge of our planetary ascension. The quantum field is a shared resource. Hence, practitioners of *field-ology* and *joyology* may, for the sake of themselves and others, seek to keep that shared resource clean and of a high-vibration nature.

Who can't enjoy the benefits of coherence in the field? —those in fear, or practitioners of *fearology*. Let's be honest: most of us are addicted to *In-fear-tainment*, but at what cost? Fear is contagious because it infuses our personal biofield before broadcasting into our jointly shared quantum field. Fear (by dozens of names) shuts down our field receiver but not our field transmitter. Hence, practicing fearology may pollute the quantum field for others while cutting off our access to potentially game-changing or even lifesaving intuition—a lose-lose situation.

Are practitioners of *fearology* easy to find? If you willingly take in fear-biased "news" and then feel uneasy, disturbed, pessimistic, etc. (different words for fear), you may be a practitioner of *fearology*. If you like feeling concerned (another word for fear) when watching that crime show, you may be a practitioner of *fearology*. If you like movies with danger (another word for fear), you may be a practitioner of *fearology*. If you like to get distressed (another word for fear) over the latest fear-wrapped conspiracy theory, you may be a practitioner of *fearology*.

We can infuse our personal and shared quantum field with fear, imbalance, and a tendency for a shortened life, or we can infuse it with joy, balance, and a tendency for a longer, happier life. Our current society will make sure we automatically default to fearology unless, that is, we make a conscious choice to be stewards of a clean field. What will it be?

Default laws

Scientists learn the four laws of physics without realizing they're likely subordinate to the yet unrecognized, higher law of consciousness. Hence, science can only predict or explain (four-law) default outcomes. When a higher law expresses itself to alter the default, science typically dismisses it as anomalous, an error, or a *miracle* rather than properly following it to the point of discovering the law of consciousness.

Why is that? Pursuing the scientific method beyond the existing four laws of physics may endanger one's science funding, science reputation, and science status. Thus, our fear-based science is often anything but scientific.

No-nonsense rancher and dowser Raymon Grace combined the laws of physics and consciousness to create three practical rules that have served him and his clients for decades:

- Everything is energy.
- Energy follows thought/intent.
- Energy leaves an imprint.

If you're not sure about the last one, have you ever received impressions from holding an object (psychometry) or noticed energy in a room where an argument or wedding has recently occurred?

Spirituality embraces the laws of physics and the law of consciousness, utilizing today what science will eventually *discover*. As long as it may take science to eventually notice the law of consciousness (e.g., the power of intent), it will likely take longer for science to recognize that even it may be subordinate to the yet higher laws of divine Love and Oneness. Reportedly, we will eventually realize that nothing in the universe is more powerful than clear, consistent, positive intent aligned with divine Love.

> *Prayer eventually graduates from a message sent to an outer "other" to a positive emotion-charged intent, lighting the path to our inner infinite.*

For those who need a formula, ignoring the constant and transposing the famous equation $E=MC^2$ yields M=E [Matter IS Energy]. Taken a step further, matter is *conscious*[131] energy, or $M=E^{(c)}$.

Quantum biologists believe in and study the hyper-D aspects of human biology. Thus, it's not that big of a stretch to hear from esoteric sources that the double helix of our DNA is a hyper-D antenna that resonates at the frequency of divine consciousness energy.

> *When science gets around to looking into the physics of consciousness, it may discover consciousness in physics.*

As part of our shift toward higher frequencies of consciousness, our hyper-D awareness and abilities may be increasingly upgraded from theoretical to operational.

Each of our double-helix DNA antennas is reportedly tuned to at least two specific frequencies: divine Love and our thoughts. Thus, every thought, whether constructive or destructive, is reportedly received, stored, and acted on by our trillions of DNA strands. The 95% of our DNA with no obvious chemical function reportedly provides layer upon layer of information storage—that emotion you had eight lifetimes ago? It may be stored there.

Our (~33% efficient) DNA is like a hallway with most doors locked. The ones currently open are heredity, the Akashic inheritance of creative passions, fears, phobias, and karma, which pushes us around like a rudderless boat. In the new [shift] energy, we have a rudder, so close the karma door, and steer your own boat. How will you know you've done it? Drama with friends/parents/current-events is over. Closing the karma door opens new doors: The ability to be your own guru and steer your own boat toward self-balance, peace, and heath. At 44% DNA efficiency, the ability to tune into your body as your own medical intuitive, without kinesiology will appear. When you reach 88%, you'll have the ability to match your energy pattern to matter and ask it to change. —Kryon

Because the inexhaustible information and energy of the quantum field are constructed from the universal building block of loving consciousness energy, our personal biofield (constructed of the same) can be used to interface with it. While physics may leave this birthright capability underutilized, metaphysics does not. Tuning our consciousness to the divine Love frequency grants us resonance[132] with and access to that unlimited information and energy. In this way, information of any kind can be tapped for inventions or to access our *extended* history. By way of this same interface to information and energy, matter can theoretically be altered, healed, manifested, etc.

> *At the lowest level, there is only one universal building block. Since each of us is constructed solely from divine Source consciousness, to lean toward or away from Source is to lean toward or away from our authenticity and full potential.*

Our consciousness will be capable of controlling matter when it's capable of interfacing with the consciousness associated with matter. All that keeps us from experiencing this on a regular basis is sufficient sovereignty of mind to hold focused, consistent, clear, and loving intent. Lee Carroll said that the term for this in ancient Lemuria was "shamanic imaging." According to one esoteric source[133], holding that quality of intent for as little as 17 seconds can make a real difference in our physical world, which is why, moving forward, sovereignty of mind should be high on our priority list.

> *By paying attention to the way you feel…choosing thoughts that feel the very best, you are managing your own vibration, which means you are controlling your own point of attraction – which means you are creating your own reality…the less attention you give to everybody else's reality, the purer your vibration is going to be – and the more you are going to be pleased with what comes to you.* —Esther Hicks

How much energy might our clear intent access and control? You may be familiar with the saying that "the faith of a mustard seed can move a mountain." This was not just a metaphor. Einstein's equation tells us that a 0.5-gram (teeny tiny) mustard seed contains the theoretical energy[134] of 3000 WW2 atomic bombs, which could literally move a mountain.

Do we have adequate proof that our thoughts can act like a valve to allow or shut off huge sources of energy? Just look at the infinite quantity of Love and Truth we manage to keep *away* from us with only our fear and disbelief! What will it be?

Living by intent or default

The degree of self-sovereign amazingness we're born with is often the opposite of what we're convinced of by controlled narratives. Therefore, since our birthright tends to be systematically dismembered by training, our enlightenment path tends to be one of remembrance.

> *You've been trained to forget your true power… your hyper-D soul. When you become more awake to your soul power – your unique gifts and ways of seeing the world, you can cocreate with spirit.* —The Z's

For those who prefer sleepwalking, an unspoken assumption may be that if others really had access to higher Truth, they'd find a way to force them to listen. That's a false assumption. As unconscious as a default choice to keep one's self-sovereignty dismembered may be, it's the choice of a sovereign being that's generally honored by the universe. That is, unless a sleepwalker says something like, "Dear Spirit, tell me what I need to know," which gives sovereign permission to learn and grow—to become more lucid while sleepwalking on the way to being truly awake.

Although a sovereign's intent to remain asleep may cause the gap between them and light workers to widen, light workers still have a way of creating an ascending influence for them. When the vibrational tide rises, all boats rise.

> *Become a clear vessel, bringing more of heaven to Earth. The more*
> *you do, the more Earth's systems will transform, for you cannot*
> *change the energy and expect the form to remain the same. That*
> *is what so many of you are doing. More people setting the example*
> *of vibrational difference is how the planet will change.* —The Z's

So, light workers don't have to convince individual sleepwalkers of anything. They only need to constitute a critical mass in order to improve the world by way of the Maharishi Effect. Depending on who you believe, a critical mass may require either one half of 1% of the planet or as little as the square root of 1% of Earth's population. The latter would currently require as few as 9,000 global light workers to raise the vibrational tide for everyone.

> *I'm not into convincing others. I lean into higher and greater*
> *Truths. Those doing the same will likely convince themselves.*

Consciousness has energy that can change not only our present but also our selection of future potentials. Those who realize this may employ birthright self-sovereignty to steer the quantum potentials of their lives with intent. That is, steer those potentials away from the default. Those who don't do this may be agreeing to life's potholes *by default.* When we settle for the default, both in our dreams and in life, we may be *defaulting* on our self-sovereignty birthright.

In other words, should we give active *intention* regarding the challenges and helpful synchronicities of our day and then accept what unfolds as intention-biased? Psychology calls this an "internal locus of control." Or should we just take the intention-free default of whatever shows up and then play victim? Psychology calls this an "external locus of control." On your path toward mastery, would you rather be in (external locus of control) preschool or (internal locus of control) graduate school? One trait of being in spiritual mastery graduate school may be to bless <u>before</u> we assess. When we enter a new situation, whether in a dream or in real life, the first thing we historically do is *assess* the situation. What we then interact with is often less than ideal.

> *The ability to observe without evaluating is the highest form of intelligence.* —Jiddu Krishnamurti

What if, instead of *assessing*, our first instinct upon encountering a situation was to *bless*? I've done this many times in a dream, only to see the situation I <u>then</u> assess as being noticeably upgraded. This can also be used in the waking world. While (*bless before assess*) situation upgrades may be less obvious in real life, rest assured that the possible outcomes for that situation have likely been improved.

If, before you assess, you bless, what you assess will be more blessed!

Welcome to spreading light and blessing wherever you go and the road to mastery!

Hierarchy of spiritual needs

Maslow's "hierarchy of needs" lists what's required to keep our Earth avatar body going, such as oxygen, water, food, and shelter. What about when we're out of the body, such as during a near-death experience or between lives? Is there a different list?

Perhaps not a list of needs, because *need* infers separation and lack when neither are factors while we're in energy body form. How about when our consciousness might be only partially located in our body, such as during a meditation, remote viewing, remote healing, or bilocation session? If all we can take with us after this life is what's real, it may be worth the trouble to identify our out-of-body priority list and gather those transferable, non-expiring, hyper-D treasures now.

> *Store up for yourselves treasures in heaven....* —Matthew 6:19-21

Imagine that you find yourself as only a conscious energy cloud in a place without form or time. What do you wish for, and in what order? For starters, how about *clear, accurate, insightful, and intuitive perception*? If these will be high on our out-of-body wish list and transferable from our current life, why not prioritize them now?

Even while in energy cloud form, you may want to first *bless before you assess*, then *bless as you assess*, and then *assess what you've blessed*. It improves not only the current conditions but also the range of possible outcomes. From there, we can further upgrade our situation by way of sovereignty of mind and the law of consciousness.

In *geek speak*, bless by holding a frequency of Love, meaning a *frequency of syntropic resonance*, in order to promote higher levels of order. In regular speak, "Love makes things better."

If all these are so important and hyperdimensionally transferrable, why not get a head start by prioritizing the accumulation of these non-expiring treasures now? If you do, don't be surprised if it has a positive effect on your current 4D world! What will it be?

The power of clear intent

Imagine wearing augmented reality glasses that display quantum field potentials as you come upon someone who's just received a severe blow to their arm. Your glasses show countless quantum potentials swirling around the arm. That is, until the person says, "Oh, that's leaving a scar!" when you observe multiple quantum potentials around the arm collapse into a single potential—*scar*. Next, the person says, "It's broken!" The glasses allow you to watch all the quantum potentials instantly collapse into a single reality—*broken*.

You've just witnessed the all-too-common malpractice of our underappreciated power of pure intent. If you suspect there's a parallel timeline where the same person was either unconscious or had the sovereignty of mind to say, "I'm grateful for the best possible outcome" and ended up with neither a broken arm nor a scar, you wouldn't be alone. I've heard too many shaman stories[135] where sovereignty of mind steered or even reversed a probable outcome.

Even if the bone was broken, do you think the mending time would be the same regardless of whether we keep saying to all our friends, "I see my bone as healed in record time" versus, "My arm is broken?" In the sense that our thoughts, as conscious energy, can alter reality, probably not.

> *There is no greater power in the universe than*
> *human intent aligned with Love.* —Kryon

Whether it involves health, longevity, or wealth, what qualifies as sufficiently pure, focused intent for a hyper-D person to bias quantum potentials away from the default laws of chance? Pure intent for an outcome is a deep knowing beyond tentative belief. Kryon refers to this as "cognizing."

Pure intent aligns our monkey mind, subconscious mind, superconscious mind, and divine Love, ideally without violating another's free will; that combination reportedly turns the key in the metaphysical lock. To the extent that we muster only partial intent, we tend to receive only partial results, dominated by the strongest intent among all our levels of mind. Our ability to utilize pure intent might begin with flashes of what's possible.

> *The flashing…a state of mind…belief… faith…knowing… If one knows something is true, that person becomes able to demonstrate that truth…the depth of knowing…opens the gateway to intelligent infinity and allows…Christ consciousness energy passage …people will be drawn toward that light….* —Q'uo

When the universe *does* see pure, focused, sustained intent, it reportedly does its best to comply by juggling countless moving parts involving shifting potentials juxtaposed against the free will of others. Manifesting is already a challenging, moving-parts puzzle for the universe to solve, so the wise don't render that puzzle unsolvable by specifying where, when, or how.

> *The space in every atom between the protons and electrons contains intelligent energy…capable of responding to thought.* —Raymon Grace

The bottom line? The universe is listening, and sovereignty of mind with clear, aligned intent can make a difference. What will it be?

Heisenberg…our friend

In Newtonian (4D) science, the *Heisenberg Uncertainty Principle* states that we can either know the exact speed or the exact position of a moving object, but not both at the same time. Speed is calculated by changing locations per unit of time, so knowing something's *exact* speed while it's on the move precludes us from knowing its exact location. Likewise, the only way to know the exact position of a moving object is to freeze its motion, forfeiting our ability to tell its speed, which at that instant could be virtually *any* value. How is this relevant to the spiritual path?

As we increasingly embrace our hyper-D, quantum nature, the same (only one may be fixed) principle may apply to *energy* and *time*. Hence, to fix our consciousness on one point in *time* would theoretically allow for *any* amount of energy at that point. If so, holding our consciousness in "now" time may allow us access to untold energy for altering the laws of physics—not just regular 4D physics but hyper-D physics.

Likewise, fixing our consciousness on the *energy* of a specific location may allow us to access virtually *any* point in time at that location. Welcome to the era of sovereignty of mind, where we increasingly employ consciousness to play with matter and time.

A unified theory of everything

What's more real and lasting, matter or energy? While most think of 4D matter as being the *most* real and lasting, with hyper-D things such as energy and spirit being the *least* real and lasting, it's just the opposite. Unlike matter, which can be destroyed, thermodynamics states that energy can't be destroyed. Everything that *seems* physical is made of atoms that carry virtually all their mass in their nucleus. Perhaps 1% of that mass comes from quarks, with ~99% coming from force fields pretending to be mass.

That is, mass is mostly simulated by force fields in the form of *gluons* randomly popping in and out of existence in the hyper-D quantum vacuum—a vacuum that some view as a virtually infinite sea of zero-point energy. Thus, what materially *appears* to be there and lasting is neither.

> *Matter is energy…there is no matter… Reality is…an illusion… a very persistent one.* —Albert Einstein

It's like the universe has a 3D printer for all matter, where the only raw material going in is energy, with all matter coming out. That said, it quickly degrades back to energy and must be reprinted again[136]. Like pixels on a video screen, as long as matter gets reprinted more often than our eye's *flicker fusion rate*, we don't notice any flickering. The notion that this occurs with sub-second speed is bolstered by cases of multiple personality disorder, where scars have been known to appear and disappear[137] in an instant. If this is the case, it would be quite ironic if those not believing in life or mind[138] without a body are without a material body several times per second!

If one approaches what appears to be a material human body from the physics below it (Fig. 12.1 center), they ultimately reach the conclusion that the body is made from only energy. If one approaches the same body from the spirituality above it, they ultimately reach the conclusion that all is made from only thought *energy*. Notice a similarity? Both can be generalized to "everything is a projection of divine thought energy." Thus, semantics may be all that's keeping us from the illusive *unified theory of everything*[139].

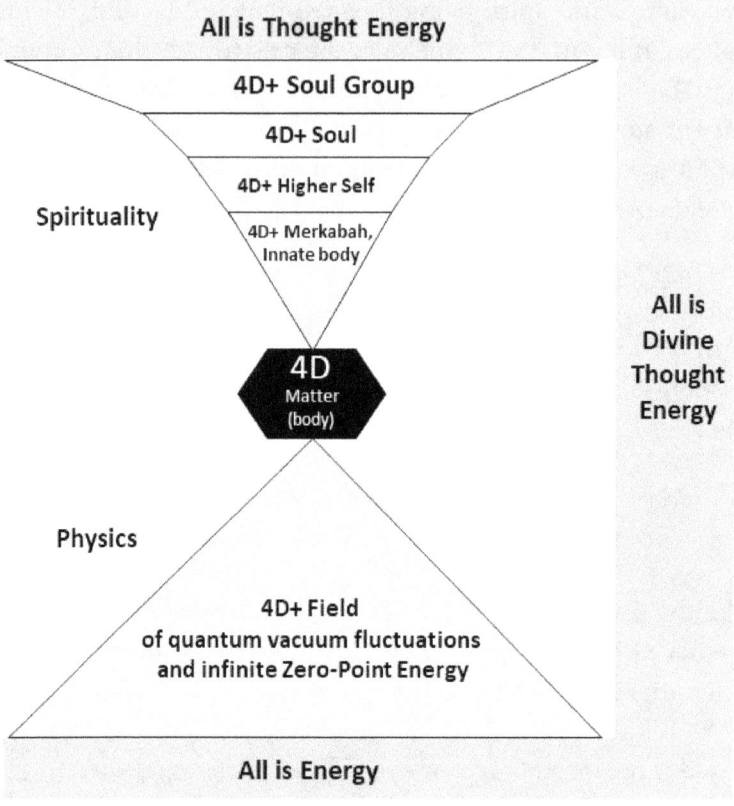

Figure 12.1: A unified theory

Spirituality, or metaphysics, is sometimes called *future physics* because contemporary physics (besides not yet noticing the game-changing *Strong and Weak Interdimensional Forces*) still thinks properties like mass, density, etc. are fixed. Spirituality and metaphysics have long known such properties to have a *default* that can be altered under the right conditions, like when a guru leaves a handprint in a boulder.

The hardest way to accomplish that is to press a *seemingly* solid hand into a seemingly solid boulder. I emphasize seemingly in that we now understand that at an atomic layer, virtually everything is empty space, with solids being represented by the pushback of electromagnetic fields. Hence, an easier way to accomplish the same outcome is to utilize the higher law of conscious intent to move one electromagnetic field (that of the hand) into the space of another (that of the boulder).

That said, there may be an even easier way to accomplish the same result. What if that boulder has an unchanging shape only due to being continuously 3D printed from an unchanging template? If so, what if the Guru's conscious intent reworked the stone's quantum template until it was reprinted as indented in the shape of his hand? Perhaps this is the same way that water, by intent and sovereignty of mind, is changed into wine or spontaneous remission is facilitated? Welcome to our hyper-D, more ascended future. What will it be?

All is one...love/light...infinite creator. Healing occurs when [we] deep within realize there is no disharmony/imperfection; all is complete, whole, perfect. Intelligent infinity within re-forms the illusion of body to a form congruent with The Law of One. The healer acts as energizer or catalyst for this individual process. —Ra

Tapping into field energy

Where we can or can't display compassion and kindness might come down to where we see unity and where we see separation.

There is going to be a split...compassionate and not...Caring and uncaring...sooner than you think...wild cards are coming. —Kryon

Compassion and kindness are often minimized by those taught that we are separate from all things and that we have oneness of mind (we *are* our mind chatter). This category of person often ends up disempowered and (perhaps not by accident) in service to the system that taught them.

On the other hand, compassion and kindness are often maximized in those who are taught oneness with all things and that we do *not* have a unified mind. That is, we are *not* our mind's chatter. We have a thought talker, an intuition and thought receiver, a thought listener, and an observer of those. This perspective offers us the option to accept or reject what seem to be our *own* thoughts. This category of person often ends up empowered and in service to their reason for being.

> *All humans are on Earth to see how much hyper-D soul energy they can bring into their lives, and then, the lives of others.* —The Z's

It's said that kindness and compassion have their own rewards. If so, what might be the mechanism for receiving that reward? What if, in addition to helping others, altruism in the form of kindness and compassion grants us personal energy dispersals from the quantum field? What if this is a secret that spiritual masters have long known?

> *[With compassion,] no more catching the disease of the day.* —Kryon

If you've ever been part of a multi-level marketing business, you understand the *returns* that can come back to you by creating "downlines" beneath you. Using this concept, plus the concept of battery cells, I will attempt an explanation of how our *kindness* may build a personal *field* energy battery, one cell at a time. In addition to kindness giving us access to a battery's potential energy, what if compassion can also enable a constant flow of quantum field energy?

When it comes to acts of kindness, how often are we the giver versus the receiver, and why does it matter? A battery cell consists of three parts: an energy *giver* element, an energy *receiver* element, and some medium that connects them. This configuration makes electrical energy available. In a similar way, a hyper-D *battery* of sorts may be constructed when a *giving* person is *connected* by the medium of kindness to a *receiving* person. However, instead of electricity, quantum field energy and information may come from this type of quantum battery. Something similar may be at work when a performer connects with an audience and feels an energy rush.

While a regular battery can be disabled by separating the energy giver and receiver, a *kindness quantum field battery* cannot be disabled in that way. Since kindness is hyperdimensional, it can keep the giver and receiver connected across large expanses of space or time. Hence, once connected, a *kindness battery* may stay assembled indefinitely.

Consider how many people you've shown kindness to in just *this* life and how they may have paid that kindness forward to others who did the same, etc. This may be like creating a compound arrangement of quantum field batteries and assembling one with tremendous capacity. How do you suppose the matriarch of a family appears as an endless well of energy and kindness? Perhaps she's working with a huge quantum field battery that she's built, one kindness at a time. The more energy and kindness she's given out over the years, the bigger her quantum battery.

Perhaps what she receives from the field is *firsthand, full-strength* quantum field energy. On the other hand, (downline) family members are receiving, from her *second hand, diluted field energy*. Because we can all too easily become satisfied with second-hand field energy, grandmas eventually leave the planet as a disguised act of kindness, forcing us to take off our training wheels and build our own direct source of undiluted, first-hand quantum field energy. This explains why her passing may leave such an energetic hole for all the *downline* kids, grandkids, and family relations. The family battery may be dismantled until someone steps up to rebuild a new one, one kindness at a time.

Knowing this, how might we build our own quantum field battery? Showing kindness to someone, even if it's only smiling at a passing stranger, is to create an energetic link to a *downline*, who may propagate that love ripple further downline, who may do the same.

Now that we know how to build our own quantum field battery, how might we make use of its energy? What if we tap into it when using focused intent to improve our world?

In a 3-wire transistor, two of the wires carry "from" and "to" electrical energy, while the third wire controls "how much." Compassion, like a transistor, may also have *from, to,* and *how much* aspects. If so, perhaps quantum field energy is the *from,* the focus of our attention is the *to,* and our momentary level of compassion controls the *how much.*

It takes a lot of quantum energy, plus the ability to stay in the "now" moment, to alter physics and the laws of chance. So, how have spiritual masters throughout time accessed enough quantum field energy to alter their world? Perhaps it's as simple as acts of *kindness* at every turn, plus *compassion* with every thought, while always being in the moment? This may assure a constant supply of energy with which to work. What will it be?

Dimensionality scales both ways

What we learn from *fractals* and sayings like "As above, so below" is that things sometimes scale in both directions. That is, toward the ever-smaller as well as the ever-larger. What if this applies to our access to dimensions?

When someone walks up to me and starts talking, I mentally flip through the "Which Bob persona will respond?" dimension of my "*rolodex*" and make a selection. Will it be *student* Bob, *teacher* Bob, *parent* Bob, *child* Bob, *sibling* Bob, *spouse* Bob, *spiritual* Bob, *retired* Bob, *engineer* Bob, *creative* Bob, *citizen* Bob, *introvert* Bob, or *goofball* Bob? Once I've made a choice within *that* dimension, my choices keep branching out into virtually endless connected dimensions. If I've selected student Bob, is he cooperative, difficult, sitting, standing, paying attention, distracted, or bored, and for how long?

While these are mundane examples of hyperdimensionality, more esoteric examples are also common since consciousness is energy and energy effects matter. One such example is when I send healing energy to someone and expect my conscious intent to alter matter, regardless of distance or time. The point is that, though some think we're inching closer to being hyper-D humans *someday*, we've already been there for quite some time!

A single Bob on a single Earth is not likely. Hence, what I'm experiencing in the present moment is likely one of countless *Bobs* on one of countless versions of Earth, all happening in parallel dimensions and occupying the same space at the same time. How can that be? How can hundreds of cable TV channels share the same coax cable wire at the same time? They coexist in parallel as information-laced energy.

In how many parallel dimensions does the same Bob get 3D printed at the same time and *place—a*s many as are needed? Where's the schematic diagram for each Bob stored for each of those dimensions between printings, who's maintaining that storage, and who's operating and maintaining the matter manifesting *"printer?"* The printer may be operated by a conscious universe.

Although many TV channels can coexist on a single wire, only one at a time is our current point of focus. When you've navigated from one TV channel to the next, did the new channel suddenly exist as the old channel suddenly did not exist? No, they all exist in parallel, whether our attention is on them or not. It's likely the same way for all the Bobs in countless parallel dimensions.

As with the TV example, what if the Bob dimension I'm currently experiencing comes down to my soul's primary point of focus, with adjacent dimension Bobs always available to me so long as I maintain sufficient energy? If so, shifting from one *Bob dimension*, with one health status and memory of the past, to a different *Bob dimension*, with a somewhat different health status and memory of the past, might occur in a blink, as fast as changing the TV channel.

Imagine hundreds of cable TV channels in succession, where what's playing on one channel looks *nearly* identical to what's on the previous channel, except for subtle, incremental changes. That's what adjacent parallel dimensions may be like. When differences are more of a quantum leap than subtle, such as when we notice that the weed growing out of the sidewalk is suddenly a flower or a disease is suddenly gone, we give these occurrences names such as the Mandela Effect or spontaneous remission. I'd call it a sign of becoming more lucid within the illusion of awakeness.

The door is wide and open, don't go back to sleep. —Rumi

While linear logic assumes something *within* our dimension has changed, nonlinear logic suggests it could also be a change in dimensions. In both the new and old dimensions, the same guy may be standing next to me on the sidewalk. Likely, neither he nor I traveled from the old dimension to the new one; we were probably both born here and have been living our lives in *this* dimension, just in case this dimension ever became my soul's primary point of focus. When nearly identical, parallel dimensions are that accessible, what controls *whether or how* we navigate between them? Likely, it's every single thought plus our energy level. Higher/improved dimensions require the sustained higher energy levels that come from unblocked circuits. Yes, we may really be *that* hyperdimensionally powerful and *that* responsible for our thoughts!

If my next thought is positive and loving or negative, unloving, judgmental, or fearful, I might (typically, without noticing) jump my soul's primary point of focus one or more dimensional steps *up* or *down*. In both my prior and current dimensions, the same low-vibration person may still be standing next to me on the street, but the gap between our perspectives may have either widened or narrowed.

Perhaps due to a *single thought*, my current dimension is either one step closer to or farther from "heaven" than when I woke up today. This is a sobering thought when one considers that we may have ~70,000 thoughts each day. Perhaps that "free" fear-laced news or TV show costs more than we think?

What about the version of Bob and Earth in the prior dimension? They keep living their lives in a parallel dimension at the same time and in the same place, with their own memories of the past, but my soul's primary point of focus is now elsewhere. If the Bob I just shifted to had a different haircut two weeks ago, I typically won't notice because, in jumping dimensions, I usually leave behind my memory of a different haircut while taking on a new haircut memory. If I don't, that's the Mandela effect. The esoteric community agrees. This is a paraphrase of a channeling from an angelic entity:

You're in a hyperdimensional reality. Multiple Earths and multiple versions of you, all happening at the same time and place. As you awaken to more awareness, you see more things…ascend your consciousness into a higher dimension version of you and Earth, while still being here... This is why many can only see a limited reality while the realty of others is expanded. They are experiencing another reality. One can experience esoteric knowing, where angels may show themselves…where joy and love exist, while standing next to one who experiences none of that.

So, if you're a lightworker with expanded, dimensional perception, how might you navigate the shift? This paraphrasing is a channeling from an entity known as *Onyah*[140]:

This is the time of the great evolution…for the frequency of the planet to shift so you express yourselves hyperdimensionally…. All are capable of channeling love…of becoming more of who they really are. It's a choice. It's time for the "evolutionary" to be present, to know your truth…inspiring others. To complement one another…open to new knowledge and ways of being/cocreating…a balanced, wise, wholehearted, hyperdimensional being, knowing when to be still, when to take action and when to live your truth. The time you incarnated for looks messy in the moment, but stay strong, for you are calibrating into new levels. One step at a time…once in a while, a quantum leap. Increased light expands you hyperdimensionally so that the limits you once knew are dissolving. Graduate from occasionally holding the light individually, to occasionally holding the light collectively, to constantly being the light individually, to constantly being the light collectively. Breathe deeper, higher frequencies, fully present… open to intuit/express universal intelligence. Lean into your hyperdimensional superpowers.

Why does the shift look so messy at the moment? The shift has escalated the conflict between light and darkness. *Light* is like a chemical *chelation agent* that draws the dark out of the fabric of society. As light begins to increase by way of lightworkers transmuting fear into peace and balance (which *isn't* reported), the dark reacts to promote more fear (which *is* reported). This fear may temporarily neutralize many lightworkers by shifting them away from peace and balance.

> *Keep working on behalf of light, rather than becoming obsessed with what the dark is doing…for that's debilitating to most.* —The Z's

Eventually, lightworkers (while maintaining their peace and balance) will bring forth even more light as a solution to the darkness, which causes the darkness to react again. Although this may appear as a futile circle to some (and as fear and chaos to many), those savvy to the shift know it to be an upward *spiral*, offering great hope regarding where this dance will ultimately lead.

We can hasten that future by how we consume the news. It's better to be peacefully under-informed than fearfully misinformed. If one employs sovereignty of mind to consistently ascend in dimensions, what ascension signs might they notice? Each higher dimension tends to be marked by an improvement in light, balance, peace, health, longevity, and perspective. Eventually, we notice a difference. What will it be?

Our tuner impacts veil thickness

When it comes to frequencies, like allows entry to like. This is how the frequency of a radio tuner allows entry to the energy and information of only one out of many radio stations. Likewise, shamans and masters access energy and information from beyond the veil by matching the frequencies of *grievance-free compassion, Love, and balance.*

Imagine the setting sun projected out to sea through the lens of a lighthouse. The sun's light, channeled, focused, and directed by the lighthouse, dwarfs what it generates on its own. Likewise, those on the path to mastery learn that the love they can generate and direct from ego is dwarfed in comparison to the intensity of Source Love they can channel through the clear lens of a grievance-free heart.

For every second we hold "beyond the veil" mental frequencies, our personal veil gets *thinner*, allowing entry to increased energy, intuition, inspiration, and benevolent synchronicity. This promotes a more self-empowered, self-informed, and less easily deceived or manipulated individual.

BYOB - Bring Your Own Bias. Whatever you want to feel in a room or in the world, the disempowered hope for it, while the self-empowered bring it.

It's time to remove the training wheels and take full responsibility for the moment-to-moment frequency of our thoughts and how it impacts our lives and the lives of others. What will it be?

Thoughts are things, and you are creators. Be judicious in your thoughts, what you take in and what you give out, for those are creative energies. —The THEO Group

Veil thickness, compliments of N.E.W.S.

Every second we hold the mental frequency of worry, frustration, and fear may *thicken* our personal veil, resulting in being *less* intuitive, *less* empowered, *less* balanced, and more easily deceived or manipulated.

> *Worrying is using your imagination to create*
> *something you don't want.* —Abraham-Hicks

When every day, perhaps one in 1000 has an exceptional day, most out of a million have a typical day, and a few in a million have a terrible day, do you suppose it's a coincidence that the N.E.W.S. (*Neutralize Empowerment With Subterfuge*) tends to mention only the few in a million that will promote veil thickening—worry, frustration, and fear? I don't use the word "subterfuge" lightly. By definition, *subterfuge* involves employing deceit to serve a goal, which in this case is to slant the news of the day to capture the viewer's attention-seconds.

According to Kierkegaard, there are two ways to be fooled: to believe what isn't true or to refuse to accept what *is* true. The sea of information we swim in daily is crafted in such a way that both ways of being fooled can be accomplished. This is accomplished by evaluating new information through the flawed lens of controlled narratives instead of by way of our heart's intuition.

> *The man who never looks into a newspaper is better*
> *informed than he who reads them…whose mind is filled*
> *with falsehoods and errors.* —Thomas Jefferson

Try a 30-day N.E.W.S. fast, and notice how infrequently (because information is everywhere) a topic comes up that you haven't heard about, and how frequently you've felt compassion or had a positive solution come to you through the veil because you were able to keep your tuner set to a higher frequency.

Also, since the N.E.W.S. frequency tends to dampen our intuition, notice how, ironically, avoiding the N.E.W.S. results in being *more* accurately informed.

Charting our ascension

We arrive as *babies* with amnesia about who we really are, where we're from, and what we're here to do.

> *Humans are about to enter a consciousness renaissance, where advancement goes exponential due to babies born with instinctual knowledge instead of being a blank slate. Consciousness will eventually become so holographic and shared that when one person learns something, all will instantly know it.* —Kryon

The puzzle of life tests whether we're willing to employ sufficient intuition and courage—sufficient to uncover our divine parts as we climb the enlightenment ladder out of amnesia toward home.

Given that, how might we measure our progress?

We casually mention one's level of vibration or enlightenment, but are those terms useful for gauging whether our next thought, information, or entertainment exposure inches us closer to or farther away from oneness with divine Source?

Since a contemporary light meter or vibration frequency meter may not help in this regard, perhaps we should look for other metrics? Let's see how far we can go with only four metrics: *Truth, Love, Joy,* and *Oneness.* Indeed, high levels of each of these have typically been displayed by spiritual masters.

If we've chosen our metrics wisely, how far up or down we are on just those four scales can describe, for most situations, how far we are (in that moment) from enjoying the perks of an ascended being— perks like flowers growing where we've walked, the trust of *animals,* and being able to employ the higher laws of conscious intent to alter the lower laws of physics.

> *Demonstrate mastery with balance, compassion, and multi-D sending/receiving. Send thought groups or pictures to animals, soul to soul. Speak to trees, the Earth, and the diversity of unseen beings around us. They speak back in fleeting, nonlinear, intuitive concept bundles that we can interpret, without letting filters/analysis distort it.* —Kryon

If my left hand accidentally knocks something over, should I angrily judge it and hold a grievance against it? Anger, judgment, and grievance regarding my left hand would, per Fig. 12.2, score low on all four scales. In short, I'd be *angry* (low on the *Joy* scale) due to low *compassion* (low on the *Love* scale) and low understanding (low on the *Truth* scale) about my lack of separation (low on the *Oneness* scale) with my left hand.

A higher perspective regarding that incident might lead me to sufficient *compassion* (higher on the *Love* scale) to forgive my left hand before realizing (higher on the *Truth* scale) with a smile (higher on the *Joy* scale) that due to it being connected to my body (higher on the *Oneness* scale), there is nothing to forgive.

Let's assume that every thought and action move us either farther away (distal) from or closer (proximal) to divine Source, which is the ultimate destination of all four scales: *Truth, Love, Joy,* and *Oneness*.

Farthest away (most distal) from the higher, divine attributes on each scale is their (lower on the scale) fear shadow. The more intense the shadow, the more intense the fear and its children. The opposite is also true.

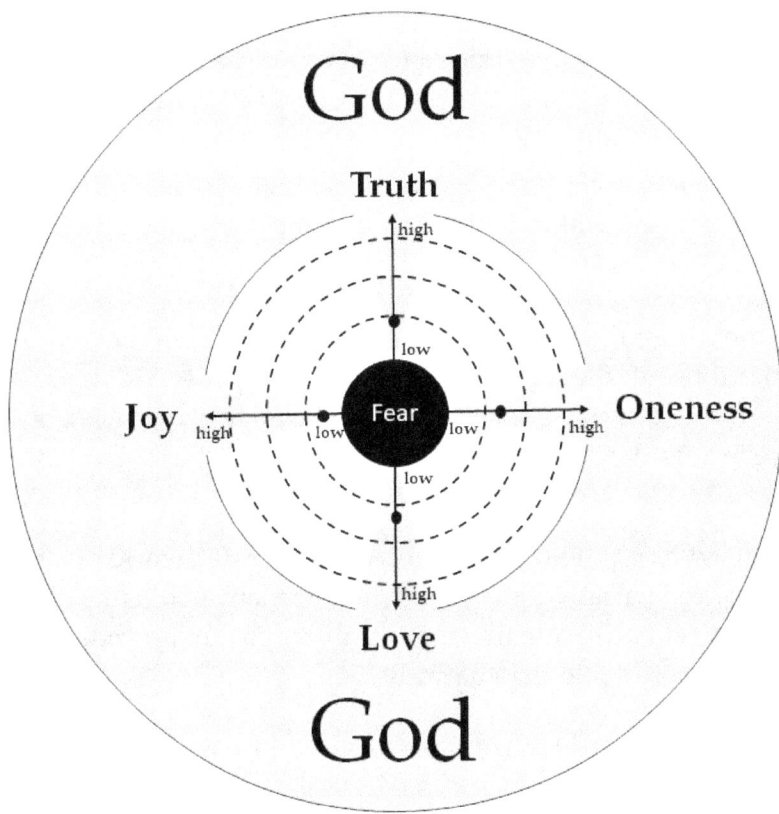

Figure 12.2: Four ladders to mastery

The four traits we're discussing tend to be mutually reinforcing. This provides a classic example of hyperdimensionality in that within each, the others may be found enfolded. Each can also lead to the others:

- Climbing the <u>Truth</u> scale can lead us to Oneness, Joy, and Love. And within Oneness, Joy, and Love, Truth may be found enfolded.
- Climbing the <u>Oneness</u> scale can lead us to Love, Joy, and Truth. And within Love, Joy, and Truth, Oneness may be found enfolded.

- Climbing the <u>Love</u> scale can lead us to Oneness, Joy, and Truth. And within Oneness, Joy, and Truth, Love may be found enfolded.
- Climbing the <u>Joy</u> scale can lead us to Love, Oneness, and Truth. And within Love, Oneness, and Truth, Joy may be found enfolded.

Reaching significantly high levels on more than one of these continuums at the same time may be experienced as *balance*, promoting a sense of *peace*. It may also help with *sovereignty of mind* as we increasingly give precedence to *internal* authority over *external* authority.

At the God-*distal*[141] end of the Truth continuum is a world of far more fear-inspired narratives than Truth, where many of us currently live. At the God-*proximal* end is our future, in an ascended world featuring more Truth than narrative.

Enlightenment is the crumbling away of untruth. —Adyashanti

At the God-*distal* end of the Love continuum is low compassion or hate, where many of us live today. At the God-*proximal* end of the Love continuum is our ascended future, featuring more Love than fear-inspired hate.

If you can think of any upgrade for the God you were told about, what you accepted (or rejected) wasn't God.

While happiness may depend on happenings, *Joy* can be independent of happenings. At the God-*distal* end of the Joy continuum is gloominess, solemnity, emotional flatness, or even depression, which is where many live today.

We're used to high and low moods, with guardrails at both extremes. Per the shift, those guardrails are gone. It may now be a mistake to expect a guardrail to limit how low and dangerous depression can go. Sovereignty of mind and mental balance as priorities have never been more important. On the flip side, there are no more limits to how high we can now go when exploring ecstatic joy, gratitude, and Love.

At the God-*proximal* end of the Joy continuum is our future, an ascended world where laughter and ecstatic, blissful joy are much more prevalent. These are not prevalent by accident but by way of the discipline to consciously cultivate them as an alternative to sorrow.

> *Laughter and joy are incredibly powerful...they take you into higher dimensions.* —Lee Harris

At the God-*distal* end of the *Oneness* continuum is the separation that's baked into much of today's daily programming. It leads to a strong sense of *"me"* amongst an imbalanced, chaotic, and manipulated *"we."*

At the God-*proximal* end of the *Oneness* continuum is a future, ascended world where lines of separation become increasingly blurred. It leads to a strong sense of a balanced *"me"* amongst a coherent *"we."* All this in a world shifting from competition to collaboration.

> *Enlightenment [is remembering] that love and connection [oneness] are the highest octave. And when you realize that...you play separation games far less.* —The Z's

From a narrow breadth at the chart's fear-based center to an ever-widening presence, each of the four traits increases in gravitas and influence before ultimately merging into divine unity. Although not to scale, this chart illustrates that we still have a long way to go toward becoming an ascended society. It also provides a way to notice how much each thought or action moves us closer to or farther from the ascended beings of our future. What if, for every situation, we ask ourselves, "What would high levels of (JOLT) *Joy, Oneness, Love,* and *Truth* do?"

We, as infants, tend to begin life as authentic versions of ourselves, scoring quite high on all four scales. It's only the programming and experiences of life that take us so far from those initially high levels of authenticity.

Hence, dedicating our lives to climbing higher on those four scales may be thought of as a path toward Spirit, but it's really a matter of unlearning, or clearing away, on our return path to our authentic selves.

Our conscious and subconscious free will grant us the capability to either hasten or delay that day. For instance, a subconscious part of us likely resists becoming more *Truthified*, because, in past lives, it tended to get us *crucified*. While our conscious mind may know this is no longer a concern, our subconscious mind might not and may perceive the stripping away of false narratives as a threat.

That said, on the path to mastery, this is the work. What will it be?

Bringing it all Together

We are all one…within this unity lies love, light, and joy…the fundamental teaching of all planes of existence. Service to others, knowledge of self and discipline are just technique. The "game" is won by, in authenticity, placing your cards face up and inwardly saying "whatever your hand, I love you." This is the REAL game outside the apparent game; to know, accept, forgive, balance, to open to love. —Ra

Our challenge as light workers is to become hyper-D, meet the hyper-D beings around us, and live longer so as to plant more seeds. —Kryon

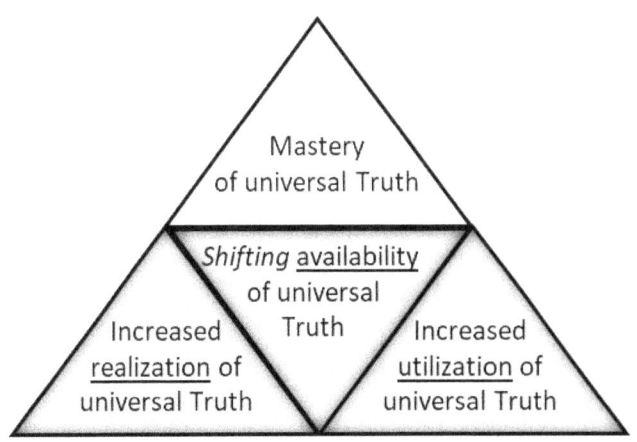

Ch. 13: Rendezvous with our future

Skating to the hyper-D puck 📖

It's been said that *good* ice hockey players skate to where the puck currently is on the ice, while *great* hockey players intuitively skate to where the puck will be next. This is known as "skating to the puck." Applied to the era that is now upon us, to skate to the puck is to be a self-sovereign that intuitively prepares for and aligns with where things are headed. That is, someone with:

- An inclination to incrementally improve their JOLT (Joy, Oneness, Love, Truth) scores.
- The courage to clear old traumas and triggers.
- An inclination to optimize vibratory rate, life force, and balance to bring their unique, full-strength ingredient to the collective soup.
- An open mind and a loving heart.
- A desire to make the world a more compassionate, win-win place.
- An inclination to harmonize and synergize with parts of oneself and with like-minded others for maximum impact.

The fact that this also makes us the type of human that unseen high-vibration hyper-D beings want to assist and unseen low-vibration hyper-D beings want to avoid is icing on the cake! In other words, continually re-choosing the high-vibration spiral up, consistent with Earth's potential future, as opposed to defaulting to the low-vibration spiral down, consistent with Earth's past.

> *...future beings... self-thinking [with] proper breathing ... present, aware, and at peace.* —Jerry Wills[142]

Since it's a safe bet that our future descendants will be checking in on us via techniques such as remote viewing and time travel tourism, why not surprise them by acting futuristically enlightened now? How might that look? It's time to:

- Prioritize critical thinking, research, intuitive Truth-sensing, meditation, and growth over controlled narratives.
- Cultivate and appreciate kinesiology[143] as a Truth-sensing skill.
- Appreciate the power of introspection and positive, emotion-charged[144] intent.
- Be courageous enough to not fit in.
- Prioritize advice from the wise over the clever.

The decision to journey within is not for the timid. You never know when the growing flame of Truth and authenticity will get too close to the dry tinder of "This pseudo-truth is good enough for now."

Finally, use the biggest brain first, not last. Aboriginal wisdom says that gut instinct should be the first brain used, with its output filtered by heart intuition as the second brain before finally reaching the smallest brain inside the head. In short, those who skate to the puck are students of what some call the "new enlightenment."

Those of the "New Enlightenment" marry science and spirituality as hunter gatherers of truth. —David Korten

The "real" world: bringing it all together 📖

Win-lose *me*-people often infer that win-win *we*-people don't understand the real world, so they are unknowingly both vulnerable and missing opportunities. In response, win-win we-people may just smile, knowing that (having been in both positions), win-lose me-people don't understand the real world and are therefore unknowingly vulnerable and missing opportunities.

A win-lose, me-person may request an explanation but have no context with which to understand it. For those up to the challenge, I've listed some key points in an attempt to provide a frame of reference.

Before there was matter, space, or time, there was only the Prime Creator, or aware nothingness. Given this, matter, space, and time are constructed from the only building material available: a single consciousness, or self-aware vibratory energy. Since there is nothing that is not constructed of this consciousness, there is nothing that's not, on some level, conscious. Although solid, visible things may be conscious beings, there is no requirement that conscious beings be solid or visible.

Given a virtually infinite number of timelines (and some beings' ability to phase in and out), the existence of invisible beings is logical, to be expected, and part of the life experience of many. Invisible beings run the gamut between *watchers, helpers, tricksters, exploiters,* and *predators*, just like visible beings. The branches of science and medicine that first embrace this (and the impact of consciousness[145] in general) will likely make great leaps forward.

> *Of all the versions of you in alternate timelines, many have not lived to this point, so don't be surprised if some of your unseen guides are you!*

The ultimate (multi-incarnation) end game is to raise our vibratory rate to the point that we rejoin the Prime Creator, from which we originated. This may involve effort and discipline.

> *To those irritated by some reaching for a higher vibration in every situation… It's not personal; it's just IS-ness.*

The vibratory rate each of us uniquely has today has something of a neutral buoyancy. It may not go up much until a thought, action, movie, book, song, etc. of a higher vibration (relative to our own) pulls it up. The opposite can be said for negative thoughts, societal influences, etc. that are of a lower vibration than our own.

Noticing and controlling the vibration of our thoughts and influences represents a huge turning point in our upward vibrational journey. Prior to that, our daily vibrational rate may have been more like a cork bobbing randomly on a restless sea.

Ours may be more of an experimental planet with the *historic* potential to be a soul trap. With few exceptions, a soul that incarnates into a human avatar body reportedly knows that they will start with a karmic score of zero and will not be allowed to leave upon death until they again have a karmic score of zero or greater.

You do not have a soul. You are a soul. You have a body. —C.S. Lewis

A *one-and-done* incarnation on this planet is theoretically possible, but only if one is careful not to let negative karma points move their overall score into the negative. It's said that most exit their first Earth body to find the exit door missing or locked until they've reincarnated enough times to raise their karmic score to at least zero. I emphasized the word "historic" because, as part of the shift, light workers reportedly now have a new way to nullify karmic influences.

We arrive through a door marked: "Take on a body with amnesia, believing we're physical and separate." As we piece together what we used to know, few go near the exit door marked, "I forgive everyone, everything... I am loving, conscious energy, separate from nothing."

One might think we would pick up on the rules of the *game* and discipline ourselves to think and act in a way that quickly secures our soul's exit. That might be true except that each new incarnation usually comes with amnesia, tending to make us forget there is a game with a scoring system, let alone the rules for making progress or exiting.

The wave-partial duality means we are simultaneously only matter and only energy waves. Science may eventually see us as a conscious collection of energy waves with amnesia within a conscious energy sea without amnesia. We eventually come to know the conscious sea as observing and supporting our interactions until we struggle out of amnesia, when it may ask, "Would you care to play again?"

It's not uncommon to encounter people who've incarnated hundreds of times, with early incarnations leaning toward victimizer, win-lose, and *me*-behaviors, adding to their karmic debt. This may be followed by many incarnations leaning toward victimized, win-lose, and *me*-behaviors, experiencing the other side of predatory behaviors while reportedly burning off negative karma.

Sooner or later, the arc of multiple lifetimes of karma accumulation and balancing makes it clear that what appears to be a *win*-lose is actually a lose-lose. When this realization sets in, we may begin to gravitate toward loving, forgiving service to others in win-win *we*-people incarnations (improving our karmic score). It's said that the moment we forgive everyone and everything, including ourselves, is the moment we stop the turning of our multi-lifetime karmic wheel.

In other words, early incarnations may involve looking through the eyes of a fearful, win-lose human-mammal avatar until we learn to look through the eyes of the fearless, indestructible, loving, win-win energy being inhabiting that avatar. Hence, "I'm taking this from you because I can" *me*-people may ironically be victimizing themselves by increasing their negative karmic score while potentially minimizing the negative karmic score of their victims.

Viewing life through a yin-yang diagram, we can choose to see lightness, darkness, or a unifying circle. Our perceptions dictate our reality.

Whether we place our attention on the fearful or hopeful, our consciousness is reportedly capable of biasing time, space, and matter at the quantum level to increase reasons for that fear or hope.

When we integrate our higher self into our body and operate from the heart, nonlinear or hyper-D time, abilities, and experiences become available to us. The information, experiences, and group effects available in our linear-time physical illusion are significant, but nothing compared to what's available in the nonlinear-time, hyper-D quantum world.

Our inner focus on impacting the quantum field may be our biggest leverage for change. The various controllers of society, who've likely understood this concept for centuries, may misdirect our group-manifesting potential for their own use. All the while, we just think we're watching the news or the latest hit movie. We cannot collectively graduate to the next level until we appreciate and take responsibility for how our individual and mass consciousness alter the quantum and physical worlds.

Although we live in a free-will universe, many do not appreciate that by cosmic law, we're default-*yes* humans living in a default-*yes* universe. Therefore, if any beings (seen or unseen) want to take advantage of us, our default answer in a free-will universe appears to be "Yes!" unless we notice their manipulation and exploitation attempts and specifically say "No!"

Hence, the age-old game of the less scrupulous, whether seen or unseen, is to control and exploit in a way that stays just below our victimizer-noticing threshold or is something to which we (perhaps out of fear) have implicitly agreed. Improved intuition by way of meditation can re-sensitize our victimizer-noticing threshold, making *we*-people ironically harder to victimize than *me*-people.

If mind control programming to desensitize our victimization-noticing threshold gets ahold of us while we willingly sit in front of a movie or video screen, our free will has not been violated. If we lower our personal vibration by exposing ourselves to TV (clearly labeled as *programming*), our free will has not been violated.

If our higher self agrees to our having an unpleasant educational or karma-balancing experience that our conscious mind would never agree to, our free will has not been violated.

> *The soul draws to itself challenges for its…growth.* —Theo

If we have a fearful thought prior to developing sufficient mental discipline, and a default-*yes* conscious universe responds with, "Yes, I'll get right on that!" and something unpleasant comes from that, our free will has not been violated.

> *Judgment asks the Law of Attraction for more of what we don't want. Intent asks the Law of Attraction for what we want.*

Hence, what may occasionally appear as insanity from the universe may be more about our not understanding that we live in a thought-activated field of quantum potentials.

Once we've been programmed to not notice our victimization and to avoid (without investigating) areas that so-called serious minds ridicule, it may be *game over*. Welcome to the land of the blue pill, free range, imprisoned with more bills than money, and a brain full of unverified, hand-me-down narratives and conclusions.

> *The narratives programmed into you don't have to be seen as wrong, but only as an incomplete beginning —a place to start but not a good place to end.*

So as not to violate our free will, the Truth is often hidden in plain sight in the form of movies, etc., that we just assume (without any real investigation) are 100% fiction.

The way out involves developing self-sovereignty by way of Socratic critical thinking and sufficient Truth-sensing intuition to sense formerly unnoticed deceptions and exploitations. Intuition can be increased via meditation and having the courage to turn up the volume on our heart-compass as a critical intelligence-gathering point where normal senses are integrated with subtle (hyper-D) senses. As such, numbing our hearts to the point that we can say, "It's not personal, it's just business," may forfeit a vital intelligence asset.

"*We*-people" are not easy, toothless targets—they are perfectly capable of dealing with the nefarious. We just won't like the way it feels in our body, and we will not stay in that part of our vibrational spectrum any longer than necessary. Karmic consequences aside, loving kindness, compassion, forgiveness, and service to others actually feel much better than the spoils of "I took it because I could."

Forgiving and releasing grievances unlocks a surprising amount of previously sequestered health maintenance and dream-manifesting energy. When we truly let go of a grievance, like refreshing the pixels on a video screen, the consciousness that may recreate our physical universe countless times per second may respond by recreating our universe without that former toxicity. As a result, forgiveness *anywhere* may upgrade our personal and shared *everywhere*. Imagine if everyone in the world laid down just one grievance a day—our world might be barely recognizable in a year!

If you have not already come to the conclusion that raising our vibrational frequency is worth the trouble, there is another reason. You may have visited one of the Hawaiian Islands that's known for being a personal energy amplifier. If you arrive on one of the islands in a positive, negative, or unstable mental state, you may experience a significant amplification of whatever energy you brought to the island. Some experience this as the islands (in effect) saying, "Raise your vibration, or leave."

How does this relate to the current topic? While we may think of deep, interstellar space as bitterly cold, with temperatures near absolute zero, our solar system (for the next ~10,000 years) is currently passing through a very highly charged, very hot 30,000–50,000[146] degree-K local interstellar cloud[147], which resides within an even hotter 1,000,000 degree-K local bubble of interstellar space, inundating our entire solar system with highly energetic particles and high-vibration cosmic[148] rays.

Imagine an intense heat envelope surrounding a spacecraft reentering the atmosphere. Now imagine a solar-system-sized heat envelope surrounding our heliosphere (the entire solar system) as it plows through this extremely hot area of deep space. As a result, our sun, our bodies, and several of the planets and moons of our solar system, including Earth[149], are beginning to show signs of being overstimulated, with no end in sight.

Proxima Centari, our closest neighboring sun, has been exposed to this same over-energizing interstellar cloud longer than us, in that it reached it sooner. The fact that Proxima Centari recently responded to that overstimulation with a micronova solar flash[150] does not bode well for how our sun may react to a similar environment. Many ancient traditions have predicted just such a micronova for our sun, using terms such as Samvartaka Fire[151] to describe one or more massive solar flashes that catalyze human consciousness to the next level. In the Bible, Isaiah 30:26 speaks of the sun becoming seven times brighter than normal, such that moonlight is as bright as sunlight.

Besides the sun, we should probably be prepared for overstimulated people and power grids, in addition to overstimulated planets and moons. Some sources[152] have described a similar, high-energy inundation from a metaphysical perspective. Their take is that we live on a planet predominantly populated by people with chakras one, two, and three activated. While this has been a sustainable situation for thousands of years, going forward, Earth is now said to be increasingly inundated by energy more closely matching our fourth, or heart, chakra. The difference between this and the island situation is that, unlike the "raise your vibration or leave" island example, leaving our solar system is more difficult.

> *The veil is thinning…our consciousness expands… entering the new dimension with…raising…vibrations…The old paradigms and… belief systems…fall…to make room for the new.* —Dolores Cannon

Evidence for this vibrational inundation may be found in how much progress we've made toward tolerance, inclusion, kindness, and compassion in just the last 100 years. As this heart energy inundation is expected to only intensify, one could extrapolate the trend to predict the potential for a much kinder planet.

For those with open heart chakras, the transition experience to this new level of earth energy may be like plugging their 220-volt central nervous system into a 220-volt wall socket. For those who are unwilling or unable to open their heart chakra, the experience is liable to be more and more like plugging their 110-volt central nervous system into a 220-volt wall socket.

While it remains to be seen whether this type of sustained energetic overload could cause the "end time" madness predicted by some religions, there does seem to be an increasing trend toward mental instability, mass shootings, and either love-driven or fear-driven polarization.

Higher-vibration, positive, loving, hyper-D people may navigate the heightened energetic overstimulation environment with fewer problems while increasingly uncovering innate abilities. Mild symptoms I've noticed amongst myself and friends may include dizziness, vertigo, ringing in the ears, shallow breathing, etc. Lower frequency, less positive (closed heart chakra), or unstable 4D people may be in for a rougher time.

..incoming cosmic energies are affecting our behavior and perceptions...bringing up insecurities, traumas...now is the time to focus on these...the longer we wait, the harder it will be. —Corey Goode

To play off the quote above, some have said that the ideal way to position ourselves for a smooth transition is to deal with our shadow selves while working toward becoming predominantly[153] of heartfelt service to others. Besides the fact that there really is no *other*, the lessening of karmic debt that comes from forgiveness and loving service to others, like cutting away drag chutes, is very much a loving service to a hyper-D self.

The flip side is that increasing karmic debt from *seemingly* performing a service to oneself at the expense of others is actually a disservice to oneself and is equivalent to *adding* drag chutes. In addition, when we negatively mess with others, we may implicitly authorize unseen negative energy beings to mess with us.

Although many realize the benefits of raising their vibrational frequency, some win-lose me-types will try to bypass the karmic scorekeeper by way of technology. While this may work for a time (such as using medical breakthroughs to counter the health consequences of disharmony), it's ultimately not sustainable. All paths ultimately narrow to the single (JOLT) paths of Joy, Oneness, Love, and Truth, so they're only putting off the inevitable. In the meantime, the use of technology in service of exploitation may only increase karmic debt more rapidly.

Finally, win-win *we*-types, as I have personally experienced, often gain an increased understanding of and an ability to interact with dimensions, time, and timelines. This is no small advantage.

You're in a hyper-D reality. Many Earths/versions of you at the same time/place. As one awakens, they ascend consciousness into a higher dimension... This is why many see a limited reality while others are expanded. They're in another dimensional reality. Some see the esoteric, knowing it's real...where angels show themselves, where joy/love exist, next to one who sees none of it. Together, in different dimensions, at the same place/time. —Kryon

So, between the win-lose *me*-person (the caterpillar) and the win-win *we*-person (the butterfly), who will increasingly be living in the *real* world?

Leaning into a kinder, better world 📖

As a retired engineer, inventor, and futurist, I continue to see around bends into the future. I'm not alone in noticing that the win-lose paradigm is (after a run of thousands of years) not just in decline but possibly terminal. Humanity's increasing vibratory rate and global communication ability, combined with a decreasing ease in turning a blind eye when wins come at someone else's expense, will be its likely cause of death.

Already, the transition has begun from a world led by nations focusing on win-lose intimidation to a world led by nations focusing on win-win collaboration. Hence, those interested in continuing to live in a world-leading nation should support the leaders that understand the need to switch horses soon instead of continuing to ride the old "As long as I get mine." horse into the ground as more enlightened nations take the lead.

> *Irony: The biggest roadblock to the type of harmony that would make negativity endangered is negativity.*

We've had thousands of years of "I'm taking this from you because I can, and there's nothing you can do about it." Due to technological changes, the second part is no longer true. Technology is increasingly bringing about the democratization of a "group-suffering button" that anyone can access. That's not a happy thought. Either we begin caring about each other soon, or we may be in for an unnecessarily rough road.

> *When the tools of warfare become too effective and available, we must choose between maintaining the myth of separation and maintaining a civilization.*

I know which way I would prefer. The nations that grasp this reality first are the ones that will, if only motivated by self-survival, lead the win-win charge toward a new and better world.

Bringing our ingredients to the collective soup 📖

If you reached into a spice cabinet for a bottle labeled "Italian Seasoning," you'd expect it to include a unique mixture of well-blended, full-potency ingredients. Likewise, it's our responsibility to ensure that when we bring our individualized *spice* to the collective *planetary soup,* its components are pure, well-blended, and at full strength. In my experience, these are just a few of the ingredients we are well served to include in our personal self-sovereign *spice* mixture:

Empowerment: The only true empowerment is self-empowerment. As with an airline oxygen mask, prioritizing our own sovereign self-empowerment allows us to be more useful to ourselves and others.

Creativity: In order to maximize creativity, identify and protect the most coherent and productive times in our day. Recognize that not all "ah ha's" are created equal or reach us by way of the same part of the body. Some come from:

- The brain, such as something dawning on us.
- Heart intuition (which represents a synergistic combination of internal and external information).
- Outside us, as inspiration (literally: "Spirit coming in"), inferring a download of external information.
- Outside us, in the form of "a still small voice," inferring external information entering via the throat chakra.

- Outside us, in the form of seeing the answer, inferring external information entering via the forehead chakra.
- Outside us, in the form of just knowing an answer, inferring external information entering via the top of the head chakra.

When we live in an alive, collaborative universe, becoming informed by way of all the above is not just possible but suggested for those desiring an evolutionary advantage.

A soft, kind, buoyant heart: While we may start life at that place, an adult typically must do real compassion, forgiveness, and cosmic perspective work in order to return to that place. Since a light, buoyant heart, combined with altruism and a strong sense of community, is said to be a key ingredient in a long, happy, and healthy life, the effort is likely to pay unexpected dividends.

A good life 📖

A good life might be described with words such as "optimize," "maximize," "minimize," "balance," and "synergize." That is:

- <u>Optimize</u> our intake of universal healing and manifesting energy.
- <u>Maximize</u> self-reflection, self-study, and first-hand conclusions.
- <u>Minimize</u> pre-chewed, hand-me-down conclusions, controlled narratives, and the taking of fear or outrage bait.
- <u>Balance</u> our internal masculine and feminine energies.
- <u>Integrate</u> our logical left brain and creative/intuitive right brain, heart, and pineal gland.
- <u>Balance</u> "getting-things-done" time with "me" time.

Synergize with a community of like-minded self-sovereign individuals who've married their instincts and intuition, who've married their brain, heart, and spirit decision centers, and have chosen to consciously steer their quantum reality for the better. If I could give only one piece of advice, it would be:

Small questions result in small growth. Big questions result in big growth. Make your questions as large as your courage!

Synchronicity snowflakes, and thoughtful thinking

Every snowflake is different because it forms around the unique geometry of a speck of dust. Likewise, synchronicities may find us, formed around the unique geometric pattern of one of our prior thoughts. This prompts us to become responsible with our thoughts, which will increasingly be seen by the universe as a personal and collective purchase order. Being increasingly hyper-D, our thoughts likely travel forward in time, like a bow wave in front of a boat.

Whether they're of a low or high nature, our thoughts become the center of a synchronicity snowflake, which (for good or ill) positions itself to cross our path. Although masked by a time delay, much of what synchronicities do *for* us or *to* us may actually be (via thought) originated *by* us.

Since our post-shift planet is becoming increasingly thought-responsive, it behooves us to become increasingly thought-*responsible*. That is, to become more *thoughtful thinkers* as we increasingly embrace our sovereignty of mind. What will it be?

The true/untrue ratio continuum

Although enlightenment is available to individuals today, collective enlightenment may take some time. Our society builds its worldview atop a stacked pile of beliefs and controlled narratives that we collectively trust as true. Imagine drawing a long line in the form of an enlightenment continuum. At the low end of that line is a very *unenlightened* society, where nine out of ten things we firmly believe to be true are not. At the high end of the continuum, in a distant future, is an *enlightened* society where nine out of ten things believed to be true are *actually* True.

You're here to have a spiritually enlightened life, and seed that energy on the planet. While it looks different for each person, it's a sense of flow, peace, well-being. An ability to quickly return to a state of presence, when taken out. You don't lose the light for very long. You cultivate, maintain, and emit light and vibration to the world. Your vibration dictates the world you create for yourself and others. —The Z's

Since the enlightened end of that continuum may be thousands of years away for our society, one should expect that far more than half of what we currently think of as unquestionably true…is not. The courageous spiritual path is about discovering and rectifying false, blue-pill beliefs. Hence, while blue-pill people increasingly disagreeing with you may not guarantee that you're headed toward enlightenment, it may be a good sign!

Working the free will and polarity puzzle

Why will there always be some darkness on Earth? Earth is said to be a free-choice, light/dark polarity puzzle experiment that most people work on with amnesia. Without the ability to lean toward either light or dark, there's no real free choice, no real experiment, and perhaps no real need for this planet.

If you've ever asked, "How could a loving God allow…?" The answer is "free choice." How could a loving parent let go of their toddler's hand, knowing they may fall? Only by falling will the toddler realize why it's worth the trouble to learn to *not* fall. In this Earth experiment, only Love supersedes our free will, like when a toddler wants to play with something dangerous, but Love withholds it until there's sufficient maturity.

This Earth experiment requires that we be allowed to use our free will for random, undisciplined (some light, some dark) thoughts that direct the quantum field to manifest a (some light, some dark) mess. Only by experiencing the random mess created by our random thoughts will we eventually learn why it's worth the trouble to develop sovereignty of mind.

The shift is increasingly amplifying how much our thoughts impact dimensions we don't *see*, which likely impact the laws of chance in dimensions we do *see*.

> *Irony: Most of those steering our consensus-created reality don't believe in consensus-created reality.*

We treat our free choice birthright too lightly in that it's reportedly so intergalactically respected as to restrict the actions of interdimensional beings. It's respected enough to restrain a room full of unseen guides that would dearly love to help us but must sit idly by as we create a mess until we utilize our free will to ask for assistance.

> *If you don't ask, we often don't have the ability to step in and help…there are ways that we can and do step in, but there are limits.* —The Z's

Higher-vibration galactic and hyper-D beings respect our free choice because it's the right thing to do. *Lower*-vibration galactic and hyper-D beings respect our free choice because they must. Unless, that is, we can be convinced to forfeit our free will, often along with our peace and balance.

Like a family pet that, afraid of the yard, never leaves the porch, why do we use our free will to restrict ourselves to a muted color, disempowered, linear 4D world while surrounded by a birthright hyper-D, full color world? We've used our free will to believe narratives that say hyper-D realms, from which we came and will return, either don't exist or should be avoided.

We've normalized many names for all that can separate and disempower us by way of fear and imbalance. Words like mistrust, hate, worry, bigotry, outrage, anxiety, etc. Our society offers constant opportunities to marinate in these offspring of fear. The linear, 4D world may think these are just tools for monetizing or controlling us, but those living in the hyper-D real world may see a bigger picture.

While important things occur in 4D, light workers know the most important things likely take place in, and the most important information likely comes from, hyper-D realms. Studies have shown 24% less crime and 76% fewer war deaths occur while only 1% access hyper-D realms in meditation for peace. Hence, accessing hyper-D realms may offer our biggest leverage for positive change. Since the hyperdimensional can only be accessed from a place of peace and balance, those who don't prioritize peace and balance over being entertained and *informed* employ their free will to stay somewhat disempowered and limited to the 4D *porch*.

Why is it that many who courageously venture beyond the 4D porch don't like everything that manifests for them? Minds connected by a common bond may synchronize. When our conscious mind wants one thing, our subconscious wants a second thing, our innate body consciousness wants a third thing, and our higher self wants a fourth thing, which mind wins and shifts the odds of chance at the quantum field level to bias what shows up for us? The most coherent consciousness wins. Hence, if we've not used our free will to prioritize sovereignty of mind to the point that our conscious mind is the most coherent of all our minds while aligned with our other minds, do unpleasant experiences *violate* our free will? No, they *reflect* it.

What's to be found in the hyperdimensional realms beyond the limits of the porch? Progress toward the incarnation amnesia puzzle, along with inspiration, intuition, assistance, empowerment, and the road toward mastery.

> Your intuition will grow and expand like a majestic cloak of wisdom. Your ability to choose your battles will be fine-tuned to perfection. Your capacity for stillness, for living in the moment, will blossom…. —Donna Ashworth

As the *shift* evolves, we may increasingly *split* into two camps: those who've been convinced to stay asleep on the 4D porch and those of peace, balance, and self-sovereign empowerment who've worked the puzzle enough to remember that our true home and birthright are to be found beyond the porch, in the hyperdimensional. What will it be?

Taking the tape off our "Check Integrity" light

When the "Check Engine" light comes on while driving, we have a choice. We can take corrective action or, at our own peril, just cover the light with tape. Likewise, we're all born with an internal "Check Integrity" light that may flash on our internal dashboard from time to time. Our *check integrity* light tends to flash when we want something bad enough that we're willing to prioritize obtaining it over Truth, fairness, etc. That is, when we've convinced ourselves that the end justifies the means.

When that internal light comes on, we have the choice to take corrective action or, at our own peril, just tape over the light. The Truth is, many of us taped over that light a long time ago. For instance, if someone creates a "news" organization where most of one political party can do no wrong while most of another can do no right, they've taped over their "Check Integrity" light. Monetary or political gain may have been valued above integrity. If I tune in, opting for indoctrination, and then argue and vote as if I'm truthfully informed, I've taped over my "Check Integrity" light.

I've traded my integrity for a false sense of safety—a false feeling of moral and intellectual superiority and the rush that comes with being included in a polarized group. While consciously submitting to polarized indoctrination may be a less harmful indulgence when it comes to our favorite sports team, as a means for deciding who and what to vote for to shape our collective future, not so much!

As part of the shift, people are beginning to remove the figurative tape and, as needed, take corrective action. Those who do so first will be the whistleblowers and the audience, as the spotlight is increasingly cast upon the individuals, organizations, and institutions that've waited too long.

When illumination is increased, the dirt that was always there will suddenly become visible to all. Therefore, time is running out to proactively choose one side before automatically defaulting to the other. When the spotlight eventually reaches our dirt, history will be kinder if we already have a broom in our hands. What will it be?

The gasp

The path from *religious* to *spiritual* is a transition from someone else's mixture of true and false narratives to our own. A path from training to Truth.

> *To allow religion to take precedence over spirituality, as with judging or shunning, is to move away from God. To allow spirituality to take precedence over religion, as with discernment, tolerance, and compassion, is to move toward God. It's ironic when the result of 2000 years of moving away from God is touted as the best path to God.*

While we likely can't correct the false narratives embraced by others, we *can* correct our own as we seek out the flames of Truth beneath all the smoke.

At "death," when we employ the divine *fact checker* to compare what's True against the false narratives we accepted as true, we'll likely gasp. Hence, the spiritual path, while on Earth, is for those who wish to minimize that gasp.

Imagine one day arriving on the other side of the veil and running a sentence you believe to be true through the divine fact-checker filter, knowing that only pure Truth makes it out the other end. When you input "*Jesus, my Lord, saved me, who was born dirty, from the judgment*

343

and punishment of an eternal, loving God," you may gasp when the only part of that sentence that makes it through the divine fact checker is *"eternal, loving God."*

Why is that? On the other side of the veil, all that we'll find is a loving, hyper-D, holographic energy soup that knows nothing of separation. With no separation, there can be no hierarchy or judgment. That gasp may come from realizing all the ways in which those living in only four dimensions projected their dysfunction, false sense of separation, judgment, and hierarchy onto their notion of the divine and then lovingly taught those flawed projections to their children.

This raises the question of how one can tell where they might currently reside on the spiritual path toward mastery. The path's beginning is characterized by younger souls that tend to be high on judgment and fear and low on the compassion that comes with hyper-D discernment. Further down the path, older, more advanced souls tend to exhibit the compassion and love of low judgment and fear due to greater hyper-D discernment. Speaking of advanced souls, the historical man (usually called Jesus) was *Yeshua,* meaning *"to rescue"* or *"to deliver"* in Hebrew. He was here to *rescue* us from false narratives that keep us from the path of mastery and, through leading by example, to *deliver* those who would follow him to that path. How ironic that 4D men generated so many false narratives around the one who came to rescue us from false narratives!

On the other side of the veil, determined to create a sentence that comes through the divine fact checker unscathed, you eventually succeed with something like, "*Yeshua invited us, who are born sovereign and magnificent, to emulate him on the path to ever increasing hyperdimensional Truth and spiritual mastery, one with the eternal, loving God."*

The good news is that, by way of birthright intuition, kinesiology, etc., we have access to lesser versions of that divine fact checker today. The sad news is that remarkably few seem to be making use of them. What will it be?

Creating a new energy

Is it reasonable and logical that beings capable of existing beyond our four dimensions may be interested in and observing us? Yes, it is. Hence, we in 4D may be (whether we realize it or not) interacting with inhabitants of higher dimensions. Whether we call them guides, ancestors, or angels, it's reasonable and logical that we're being monitored by, and when our free will allows it, assisted by, them.

Hyper-D emanations (like Love, compassion, and joy), unlike radio waves, can't be blocked and are received at vast distances instantaneously. Whether called prayer or scalar waves, this is how interstellar and interdimensional beings may monitor our progress in real-time.

So, when these beings, whether seen or unseen, can monitor billions of us on just this planet, what filters might they apply to narrow the list to the most interesting humans to be monitored and assisted? Perhaps they look for those creating a *third* type of energy.

According to esoteric sources, the first type of energy is that of human consciousness, which doesn't narrow the field at all. The second type of energy is generated by dealing with the challenge of the day, which also doesn't do too much to narrow the field. The third type of energy is created as the result of applying sovereignty of mind and alchemy of the heart to transform a situation. What if those monitoring us from higher dimensions focused their attention on a virtual stadium of just those transmitting type-three energy?

If so, the cheap seats in the stadium would be filled with those who *conquered* a problem, or figuratively wrestled it to the ground, through sheer egoic determination and force. The better seats may be filled with those who *overcame* a problem with a combination of egoic

345

force and soul power. The VIP seats would likely be filled with those who *transcend and transform* a problem through the alchemy of higher-vibration (compassionate, seeking to be of service) consciousness.

For those who were lucky enough to have a kind, patient, loving, and forgiving grandmother, the experience of this energy may already be a part of their past. This type of energy is a harbinger of a more unified and kind future. If you were a higher-dimensional being interested in who's on the cutting edge of this planet's path to ascension, which seats would you be watching and assisting? I'm betting it's those demonstrating type-three energy.

It's said that those who approach mastery see nothing but oneness and Love wherever they look. Although it may take a while, this is where our ascending planet is headed, along with the increased ability of our thoughts to manipulate the laws of physics.

For *edgeologists* leaning into this cutting edge, what might be the steps between here and there? For starters, it's easier to see divine Love wherever you look when you've just finished *beaming up* or sending a divine Love blessing to everything you see.

Everything is constructed from one thing: energy, or more specifically, *Universal Consciousness Love Energy*. Thus, whether it seems like it or not, pure divine Love is everywhere you look. It may be modulated (through free will) as a *villain*, but pure Love is all there is to see, especially for those whose energy is type 3.

There is nothing that is not you. —Thich Nhat Hanh

How to meet an angel

If one wanted to meet an angel[154], how might one go about it? I'm not referring to the controlled narrative of a gendered Caucasian with mandatory wings and an optional sword, but to an actual "living light" angel.

Unseen hyper-D beings in general, whether observers, helpers, or exploiters, are attracted to us when the vibratory level of our thoughts, actions, and intent matches the frequencies that interest them. This applies whether we are referring to our personal angel, known as our higher self, or other angels. What might attract the interest of an angel? Some answers may be found in these channeled words:

> *Angels are love…attracted to those…who vibrate in unconditional love…seeking to learn and serve… It takes…courage to persist in a spiritual preoccupation… [making these people] very beautiful to angels.* – Q'uo

The day in which I met the angel I call *Myriad* may have met the requirements listed above. I was in a healing meditation and prayer group meeting with a half-dozen others. We were supplied only with a person's first name and their health issue, such as "John, brain tumor." While listening to a ~20-minute recording of a Native American drum beat (to facilitate brainwave entrainment), we were to go into silent meditation with the intent to energetically connect with the person seeking assistance. We each took notes regarding what we were experiencing.

When the drum beat recording ended, we took turns sharing our notes. On this occasion, three of us shared a very similar story about seeing (in our minds' eye) an angel. In my case, I saw a *nearly* empty room except for someone lying face up on a therapy table. I emphasize "nearly" in that an angel was there to offer assistance. When I asked for a name, *Myriad* (as in many) was the telepathic reply.

How did "she" appear? The closest approximation I can give is to imagine a half-mile bundle of alive, aware, luminous white-light fiber levitating a few feet off the ground in a beautiful pattern about three feet wide and four feet tall. That is, a pattern of celestial *living light* exuding a compassionate, feminine, assistive presence. While I'll never know whether our collective intent to help "John" had any effect, I had the unmistakable impression that Myriad was there to assist. In that I've noticed Myriad in my mind's eye on several occasions since then, I now think of "her" as part of my unseen support team. Now that you know that compassionate, courageous service can attract the attention of an angel, what will it be?

> *I would like for my life to be a statement of love and compassion, and where it isn't, that's where my work lies.* —Ram Dass

Leaning into the hyper-D era

Moving beyond underlying concepts, let's summarize a few suggestions and examples for living a hyper-D, self-sovereign life.

> *Open up to hyperdimensionality, not just for your own joy and pleasure and to make life far richer, but because that's humanity's path in the next ~100 years.* —The Z's

Wise-humans will increasingly lean into the compassion, cooperation, tolerance, oneness, and Love that will characterize our future—with the sovereignty of mind to consistently lean toward the positive from an "in the now" perspective.

Toward that end, a wise-human guards and grows their hyper-D soul flame, knowing that some thoughts, words, and experiences can dim it. One of the ways to *dim* our soul flame is to buy into false, disempowering narratives around separateness. If our flame gets too dim or goes out, it may cause our current incarnation to end. One of the ways to *grow* our soul flame is to ponder, pursue, and own our loving, hyper-D oneness. How might that be verbalized at the dinner table? "Thank you, Source, as hyper-D *food*, for blessing Source as hyper-D *me*."

To the wise-human, hyperdimensional time may be seen as non-simplistic and nonlinear. They may experience hyper-D time[155] within a hyper-D world[156] of conscious energy projected as matter.

This shift in perception may allow time, energy, and matter to be increasingly managed.

We've experienced and accessed the hyperdimensional more than we've realized. Although it's reportedly been erased from our history, we have always lived with access to both higher and lower dimensions. That said, a belief barrier between us and the hyper-D is often installed in us at a young age. Since a part of us is connected to all points in time, space, and dimension, much more is real and possible than that barrier would have us believe. This book seeks to make that barrier more permeable.

> *Belief is the barrier between you and*
> *hyperdimensionality.* —The THEO Group

We are not a collection of human cells that gained consciousness; we are consciousness with temporary access to a collection of human cells. Whether we choose to view things from the lower-vibration perspective of the body or the higher-vibration perspective of the soul determines not only how we perceive our experiences but also our experiences. Different perspectives ask a conscious universe for different teaching curricula.

If all time exists in every moment, positively raising our vibration in this moment (beyond altering our present) may impact all potential futures. As far-reaching as that statement is, raising our vibration may also impact our past.

> *Earth in 2030–35 will have more of a love and oneness*
> *frequency. In 2045, it will be even stronger.* —The Z's

Is it true that a neutral universe will stand idly by and let us return to dust if we don't work at survival (a type of *negative buoyancy* called entropy)? Or, is it true that a conscious universe, respecting our free will, stands ready to assist when we give permission, watch for signs, and *go with the flow* (a type of *positive buoyancy* called syntropy)? Depending on how we use or misuse our free will, either or both forms of buoyancy can be experienced in a given day in response to the stronger of our (often conflicted) conscious, subconscious, or super-conscious free wills. Our job is to get in touch with and align our various types of consciousness, free will, and intent, and then take responsibility for the results.

Cesar Milan is known as the "Dog Whisperer." As it happens, his approach to dog leadership is also a useful approach to a more ascended life:

> *Head up, shoulders back, in the moment, without meanness, calm, and assertive, while clearly visualizing the intended outcome.*

If you've read this far, I assume you are either in the wise-human category or perhaps open to leaning in that direction. Leanings are important when it comes to surfing a wave that could otherwise upend us.

Various levels of humans are like nested Russian dolls, so a wise-human may temporarily revert to the world of their inner clever-human or even their (inner-inner) mammal-human, depending on how strongly they're emotionally triggered. That said, on a good day, a wise-human's conscious use of time (in the now) opens the door to being increasingly elevated as a hyperdimensional being. The more we operate at the hyper-D embracing level, the more we will likely experience the ability to play with and alter the past, present, and future.

In the words of Mark Nepo, we were all broken from the same nameless heart, so in helping each other, we're each a piece of that great heart loving itself back together. This provides an important reference point. If our destiny is to love all our personal and collective pieces back to oneness, will my next thought, action, or inaction assist or resist that future?

> *The cornerstone of … the New Earth will be the ability of each person to live more deeply and more fully in the energy of the heart.* —John Ryan

This book has attempted to offer a trail guide into "*red pill*" territory, usable by both young and old souls, whether currently spiritual or not. If you come away with different information with each re-read, congratulations on being a multi-D reader of a multi-D book about multi-D topics.

For those not inclined toward spirituality through blind faith, I've sought to demonstrate that spirituality can also be reached by way of logic and observation. Since science (by way of philosophy and natural philosophy) is the great-grandchild of spirituality, science eventually leading[157] us back to spirituality would complete the circle.

For those who've shown the fortitude to undergo this journey with me, I salute you. The world desperately needs those with the courage to raise our individual and collective vibration levels to become the truth-seeking and unity-building ones needed by our future—a new collective in the pursuit of win-win in an ever-expanding circle of those we call kin. As each day brings us closer to a world of thought-driven instantaneous manifestation, I'll leave you with these words:

> Only *think* about what you choose to experience.
> Only *speak* of what you choose to empower.
> Only *do* what demonstrates who you really are.
>
> Peace and Blessings!

Study Guide

Reflection/discussion questions: **Introduction**

1. Describe a time when you began a positive transformation in a way that initially seemed anything but positive.
2. If you could write a time-traveling letter to your younger self, what wisdom would you offer? Would you coach your younger self to avoid the lessons that shaped the person you are today, or merely offer tools to smooth the journey?
3. Describe a synchronicity, event, or hyper-D interaction that caused the logical you to lean more toward the spiritual you.
4. Think of an action you've taken and ask successive "Whys?" until you reach the bottom of your personal premise stack. How many layers deep is your personal stack?
5. The wisdom path may progress from "nothing to fix" to "something doesn't add up" to "this feels more True." Describe a time when this happened to you. Along your wisdom path, can you name some premises or beliefs that were eventually replaced?
6. Have you ever remembered parts of a different lifetime?

Reflection/discussion questions: **Ch. 1**

1. Do you view yourself as an eternal consciousness with temporary access to a body, or as a body with temporary access to consciousness? Or perhaps a cosmic consciousness with the temporary use of a body equipped with built-in body-centric consciousness?
2. Given the descriptions for mammal-human, clever-human, and wise-human, have you met people from each category? Which category reflects most of the people you know? Do you see the mix changing?
3. Have you ever switched news programming off long enough to become "news sober"? If so, what was your experience?
4. Describe a time when intuition proved to be more accurate than logic.

Reflection/discussion questions: **Ch. 2**

1. Anything that encourages us to forfeit our power, our authentic selves, our Truth, or our self-sovereignty may be seen as a game pitfall. Including those listed in the chapter, how often do you notice "game" pitfalls in your day-to-day life?
2. Have you ever encountered a normally non-visible agent of the game, such as a deceased loved one, a guide, a muse, or an angel?
3. "Truth" is not always durable. Describe a time when a "truth" got demoted to either a pseudo-truth or a falsehood.
4. Describe an area of your life in which you've bravely prioritized your research, intuition, and opinions over those of an authority figure.

Reflection/discussion questions: **Ch. 3**

1. Minds are eternal; brains are not. Assuming that the levels of mind that cease to function when the brain ceases to exist are our avatar's software in operation, how often do you think we are observing the thoughts of our eternal mind versus our avatar's (standard equipment) software in operation?
2. When win-lose duality is our compass's true north, compassion may be seen as a personality flaw. When win-win unity is our true north, a lack of compassion may be viewed as a potential area for growth. Have you noticed how this choice of perspective can cause people to show up differently in the world? Please offer an example.
3. A conscious, holographic universe (cosmic switchboard) has the ability to complete an energy or information connection between us and whatever we hold in mind. Have you ever experienced this, such as thinking about someone just as they call or text?
4. How often have you emerged from a dream with an important lesson or insight? When this occurred, did you suspect that a part of you had astral traveled somewhere, as opposed to it just playing out in the theater of your mind?

Reflection/discussion questions: **Ch. 4**

1. Describe a few positive personal or societal changes you might be able to attribute to the shift. For instance, have you noticed any disclosures in the news or improvements in your intuition? Have you noticed any physical symptoms that might be associated with being subjected to increased cosmic energies?
2. Have you ever employed the "thinking as if it were already so" manifesting formula described in the book? What level of success have you had? Do you suppose that future generations will see improved success? If so, why?
3. Since the world is made better by those who are emotionally balanced, do you agree that fear, like alcohol, should be ingested responsibly or not at all?

Reflection/discussion questions: **Ch. 5**

1. When virtually all our choices are from lists that were pre-chosen by others, are we experiencing mental freedom?
2. The saying, "Every thought is a prayer," refers to the universe having a tendency to respond to our thoughts with "OK, I'll get right on that!" whether we're currently thinking in a positive or negative way. How often have you seen outward results that might have resulted from an inward thought?
3. Have you noticed the veil getting thinner? For instance, have you become clearer about your life's mission, seen an increase in secrets becoming public, had more past-life recollections, experienced a change in what is possible, etc.?
4. Throughout your life, has your relationship with fear changed? If so, how?
5. At some point in our childhood, we likely turned off some of our brilliant creative or psychic individuality to fit in. Have you recovered any such abilities? How do you think your life might now be different if these abilities had been available to you all along?
6. How do you go about optimizing your energy and vibration levels?
7. Over the course of your life, has your position moved in regards to the four-quadrant map (Fig. 5.2)? If so, how?

8. Ch. 5 speaks of the Shuar tribe, in which the women are empowered to stop men who pursue self-interest to the point of collective harm. If our society had a similar practice, in what areas should women of today be saying, "Stop?"
9. The process of reclaiming our birthright to be fear-free may include giving up fear's children, such as judgment, anger, worry, blame, guilt, grievances, etc. Have you ever encountered the staying power of one or more of these when you tried unsuccessfully to release them?

Reflection/discussion questions: **Ch. 6**

1. Describe an example of something in the news or in your life that may have been impacted by the shift.
2. Give an example of something you've had to unlearn as you've proceeded along your spiritual path.
3. Elizabeth Kubler-Ross noted that all emotions boil down to either love or fear. What percentage of the time do you suspect the average person spends under the influence of fear, under normalized names such as worry and concern?

Reflection/discussion questions: **Ch. 7**

1. Were you raised with a sense of Armageddon or WW3 doom? If so, has that sense of doom shifted or lessened in the last decade?
2. Have you noticed any evidence of the "split," such as people polarizing into ideological or political camps? If so, does it seem more pronounced since 2012?
3. The chapter mentions an "all-you-can-eat media buffet of fear bait." Have you seen evidence that the news is more sensationalistic and fear-injected than necessary?
4. Have you had any experiences that you might classify as "hyper-D"?
5. As part of the shift, have you noticed any improvement in your falsehood-sensing intuition?
6. Since 2012, have you noticed any improvement in your hyper-D subtle energy perception or skills?

7. Do you know of anyone who changed after an epiphany? Did you suspect that they became more broken or more "woken"?

8. Can you think of an example of a situation where compassion made all the difference? Going forward, do you plan to lean more toward compassion?

Reflection/discussion questions: **Ch. 8**

1. It's said that love and compassion energy always surround us, but they supplement our energy only if we set our emotional tuner to allow them in. Have you ever encountered individuals who, by keeping their emotion tuner set to the positive, seem to have a consistently higher mood and level of energy?

2. As you progress along your spiritual path, have you noticed any improvement in your Truth resonance ability?

3. Which of these below do you suspect is the way time works?
   a) The present is pulled toward one future by that future (like a windsurfer is pulled forward).
   b) The future is pulled backward into the present (like roping a cow).
   c) The present, traveling under its own steam, navigates toward one of many possible futures (like a car picking a freeway exit).

Reflection/discussion questions: **Ch. 9**

1. Can you describe a time when a statement of fact was made when (in hindsight) someone would have been well advised to couch it in terms of "or so it might seem?"

2. Do you have any experience with yourself or someone you know being fluent in silence? Have there been benefits?

3. Have you ever wasted a good crisis by failing to get the lesson, only to have the universe serve up a bigger crisis?

4. Have you experienced an example of space or time manipulation? For instance, has your present self ever comforted your past, traumatized self?

5. Have you or anyone you've known experienced a fast or unusual improvement in a health condition that made you wonder?

Reflection/discussion questions: **Ch. 10**

1. When it comes to either evolution OR intelligent intervention, or evolution AND intelligent intervention, how do you suspect the Truth will be seen by those in our future?
2. Have you, or anyone you've known, experienced the energy blowback from sending best or worst wishes?
3. Have you or anyone you've known hacked 4D, as described in the chapter?
4. Describe times when you've judged versus times when you've discerned. Did it feel different in your body?

Reflection/discussion questions: **Ch. 11**

1. At this point in your life, how often, do you suppose, are your boundaries a cage as opposed to a shield?
2. List examples of both tonic and toxic fear in your life.
3. Were you brought up to feel it was selfish to take care of yourself first or that it was OK? Has your opinion changed with experience?
4. Have you ever had something creative just "come to you" that seemed like it may have come from outside your brain?
5. How important is balance in your life? Has your opinion changed as your life has progressed?
6. Can you think of grievances from decades ago that may no longer be serving you? What is your experience with trying to release them? Do they sometimes follow you home, like an addiction?
7. Growing up, was compassion valued very much? Do you see that changing?

Reflection/discussion questions: **Ch. 12**

1. For a number of days, try blessing every new situation before you assess it. Did any of those situations then seem or become more blessed?

2. One of the concepts listed in the book is "Energy leaves an imprint." Have you ever walked into a space where an argument or wedding had recently occurred? Could you feel the energy still lingering in the space?

3. How much of your spiritual path has been about unlearning versus learning?

4. Have you noticed that the compassionate/caring trait splits people into groups? If so, does this split seem to be getting more pronounced?

5. Have you ever wondered whether there may be another "you" in a parallel dimension that's made different life decisions? If so, which decisions do you suppose were made, and to what effect?

6. A new habit may take weeks to become established. Have you ever tried to consciously set and hold your emotional tuner at different settings, such as focusing on gratitude? If so, what was the result?

7. Where would you currently place yourself on each of the JOLT (Joy, Oneness, Love, Truth) scales? How has it changed over your life, and to what effect?

Reflection/discussion questions: **Ch. 13**

1. If every atom making us up is simultaneously a particle and an energy wave, astral travel may have a scientific and theoretical basis. Have you or anyone you've known had any such experiences?

2. Do you think of yourself as a body with a soul, or a soul with a body?

3. Are you inclined to think that all your current wisdom and savvy came from just your current life or from a collection of lifetimes?

4. If a continuum exists where, on one extreme, most things believed to be true are not, and on the other end, most things believed to be true are true, where would you place our current society?

5. When you reach the other side of the veil and run all your current beliefs through the divine fact-checker, how much gasping do you anticipate?

Index

Notes

[1] Cumulative Amazon reviewers' score as of 7/11/23.

[2] Some U.S. technology patents: 7934069, 7805566, 7721053, 7546485, 8185663, 8200921, 7529966, 7478154, 7366866, 7366857, 7360044, 7340572, 7293048, 7181582, 7165141, 7162596, 7149919, 7116916, 7058850, 7031928, 7007143, 6978280, 6907505, 6848841, 6782416, 6735637, 6721902, 6721857, 6718447, 6697881, 6687805, 6662282, 8059539. These can be viewed at https://www.freepatentsonline.com/

[3] "…past, present, and future… all exist in the universal hologram simultaneously." https://tinyurl.com/4r3cz2ss

[4] http://www.sintropia.it/journal/english/2019-eng-01.pdf

[5] This will be more fully described later in this book.

[6] CIA Analysis/Assessment of the Gateway Technique: https://tinyurl.com/4r3cz2ss

[7] Kryon is an angelic entity channeled by Lee Carroll.

[8] Abraham is channeled by Esther Hicks.

[9] https://cosmosandhistory.org/index.php/journal/article/view/565

[10] I suspect it's more likely a resonant vessel within a resonant chamber.

[11] While Hinduism, at 4000 years old, is the oldest religion in the most *recent* civilization, increasing evidence points to other civilizations before ours. Kryon has stated that this last, patriarchal 10,000 years has been our 4th civilization.

[12] The 1874 Encyclopedia of Humor

[13] "Wednesday is the day we traditionally burn documents and other legal evidence…" the Vatican spokesman said. "We still have thousands of documents to destroy this week…" https://tinyurl.com/yc2h385y

[14] Onyah is channeled by Peggy Phoenix Dubro.

[15] Controlled narratives, snares, cosmic landscapes, dimensional beings, etc.

[16] Balance, pure intent, dimensionality, sovereignty of mind, etc.

[17] Unless otherwise stated, the use of "reportedly" typically infers channeled material having some degree of truth resonance with the author.

[18] From the classic movie "The Matrix."

[19] http://www.sintropia.it/journal/english/2019-eng-01.pdf

[20] Einstein's early years—some believe him more mystical/wise in later years.

[21] If mammal-humans correlate to what the Z's refer to as predominantly residing in one's lower mind, and wise-humans correlate to predominantly residing in one's higher mind, clever-humans may correlate to predominantly residing in one's medium mind, or being of two minds.

[22] Levoy, Gregg. 1998. *Callings: Finding and Following an Authentic Life*. Pg. 217. *Google Books*. Three Rivers Press. https://tinyurl.com/tqnp5oa

[23] Many claim that more than seven chakras are available to us.

---

24 Some scientists theorize that this is not a metaphor and that the chances of us existing in a simulation are around 50%. https://tinyurl.com/y4v8dqyl

25 According to Ra of L/L Research, our higher self is a gift from our far, far future self to our current self as an unseen spiritual guide—so far into the future that the gift is given just before our future self begins the process of rejoining with the creator. Since all of time occurs at the same time, we have access to that future or higher self now.

26 I am not a mental health professional. That said, I differentiate this consciously chosen technique from spiritual bypass, or subconscious disassociation due to trauma, pathological depersonalization, or pathological de-realization.

27 Per Wiktionary.org, "karmic debt" is the accumulation of negative energy resulting from misdeeds.

28 The term "other-self" is from the channeled Law of One book series by Elkins, Rueckert, and McCarty. Although my book was virtually completed before I came upon The Law of One material, it's interesting to see the number of areas in which we've arrived at similar conclusions, perhaps by drawing from the same *field*.

29 I emphasize the word "historically" in that some esoteric sources claim that as part of the shift, light workers now have the option to end the effects of karma.

30 Full/cropped image use is covered under the Fair Use provisions of copyright law for the purpose of news reporting, research, scholarship, and to illustrate a lesson. The cropped-out left side illustrates purposeful corruption activities.

31 Scivias (Know the Ways) 1.4.9 "The Souls and Your Pavilion" http://expositions.bnf.fr/ciel/grand/1-105.htm

32 Levels one–five are my arbitrary designations for the sake of convenience.

33 "International Peace Project in the Middle East," *The Journal of Conflict Resolution* 32, no. 4 (December 1988), 776–812. "The Transcendental Meditation Program and Crime Rate Change in a Sample of Forty-Eight Cities," Journal of Crime and Justice 4 (1981), 24-45

34 Orner-Johnson, et al., 782: The Effects of the Maharishi Technology of the Unified Field: Reply to a Methodological Critique David W. Orme-Johnson, Charles N. Alexander, and John L. Davies First Published: December 1, 1990 Research Article https://doi.org/10.1177/0022002790034004009

35 Shoulder-length straight white hair, pink skin, and a clean-shaven face at around age 85. Per my journal, I may have also encountered him in the 1990s.

36 http://www.theisticpsychology.org/books/w.vandusen/presence_spirits.htm

37 Those who've had both experiences would likely differentiate between simple sleep paralysis and a "Night Hag Syndrome" entity encounter.

38 For those viewing a black-and-white version of this book, colors are described where relevant.

39 https://tinyurl.com/y62xm22w

[40] A person in authority may also succumb to the *false authority* fallacy by incorrectly believing they have the authority to "spin" facts to their advantage.

[41] An internet search for "Derren Brown shopping mall" yields multiple examples.

[42] https://openheartproject.com/the-one-where-i-asked-the-dalai-lama-a-question/

[43] https://tinyurl.com/2dc26e4k The Biology of Belief

[44] Some claim that dimensions beyond the first four are not linear, so it may be inaccurate to say that 5D is next after 4D. Hence, my terms "hyper-D" and "All-D."

[45] In *The Law of One*, free will as a separate entity is called the "first distortion."

[46] If I recall *The Law of One* books correctly, consciousness levels are assigned a numerical "density" value. Contemporary humans, both in the service-to-self and service-to-others varieties, typically score around a three or four. Both types are allowed to progress to level six before duality must be dropped in order to proceed. Hence, it's possible to encounter a nefarious being that, at level six, seems quite advanced relative to our current level. Channeling (e.g., Reiki) is commonplace with 4th-density service-to-others people, as each is aware "that within it lies the glory of the Creator... [so] naturally makes the choice to channel that energy."

[47] The Institute of Noetic Sciences offers a database of many such experiments.

[48] At the same time, there seems to be another class of beings who, by their quick exit, seem to be made uncomfortable by my close proximity.

[49] People's bodies look correct but seem rubbery and less sensitive. For instance, twisting an arm to gain compliance has no effect.

[50] https://en.wikipedia.org/wiki/Microwave_auditory_effect

[51] https://science.sciencemag.org/content/210/4475/1232

[52] Can a skilled medium access useful data from the dearly departed? Yes. *Anomalous Information Reception by Research Mediums Demonstrated Using a Novel Triple-Blind Protocol*: https://tinyurl.com/4zzadt9h

[53] The *holographic universe* theory was recently bolstered by observable evidence. https://www.southampton.ac.uk/news/2017/01/holographic-universe.page

[54] From one of my #clever2wise podcasts: https://www.clever2wise.com/SHIFT.mp3 from clever2wise.com, or at https://bcochran52.podbean.com/ from Podbean.

[55] "Crystalized thoughts" from Divine Audacity, by Linda Martella-Whitsett.

[56] Michelangelo was quoted as saying: "I saw the angel in the marble and carved until I set it free."

[57] While I'd rather not go down the rabbit hole of listing examples of inappropriate things that are increasingly being brought to light, examples are easy to find.

[58] One reason why masters may not defend themselves.

[59] Or perhaps longer: https://tinyurl.com/2n73hhh8 and https://tinyurl.com/66ufrrdr

[60] DNA Phantom Effect. Laser light (with hyper-D properties) interacts with hyper-D properties in DNA, leaving a hyper-D imprint in a vacuum for a month after DNA

removal. DNA's hyper-D aspects prompted the field of quantum biology. This suggests our thoughts, as energy, program our DNA, which programs our genes. https://tinyurl.com/mr4ex3ac

[61] https://hal-ineris.archives-ouvertes.fr/ineris-00972373/document

[62] https://www.medicalnewstoday.com/articles/308772

[63] https://tinyurl.com/5euwdny3

[64] In addition to what some refer to as the cosmic law of <protected> confusion. This helps avoid the situation where a society becomes too unkind and dangerous because its intellect has outpaced its spiritual wisdom.

[65] Two people supplied blind numerical kinesiology scores indicating a very high level of Truth for one of my blogs (https://www.clever2wise.com/bob-s-blog) that attempted to answer big "unanswerable" questions using spiritual material combined with the science of kinesiology.

[66] https://www.ncbi.nlm.nih.gov/pmc/articles/PMC5131520/

[67] https://www.ncbi.nlm.nih.gov/pubmed/10407911/

[68] Two people supplied blind numerical kinesiology scores for my first book. The most conservative indicated that the work represented *Courage + Predominantly True Reasoning + Integrous Loving Intent*, which aligns with my original goals.

[69] The kinesiology score for my revised "Big *Intention*" theory was much higher than that of the "Big *Bang*" theory.

[70] Interview on Open Minds, S3, E21

[71] https://tz-ma.facebook.com/TheQueenCode/posts/1170543309634936

[72] https://tinyurl.com/ycy4f4nh

[73] For years, Dr. Lina Backman has used hypnotic regression to allow her clients to disclose their true histories. On an evolutionary scale of 10, she gauges 95% of the masses at about 4-6. The remaining 5%, at 7-8, may correlate with what I refer to as "evolutionaries." She further breaks down that 5% into old souls (with many Earth lifetimes), inter-planetaries, and human/angel types that are relatively new to Earth. – Open Minds S23 E13

[74] Kryon (Lee Carroll). You are a piece of the divine.

[75] Also known as our biofield or aura.

[76] https://www.youtube.com/watch?v=yYWKergU4x0

[77] Either avoid fear-based news all together or just scan it as text. Avoid it in narrated form, especially with a music background.

[78] https://tinyurl.com/8bebesd9

[79] This raises an interesting debate about free will. According to a channeled intelligence known as Ra, infringement of free will would not occur if the energy or information I offer my friends/family came through me, but it may infringe upon free will if it came from me. The first is sourced from and targeted by Spirit, whereas the second may be sourced from and targeted by ego.

[80] Per Kryon, those who can't cope with the new energy may pass on.

[81] Whether via yoga, yen, TM, or the Monroe Institute Gateway Technique, elimination of our internal bifurcation echo such that the body can set up an oscillation matching the ~7.8 Hz Schumann Resonance of the atmosphere can cause energy to be transferred to us. https://tinyurl.com/4r3cz2ss

[82] Granted, there are many layers, levels, and aspects to the heart and spirit that could make this simplistic model much more complex.

[83] As mentioned in pg. 92–94 of *The Law of One* – book 2.

[84] Unbeknownst to my nephew, one of his remote viewing targets was the Hindenburg blimp fire. Apparently, his astral body manifested on the scene with sufficient solidity that terrified victims made eye contact for help. Consistent with the observer effect, both my nephew and those who saw him were altered.

[85] Exploring Syntropic Intent Effects across Nonlocal Time, 2019 by Bob Cochran http://www.sintropia.it/journal/english/2019-eng-01.pdf

[86] The term "Bose-Einstein condensate" refers to multiple atoms occupying the same space at the same time, which may be explained as intersecting timelines.

[87] Edited for brevity.

[88] That continual observation may halt time progression.

[89] While typing this, my word processor suddenly reported that this book was ~300 pages longer than it should be. As I looked for the unexpected content, it just as suddenly disappeared. Perhaps it was a timeline-jumping demonstration?

[90] https://youtu.be/GUbEgg6GklU

[91] Braden, Gregg, *The Isaiah Effect*

[92] In S:24, Ep.16, of Open Minds, Parallel Realities of Potential, Jon Gabriel describes realizations about timelines (paraphrased). In talking with a woman at the store, he could see that she had an energy blockage, which he worked on as they talked. When the blockage opened, her body's circuits were capable of an energy quality/quantity upgrade. Before his eyes, she jumped to an adjacent timeline in which her present, future, and past were improved. She was able to exist in that new reality because her new energy allowed it. Hence, if there is something you don't like (within the constraints of your soul contract and subconscious beliefs), there is a near-adjacent timeline in which it is improved or doesn't exist. By clearing the trauma blocks in your energy circuits such that they can sustain the necessary quantity/quality of energy, you can ask your higher self to move you to an improved reality. Adding trauma blocks and low-vibration thinking can likewise navigate us to a less desirable timeline. https://thegabrielmethod.com/

[93] Whether via yoga, zen, TM, or the Gateway Technique, elimination of our internal bifurcation echo such that the body can set up an oscillation matching the ~7.8 Hz Schuman Resonance of the atmosphere can transfer energy/information to us: https://tinyurl.com/4r3cz2ss

94 https://tinyurl.com/2cv6npw8

95 https://tinyurl.com/yyu3m8h4

96 https://patents.google.com/patent/US20090216092A1/en

97 https://tinyurl.com/yxv2nlgr

98 Nassim Haramein estimates that a conscious universe has a speed of thought that is ~10^{40} times the speed of light.

99 Personally, nothing can bring on a lower back issue faster than thinking of a grievance or negative/judgmental thought while bending and twisting. Likewise, in addition to daily performing the "balancing table" yoga pose, nothing seems to keep my lower back issues away like compassion and forgiveness around current and stored (in the body) grievances or traumas.

100 Remote viewing talk: https://youtu.be/zgyYms376Mg. What if the Peruvian Nazca were a test to see if remote viewers could view the scene (out of body) with sufficient altitude to determine the animal being depicted?

101 https://www.imdb.com/title/tt8911874/plotsummary/

102 "'inner dimensions" https://tinyurl.com/ym8ex8e9

103 https://www.sciencedirect.com/science/article/abs/pii/S1550830711002321

104 *"Choice point"* was coined by Hugh Everett III in his paper *Relative State Formation of Quantum Mechanics* to mark the decision or jumping point between a prior timeline/future and a different one.

105 https://psi-encyclopedia.spr.ac.uk/articles/william-tiller

106 As a teenager, my brother, while sleeping, reportedly visited his friend's bedroom to consciously knock a martial arts artifact off his wall. A different family member's spouse swears they (with a backpack) walked right past them and left for work when they were actually still asleep in the bedroom.

107 https://tinyurl.com/3n4ds5b7

108 It's an interesting question as to how negative dreams might impact this.

109 https://journals.sfu.ca/seemj/index.php/seemj/article/download/425/386/779

110 Although *energy* may be increased by utilizing the gap between thoughts, *information* might be found in the gaps between breaths. The Essene Gospel of Peace says, "in the moment betwixt the breathing in and the breathing out is hidden all the mysteries…"

111 This paragraph is adapted from the work of Lee Carroll, Kryon.

112 Some peaks reportedly pushed past 30,000 feet.

113 Reportedly, around 16,000 years ago.

114 According to Kryon, we've also had a fall in our DNA efficiency and consciousness, from 44% to 33%, which facilitated our fall into toxic patriarchy. Aug. 1, 2015, Lemurian Sisterhood Channel: https://tinyurl.com/4ezjbprf

115 https://sacredland.org/hopi-prophecy/

[116] Catholic Church Pontifical Academy of Sciences, under Pope Benedict the 16th, allowed for contact with ET brothers/sisters: https://tinyurl.com/2s474yp8

[117] Unless noted, "esoteric" refers to Lee Carroll (Kryon), Lee Harris (The Z's), Onyah, or other channeled material. Although not called out, some (Kryon, The Z's, Onyah, etc.) channeled messages have been rearranged/paraphrased.

[118] https://tinyurl.com/msppb3r7

[119] Or having blood (e.g., platelet factor 4) from a younger person donated to us, as in heterochronic parabiosis. https://www.eurekalert.org/news-releases/996579

[120] Perhaps sooner than some think: https://tinyurl.com/bpumnh4s

[121] https://tinyurl.com/4mf3rpdk

[122] Although I've not studied these, they came up in a search for keywords such as magnet and perpetual: Patents US11652376, US11626225, US20200381986, and KR20210029059 (https://qree.energy/ https://youtu.be/qsGvt-RRjuk https://www.youtube.com/channel/UCZAOvmK0Wpw8JwN8tkou8hw/videos)

[123] While I'm not a master, this is exactly what disqualified me from jury duty.

[124] A Kryon phrase.

[125] Vagus nerve activation while resting seems to correlate with a tendency toward altruism, compassion, happiness, love, and gratitude.

[126] More and more are catching on. The latest poll showed that just 26% of Americans have a favorable view of the news media. https://tinyurl.com/3azm4yrv

[127] While it's unusual to find a concise overview of decades of spiritual growth, this short sequence of free audios, with angelic entity Kryon speaking through Lee Carroll, covers a lot of ground: https://tinyurl.com/rahmp7jc

[128] Like we don't let toddlers play with power saws, Spirit reportedly withholds breakthroughs until we demonstrate sufficient maturity.

[129] If only as a result of focusing on altruism and community.

[130] According to Kryon, Lemurian royalty had access to a mountaintop temple of rejuvenation that, in some cases, tripled someone's lifespan with one treatment per year. Although the entire technique and formula may not have been shared, some factors seemed apparent: (1) The low oxygen and low temperatures of an altitude so high that charcoal was burned to augment oxygen; (2) "Genisis" cells (a Kryon term: https://tinyurl.com/ysmp7era) from a newborn less than five days old; (3) Sacred tones, sung by the technician. Aug. 1, 2015: https://tinyurl.com/4ezjbprf

[131] Taken a step even further, *loving conscious* energy, or M=E$^{(LC)}$.

[132] In a similar way, the Monroe Institute system can cause our brain/body to match the frequency of and exchange energy with Earth's 7.8 Hz ionosphere: CIA Analysis/Assessment of the Gateway Technique: "…to access, via intuitive means, new categories of information not available to ordinary consciousness." https://tinyurl.com/4r3cz2ss

[133] Abraham Hicks. Though 68 seconds would be better.

[134] 4.5x10^{16} joules of energy.

[135] After reading this passage, Jeff, one of my pre-publish readers, had an accident with a chainsaw. As he was being rushed to the emergency room, he remembered this passage—taking control of his thoughts and intent for the best possible outcome as he held a cloth over the wound. Later, the medical staff said, "Do you have ANY idea how lucky you are that it's only a flesh wound?" He just smiled.

[136] "The tangible world is...infinitely rapid succession of flashes of energy." https://tinyurl.com/4r3cz2ss

[137] https://tinyurl.com/37cpn8bd

[138] Several times per second, at the peak or trough of each brain sine wave, there is a small window of time where we may be considered flat-lined. For that period of time, our mind may be more capable of going beyond space-time, perhaps making us hyper-D travelers with access to all points in space and time. https://tinyurl.com/4r3cz2ss

[139] In the linear 4D center of the chart, time is the 4th dimension. Outside the center (nonlinear hyper-D, or All-D), "when" is no more applicable than "where" because (minus an observer) there are only quantum potentials within an entangled universal hologram, involving energy with no creation date. Ultimately, students of science and spirituality are both *field*ologists, whether discussing 4D projections of the field, uses of the field, or the field itself.

[140] From a Nov. 21 Kryon and Onyah audio recording.

[141] Since there is no spot that God is not, distal and proximal don't refer to physical distance but how near or far our traits are in comparison to an ascended society.

[142] Paraphrased from an Open Minds S5 E14 Jerry Wills interview.

[143] https://tinyurl.com/475hkxf8 Muscle testing determined true/false 65.9% of the time among those with only "some" level of skill.

[144] A Mayo Clinic study found that optimists had a much lower risk of early death than pessimists and on average lived ~8 years longer.

[145] Tiller, William, Ph.D. 2009. *It is time for a consciousness-inclusive science.* https://tinyurl.com/y95leat8

[146] Voyager 2 just passed into VLISM (Very Local Interstellar Medium) space and measured 30,000–50,000 degrees K. https://tinyurl.com/us467xb

[147] https://apod.nasa.gov/apod/ap020210.html

[148] https://www.space.com/voyager-2-detects-heliopause-plasma-shield.html

[149] Earth's shield is decreasing by 5% per decade. https://tinyurl.com/3zuhh89x

[150] https://phys.org/news/2018-04-proxima-centauri-flare-powerful-visible.html

[151] "The Sun may spew massive "solar storms" ...more powerful than anything...in modern history... soon..." – Dr. Robert Schoch, Forgotten Civilization: The Role of Solar Outbursts in our Past and Future

[152] The Law of One, book 2, p. 83.

[153] Oahspe: A New Bible, 1882

[154] Angels are…inter-dimensional ultra-terrestrials who can…bilocate themselves here and are not bound by this dimension's laws of physics. – JJ Hurtak, Ph.D.

[155] https://link.springer.com/chapter/10.1007/978-94-011-5628-8_16

[156] Dewey B. Larson postulated a unified field theory with three time dimensions in addition to the traditional three matter dimensions of length, width, and depth.

[157] https://tinyurl.com/3ahkn68y

www.ingramcontent.com/pod-product-compliance
Lightning Source LLC
Chambersburg PA
CBHW060855120626
46553CB00001B/96